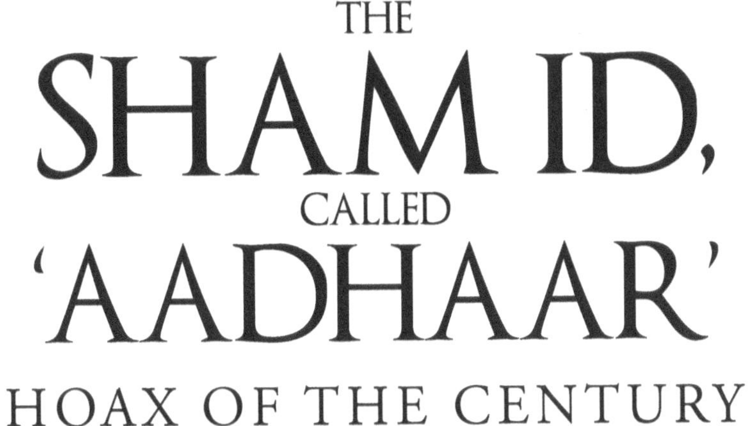

EXTRAORDINARY INDIAN DELUSION

THE
SHAM ID,
CALLED
'AADHAAR'
HOAX OF THE CENTURY

MATHEW THOMAS

ISBN 978-1-64324-909-4

Dedication

This book is dedicated to all patriotic Indians who love their motherland and have sacrificed their lives for her and those who are willing to do so in future should the call come.

Bharat Mata Ki Jai

Contents

APPENDICES

Preface

Every Indian has in some way or other been affected by a program which, goes by the brand name, "Aadhaar". The word is familiar to most Indians. Like, the poem, "The Blind Men and The Elephant" by John Godfrey Saxe (1872) in which the poet tells us how all those who touched it have a different idea of what it is; all who felt the impact of "Aadhaar" have varied views on it. (Wikisource, from which, this information is taken, calls it a "Hindoo Fable". The poet refers to the country as, Indostan)

This book looks at the blind beliefs the majority of Indians have on the program. That a billion people could be so blinded should not surprise students of behavioural sciences. We are, as Dan Ariely says, "Predictably Irrational". Our irrationality, as far as, "Aadhaar" is concerned can and must be explained. That is the purpose of this book.

The book, some may say, is late in coming. It really does not matter. Better late than never – the truth be told of the biggest hoax ever, in any nation of the world.

Its lateness many be in relation to the likelihood of the Supreme Court judgement on the Sham ID, called, 'Aadhaar' case which, was expected soon after the summer vacation. (I call "Aadhaar" a Sham ID, because that's what it is – a sham. Throughout the book that is how it will be referred to. A "sham" is something that is not what it is purported to be.)

The introduction will be brief. There is a story to tell the Indian people; a story of how they have been hoaxed as no one else, except people of a few failed states and banana republics have been, fooled as we have. It is a hoax of gigantic proportions. An entire nation is taken in, and that, for almost a decade.

Here, in this book, you will find explained for the first time that what most Indians believed to be an identity, is not an identity at all. The people of almost all nations these days have identities with which, they identify themselves for various purposes, for human transactions. If the Sham ID, called, 'Aadhaar' were to continue, all Indians will be numbered. *We will have numbers assigned to us by an authority. We cannot identify ourselves but, if we give our numbers to the authority, they will use the numbers for identification.*

This book reveals startling facts backed by incontrovertible documentary, scientific and mathematical evidence of the charade with the brand name, "Aadhaar".

No country in world indulges in such un-imaginable idiocy. Pakistan and India are the only two countries wallowing in the quagmire trap set up by foreign intelligence agencies. This is no conspiracy theory, but facts revealed in unassailable documentary evidence.

The story is being told so that people of India take action to protect themselves so that it does not happen ever again.

Some people may attempt to dismiss this as a conspiracy theory or wild allegations. I invite such people to examine the facts and evidence presented here with open minds, question them and come to their own conclusions. I challenge them to debate me in public.

Every statement in the book is substantiated by hard, incontrovertible evidence. It is also backed by undeniable scientific research at the highest levels and mathematical proof. The challenge also includes any mathematician to prove the results wrong or produce scientific evidence to the contrary.

Largely due to ignorance and partly due to greed and other unsavoury motivations, many have fallen prey to the hoax and a few have cashed in on the gullibility of unsuspecting people.

Complicit in the hoax, or victims of it, are all political parties, most politicians, state governments, media, both print and visual, corporate houses, business leaders, academicians and even social activists. Many of these people are ignorant. Many are deluded. Many sincerely believe that it will do good. There are, or must be, a small group, who are well aware of what exactly is being done and why; else, the story could not have unravelled the way it has.

This is the story of a brand name called, "Aadhaar". It is story of the use of the brand name to market a program that would pass control from people to those in power and their masters.

"Aadhaar" is supposedly a unique ID. The Aadhaar Scheme is ostensibly meant to provide unique IDs to people.

I have termed it a Sham ID and hereafter always use the word, "Aadhaar" with the prefix, "Sham ID". This is to destroy the brand name which, is used to deceive people.

Any hoax involves duplicity; deceit is the characteristic of the Sham ID, called, 'Aadhaar' Scheme. Deviousness and cunningness are combined to create an aura of infallibility, efficacy, inventiveness and use of high technology by Indian initiative. Nothing is farther from the truth.

When public money is spent, and that, in such huge amounts, it is natural to ask, "Why?"

Hence, the book begins by seeking to understand the purpose and utility of the scheme. It explains how the Sham ID, called, 'Aadhaar' Scheme cannot achieve any of its goals. Not only that the objectives are unachievable, great harm would result from it.

It is not just that there is craftiness for purposes unknown, it will be shown that the Scheme has no utility whatsoever.

The book describes the chasing after shadows, the attempt to catch the mirage which, recedes as it is approached.

A few, including the author, have questioned the Sham ID Scheme in courts and in the Supreme Court. The case has dragged on for about a decade. The book brings out starling facts which, although mentioned in the Supreme Court, did not find its way into media. The Court too may not have appreciated fully the implications of some of the facts. The torturous path of the case through Indian judicial system is described.

The book seeks to find answers to, or the rationale behind, the approach of various segments of the people of India to such a sinister trick played on them. It then hazards to predict the Supreme Court verdict and proceeds to suggest remedies to many ills that beset our nation.

The reader will find some sentences in the book in italics and some highlighted too, and some repeated, in addition. This is both for emphasis and to facilitate speed-readers to quickly note important issues that may otherwise be missed out.

Acknowledgements

Firstly, although it is unusual for an author to thank God, I am indeed grateful to God who, by His grace, has given me the health and wherewithal to pen this book at my age which, is well past the Biblical, "Three score and ten."

I am deeply grateful to my family and a number of friends and many others who made this book possible. It is difficult to name everyone of them and if I have inadvertently failed to mention anyone, I apologise to them.

This is not merely an acknowledgement of those who helped me write this book, but also an expression of my deep gratitude to all those who helped the cause against the Sham ID.

Secondly, strange as it may seem, I must thank the proponents of their Sham ID, called, 'Aadhaar' Scheme, who out misplaced zeal, overplayed it and entrapped themselves, thus facilitating this exposé; but for their foolishness, it would have been very difficult to convince people that this is indeed a hoax.

Among my friends, I must single out, Somasekhar, V.K. who stood by me and helped in numerous ways, not the least of which, was to connect me up with leaders of the BJP.

To all my advocates, starting with Venkatesh Bubberjung, who handled the case in the lower court, Gopal Subramanium, (Usha Ramanathan who introduced me to him) Anand Grover, (Indira Jaising, who introduced me to Grover), Aishwarya Bhati and her family (Father Gp. Capt. Bhati and husband, Jaideep Singh), Anando Mukherjee, Prasanna, Tehmina Arora, Talha Abdul Rahman, Pawan Bhushan and their colleagues, I owe an incalculable debt of gratitude. They handled the case *pro bono*. Apart from incurring huge financial loss, they spent considerable part of their invaluable time in understanding the case and preparing arguments.

Advocates, M.A. Sebastian & Co. and S.G. Chaitanya, handled the cases in the Karnataka High Court. They too rendered their services *pro bono*. I express my sincere thanks to them.

Although, Shyam Divan was not representing me, he made immense contribution to the public cause. To him, and other advocates, like Arvind Datar, Meenakshi Arora and Vishwanathan, all anti-Sham ID activists and I am indeed thankful.

To all activists against the Scheme, who contributed with encouragement and shared information which, was of great value I am grateful. Particularly, Usha Ramanathan, Prasanna, Anupam Saraf, Vickram Krishna, Ram Krishnaswamy, Vinay Baindur and Anand Venkatnarayanan, for their valuable contributions and activism. Dr. Gopal Krishna was of great help with RTI processes and introductions to many political leaders and functionaries. He accompanied me to meet some of them. Sunil Abraham of CIS was also very kind and helpful. The survey Somasekhar and I carried out on DBT (Direct Benefit Transfer – another misnomer in the farce), at Mysore and Tumkur were due to him. I acknowledge his help and support with gratitude.

Dr. Hans V. Mathews provided invaluable mathematical proof of the impossibility of uniquely identifying people using this biometric system. He explained to me many doubts I had. I am indeed grateful to him.

David Moss, a UK based campaigner, was always very helpful with his inputs from his knowledge and understanding of both the UK and the Indian schemes. I acknowledge his assistance with deep gratitude.

Venkatnarayanan's analysis of UIDAI's false claims were invaluable and so also were his investigations into information that UIDAI deleted from its website. I owe him a special thanks.

Harsheet Shah provided very valuable information and inputs through my WhatsApp group. I thank him for it.

Sucheta Dalal of Money Life Foundation sponsored a number of seminars of the campaign. Her website carried many articles on the Sham ID. I owe her much.

To Kshitij Urs who interviewed me and also gave me opportunities to speak at national law schools, I am indeed grateful.

Finally, I am really thankful to my publishers, their editors and staff who made this book see the light of day.

Duplicitously False Dichotomy

THE "WHY" QUESTION OF THE SHAM ID "AADHAAR"

Human beings, as distinct from animals, are rational. They have a reason for doing whatever they do. Even the insane have a reason for their actions. We may not understand their reasons, but they still have reasons. Hence, the persons who conceived and set up UIDAI too must have their reasons. The Government also must have reasons. However, the reasons publicly stated might not be the actual reasons.

Reason or rationality is the hallmark of a sound mind. The question which has intrigued me is, "Why are they doing this – setting up the Sham ID/"Aadhaar?" Are the publicly stated reasons true?

The UIDAI website says, "UIDAI was created with the objective to issue Unique Identification numbers (UID), named as "Aadhaar", to all residents of India that is (a) robust enough to eliminate duplicate and fake identities, and (b) can be verified and authenticated in an easy, cost-effective way."

The vision and mission of UIDAI, as copied from its website are as given below.

VISION & MISSION

Fig 1

Vision

To empower residents of India with a unique identity and a digital platform to authenticate anytime, anywhere.

Mission

Deliver Aadhaar numbers universally to residents with a well-defined turnaround time and adhering to stringent quality metrics.

Notice that it says that the vision is to *empower residents* of India with a unique identity.

How does the possession of a unique ID empower anyone? And why empower residents?

If a resident were a spy or terrorist who crossed the border, would UIDAI like to empower him/her?

How different is the view expressed by the present British PM, when, as Home Secretary, she moved the Bill to scrap Britain's National ID Card Act, in June 2009. This was the first action taken by the Cameron government upon assuming office. It was the fulfillment of the Conservative's election manifesto promise. It was not a "*Chunauvi Joomla.*" Referring to the ID card, she said, "It is intrusive bullying, an assault on personal liberties. It will do no good. It will cost a millennium dome worth on money." The contrast could not be starker. Between the Indian notion of people's ID under the control of government for good governance and the British perception of national ID as a tool for intrusive bullying (by government) there is a chasm. It is the difference between a mature democracy that respects peoples' rights and immature politicians beguiled by rich corporate media personalities with their pathetic notions on what is good for the country. Ms. Theresa May went on to add, "We propose to run the government as servants of the people, not their masters."

This then, is the "Great Indian Delusion" – that technology can and should be used to control people for (ostensibly) their benefit. The presupposition is that anyone could be a potential thief (politicians and some bureaucrats, exempted) and so need to be fingerprinted, numbered and the number linked to every possible database. The tragic irony is that all this is done in the name of good governance, transparency and efficiency! Astonishingly, the media and almost all political parties are silent, even acquiescing in and supporting the scheme. This could be out of ignorance or other motives or a combination of both. Ms. Mamata Banerjee alone has had the courage to call this spade [of a Sham ID], a spade.

Mahatma Gandhi opposed the fingerprinting of Indians in South Africa. He said that on checking with a friend, he found that fingerprinting was used only for prisoners. As we know, every prisoner is given a number. The Sham ID, called,

'Aadhaar' Scheme seeks to not only fingerprint every Indian and resident in India but also assign them numbers. If this pernicious evil were allowed to continue, India would be the largest open prison in the world! Sadly, those who swear by the name of the Mahatma and pay homage at his Samadhi every year are the very ones that perpetrate the evil.

The delusion of unique biometric IDs extends to UIDAI's views of itself. UIDAI has claimed to set up the largest biometric database in the world, as if it were an achievement. If only those who boast of such "achievements" pause to think, "Why have others not done so?" They may yet have not only answers, but would also prevent untold misery and colossal waste of public money.

UIDAI borrows foreign technology, hires foreign firms for structuring and managing the Sham ID, called 'Aadhaar' Scheme, and yet trumpets it as its achievement. This is the Indian version of the proverbial crow strutting with borrowed peacock feathers.

Our priorities too seem misplaced. Instead of spending scarce resources judicially, UIDAI has thoughtlessly embarked on a futile exercise.

Like the bullet train and smart cities project, we are attempting to leap (without looking) before we have learned to walk. Nothing typifies more this abysmal lack of a sense of priorities that some of the grandiose schemes touted out by politicians and "experts" of varied hues display, than a photo I received through "WhatsApp".

Here it is.

Fig 2: (Author - Anonymous)

It is both sad and sickening. Yet, it is the hard truth.

FOUNDED ON FALSE ASSUMPTIONS – "AADHAAR" STANDS ON FALSE AADHAAR/BASIS

The ostensible justification for providing the so-called unique ID number which, as we shall see, is not unique, is the false assumption that many Indians lack IDs, and hence are not able to access welfare services.

This was mentioned in earlier versions of the UIDAI website, but seems to have since been removed. It is interesting to note that the UIDAI website is constantly revised. Usually, embarrassing facts or statements or information is deleted without any explanation.

For example, there was a disclaimer in earlier versions of the UIDAI website that the ID it provides is a number, and that it does not confer the right to citizenship. I do not find the statement in the current versions of the website.

The first thing one notices about this "empowering" ID is that it is a number. What are the implications of this? If one gives the ID number to someone, as one would produce an ID card to authenticate oneself to another, the person receiving the number cannot identify the one giving the number. The recipient would have to access the UIDAI database through another agency, and that agency would have to query the database, and if the query returns a positive reply, only then may the recipient accept the person producing the ID. Hence, one cannot use the Sham ID number to identify oneself, but is dependent on UIDAI every time there is a need to identify.

Instead of being empowered, one is left to the mercy of the authentication agency and the UIDAI database administrator. Even they are not the actual persons who identify or authenticate the ID. UIDAI, as we shall see later, uses a proprietary software and hardware of foreign entities for the purpose. Effectively, Indians are placed under the sweet will and pleasure of these foreign entities for identifying themselves.

What then is purpose of this rigmarole? [Rigmarole, according to the Merriam-Webster dictionary is "a succession of confused, meaningless, or foolish statements."]

The rationale again is quite incoherent. It stems from the other unfounded assumption that the poor do not have IDs, and hence are not able to access welfare benefits. Interestingly, the enrolment form, in rows 8 a. and 8 b. asks for both proof of identity (POI) and proof of address (POA). If one does not have these, then one may be enrolled only through an introducer. Published statistics on enrolment and RTI replies reveal that only a miniscule minority of Indians did not have IDs.

When that argument sounded hollow, the theme song switched to eliminating fakes and ghosts in welfare databases to prevent "leakages" of subsidies.

Here is another assumption – that "leakages" of subsidies is through fakes and ghosts in welfare databases. The use of the word "leakages" is itself interesting. Are there pipelines from welfare databases to beneficiaries that leak? Instead, of facing the fact that subsidies are stolen, pilfered, robbed, the euphemism "leakage" is used to describe the crime. This kind of skullduggery characterizes the entire Sham ID/ "Aadhaar" Scheme. If the crime were properly stated, there would be a need to investigate it. Now, those responsible could gloss over it and pretend to be acting to prevent the theft. Then again, if at all there were fakes and ghosts, someone must certainly have made them. And, once prepared, the fakes and ghosts must be entered into the government's welfare databases. Is it not sensible to say that some government employees are the only people who could do this? Then, it is a simple matter to prosecute such government employees.

So, let's ask the question, "Why?" Why this scheme? As said earlier, UIDAI and the government say that it is to provide IDs to those who don't have any. That possibility has been discounted since almost all have IDs. Now, they use the excuse of preventing "leakages" – theft of subsidies. Hence, one should find out how the crime is committed – its *modus operandi*, before coming up with a solution. UIDAI and government have put the cart before the horse by coming up with the solution to prevent subsidy theft without any investigation of how the criminal act is carried out.

The founder of the Toyota Industries, Sakichi Toyoda, developed a problem-solving technique, "5-Whys." Simply put, to solve any problem, first enunciate the problem, and ask 5 questions, "Why?", "Why?" – 5 times, and invariably you would find a solution to the problem.

The "5-Whys" technique is used mainly for solving problems of product quality in manufacturing. It may also be applied to other situations with some modifications. For example, to apply to the theft of subsidies, one would have to ask not only the "Why" question, but also, the "What", "How" and "Who" questions.

First, how are subsidies stolen? This would depend on the type of subsidy. Let us take BPL rations as an example. Are the rations stolen from ration shops? Are they stolen from storages? Which is more likely?

Fig 3: Policeman and thief are together in it, much like what will be described shortly.

An article in 'Business Line' datelined 1 Oct 2017 says that once the DBT scheme based on the Sham ID/"Aadhaar" links becomes operational, the Center's component of the subsidy per year would be about ₹ 8,600/- 9,000/- per annum, per family. (Data is for Delhi).[1] This works out to only ₹ 3440 crores per annum taking a state with about 40,00,000 BPL families and using the lower figure in the band for calculations. One wonders how politicians claim that thousands of crores of rupees worth of subsidies are "leaked" due to lack of identification of BPL families.

It is indeed astonishing that no one asks, "How does linking to the Sham ID/"Aadhaar" numbers, or even biometric identification, eliminate 'leakages' (theft) of subsidies?" Even the simple question of eligibility is ignored. I had written to the Parliament Standing Committee on Finance informing it that identity would not prevent theft of PDS subsidies. There is discretion to decide eligibility and corruption in the process of issuing BPL ration cards, which facilitate a small part of the theft. The Committee included this in their report and said that it is not identity that is the problem but (discretion to decide) eligibility. One justification is that there are fake and 'ghost' ration cards and that these are used to "leak" (steal) subsidized rations. A simple calculation would show that the claim is ridiculous. There are about 40,000

---

[1] This is the URL link of the article. http://www.thehindubusinessline.com/economy/a-bpl-family-will-get-rs-8600-a-year-under-direct-subsidy-transfer/article3955834.ece

ration shops and 40,00,000 BPL families in Karnataka. At 25 kg per family per month of rice, with a subsidy element of ₹ 20.00 per kg, the total subsidy on rice, a major component of the ration, per month is only ₹ 200 crores. This is annually ₹ 2400 crores. Hence, this is the maximum that could be stolen per annum if there are 100% fake ration cards. Even if there is a large percentage of so-called fakes in the ration card database, it would be a herculean task to steal from every ration shop large quantities of rations. The logistics would make it simply impossible.

I had asked in an RTI query to the Karnataka Government regarding fake ration cards detected using the Sham ID/"Aadhaar". Their reply makes interesting reading. The Karnataka Government did not use Sham ID/"Aadhaar" for detecting fakes. No fake ration cards were found. Instead, using electric power meter numbers 44 Lakh "ineligible" ration cards were detected. The problem was not one of identity, but of eligibility.

FALSE CLAIMS OF FAKES AND GHOSTS

The RTI reply No: CFS/AMC/RTI/50/2011-2012 dated 22-01-2013 is in **Appendix 'List of Documents' Serial No. 1**[2] in the List of Documentary Evidence at the end of the book. It says, "There is no fake ration cards detected in Karnataka State using UID/"Aadhaar" biometric data —" Then the letter provides the number of ineligible ration cards detected using electric RR numbers (power meter numbers). The number of such ineligible persons with BPL ration cards is 44 Lakhs. The RTI reply states that Food Inspectors verify the BPL applicants. When asked as to who are responsible for making fake ration cards, the reply is, "It is the beneficiaries who are responsible for ineligible ration cards —" A word of explanation is called for here. The ration cards are issued after a physical verification of eligibility done by "Food Inspectors". There is no way beneficiaries could make fake or ineligible ration cards. It is very difficult for genuine beneficiaries – BPL families to obtain the ration cards, let alone making fake ones. There is no reply to queries on the quantum of rations drawn against the ineligible ration cards. Many people who would never take rations from a ration shop apply for and obtain APL ration cards as this is the simplest ID migrants may get.

My view is that rations are stolen in bulk at the time of procurement and they never reach the storages. Then, accounting gimmicks ensure that the theft remains undetected. Approximately ₹ 80,000.00 crores worth of food grains are

---

[2] RTI reply No: CFS/AMC/RTI/50/2011-2012 dated 22-01-2013

written off as damaged annually and declared as unfit for human consumption. It is not difficult for officials administering and accounting rations to facilitate theft of rations in bulk and then write off the stolen stocks as damaged.

Here are pictures of damaged food grains published in the media.

Fig 4: Condition of Food Storage (Author - Anonymous)

Fig 5: Wasted Food (Author - Anonymous)

The food grains are stored in the open. Instead of spending money on increasing and improving food grain storage, the government is squandering money on a foolhardy, unscientific, mathematically impossible scheme of biometrically identifying the poor, imagining that lack of identity or false IDs are the cause of food subsidy theft.

Here's statistics and a picture of mal-nourished children. These are not the lost ones that UIDAI restored to their parents, as advertised, but those living with parents and to whom, to prevent theft of food subsidies, the Sham ID "Aadhaar" rigmarole denies food.

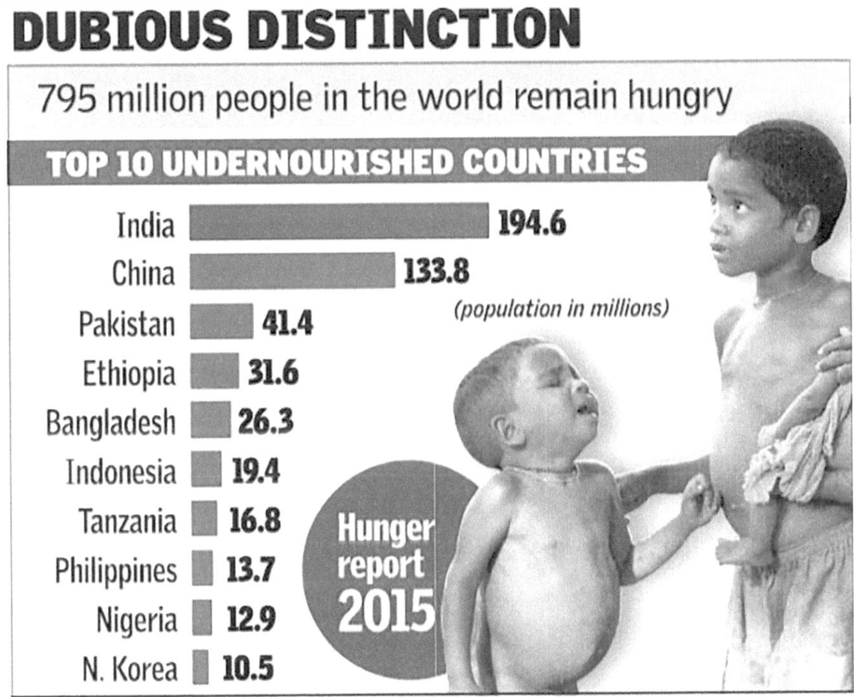

Fig 6: India tops in Hunger Index (Author - Anonymous)

Where should the priorities in spending public money lie? In preventing this crime of having about 200 million of our children undernourished, or for using allegedly "high tech biometrics to uniquely identify" them?

Fig 7: Ramshackle Housing of the Poor (Author – Anonymous)

Here's a picture I took of people living in make-shift huts in a posh area of *Namma* Bengaluru.

Again, let's ask ourselves, "Where should our priorities lie in spending public money? In bullet trains, smart cities, in biometric IDs or in housing the homeless?"

The same flawed, perverted logic of UIDAI, as for saving food subsidies, applies in the case of LPG. The "Interim Report of the Task Force on Subsidies," headed by Shri Nilekani makes interesting reading. It reads like a "Tenali Raman" fable! The fable is told to children and goes thus: To catch a crow (any bird) all you need is to place a blob of ghee on its head when it is fast asleep at night. When the Sun comes up in the morning and melts the ghee, the crow will be blinded and then the crow can be easily caught!

Here is an extract of paragraphs 6.3 and 6.4 of the Task Force Report on LPG subsidies.

EXTRACT BEGINS

"Phase II of the project will involve appending the OMC customer databases with Aadhaars and bank account details. The customers' Aadhaar Enabled Bank Account (AEBA) details will be used to transfer the subsidy.

The customers will buy all cylinders at market price while the Government will fix the subsidy per cylinder. OMCs will sell LPG at the market price and the subsidy amount will be directly transferred from the Government to the customers. The delivery to customers will be confirmed by an authentication service and the requisite amount will be transferred, on the successful completion and confirmation of delivery by the OMCs, to the residents. Phase II itself would be done in phases: authentication of delivery in the first phase and transfer into the bank accounts in the second phase.

A CSMS for LPG will be implemented as described in Chapter 4. The basic solution architecture for subsidy administration and direct cash transfer is worked out based on single pricing and proper authentication models for customers who receive subsidy either as product or as cash. The model will also consider direct customer and stakeholder involvement through relationship building elements including customer empowerment via customer education, transparency web-portal, grievance redressal, etc. With the following facets as the backbone, domestic LPG delivery system can be revamped:

1. Every customer (to receive subsidized LPG) will have an Aadhaar
   a) Aadhaar numbers of beneficiaries will be verified before seeding the database to eliminate ghost connections/registrations
   b) In order to have a wider base to eliminate duplicates, the databases of all OMCs will be pooled together. The combined database will be used for de-duplication
2. While delivering LPG, the Aadhaar number of the customer or his/her family members will be verified in order to disable unauthorized persons from receiving subsidized cylinders
3. Single price and direct subsidies will further remove the incentive for unauthorized deliveries

In the process shown below:
1. LPG cylinders are booked by customers
2. The order details are entered in the booking system (software) of the distributor
3. The delivery list for a delivery boy is transferred to handheld device
4. At the time of delivery, the device captures the authentication data from the customer
5. The device sends the authentication data to the authentication service provider to facilitate the transaction
6. The authentication service provider responds to the request received, completing the verification and enabling (or preventing) the delivery

7. The delivered data is transferred back to the distributor software

8. The cash will be directly transferred to the Aadhaar linked bank account of the customers. At the onset, each customer entitled for subsidized LPG will be given one unit of subsidy in cash directly in his/her bank account. Subsequently, when the LPG cylinder is sourced and received through the authentication route, additional units of subsidy will be credited to the bank account."

EXTRACT FROM TASK FORCE REPORT ENDS

The recommendations of the Task Force are akin to an Aesop's fable or the indigenous Tenali Raman children's story. It is astonishing that 8 secretaries to the Government of India affixed their signatures to this document. Did they apply their minds? A simple analysis of the pattern of consumption of individuals would reveal whether the LPG is used for cooking or commercial purposes. Even prior to the days before the cap on number of cylinders, one could not book for a refill until 21 days had elapsed after receipt of a cylinder. LPG cylinders are delivered at the houses of the customers. To use domestic subsidized LPG cylinders for commercial purposes one would have to take the delivered cylinder from the houses where it was delivered to the place of commercial use. In any case, common sense would tell us that biometric authentication of the customer would not prevent the use of the subsidized LPG for commercial purposes.

Pilot trials were carried out in Mysore and Tumkur and were carried out in 2014. These were not successful as biometric authentication failed. Bank transfers also caused difficulties. LPG customers were tossed around between banks and LPG distributors with neither taking responsibility for non-receipt of LPG subsidy. In one distributor's area, not one of the 300 domestic workers – women – customers could be authenticated, since they had worn out palms and fingerprints.

It is not surprising that the idea of point-of-delivery authentication has been given a quiet burial. While so, the insistence of the government on forcing BPL families to authenticate ration card holders at ration shops would appear incongruous. A deeper look would show that there is design behind this seemingly innocuous decision. BPL families are from the voiceless poor. LPG customers are mainly from articulate and vocal middleclass. Being aware of the fact that point-of-delivery authentication is bound to frequently fail, government dare not run the risk of exposing the fallibility of the biometrics. The minions of the ruling elite know that they could run rough shod over the poor who can even be starved to death, as has happened, without even a whimper of protest.

The Sham ID "Aadhaar" Scheme is founded on the duplicitously false dichotomy of either "Aadhaar" or nothing. If you don't have it, you get no benefit or service you are entitled to. The fallacy that without it (Sham ID "Aadhaar") government schemes cannot be efficient is assiduously promoted. Its many wonders are eulogized. Stories are planted in the press of a lost child being restored to its parents, as if without the Sham ID "Aadhaar" it could not have been done.

Thus, it is evident that people are not empowered by being fingerprinted, numbered and their personal data entered in all government databases and linked together. The poor have IDs contrary to claims of UIDAI. PDS and LPG examples show that subsidies cannot be saved by "targeting deliveries" using biometric IDs. This is true of all other benefits and services. There were and are no fakes or ghosts in any database. These were and are not how subsidies were or are siphoned out. It is astonishing as to why the existence of fakes and ghosts are assumed to explain away pilferage of subsidies without any investigation whatsoever. There was and is no need to use the euphemism, "leakages" for theft of subsidies. Rationality seems utterly lacking in the Sham ID/"Aadhaar" Scheme. Hence, the "Why" question continues to puzzle, as we proceed to the next chapter of the 'Great Indian Delusion' – UIDAI's Deceit.

UIDAI's Deceit

"Oh, what a tangled web we weave when
first we practice to deceive." Walter Scott in "Marmion"

Fig 8: Mixing Fact and Fiction

That the elected representatives in the world's largest democracy should deceive the people who elect them seems inconceivable. Yet, this is true of many democracies; only in the more mature ones, the deceivers are often caught and thrown out.

"Oh, what a tangled web we weave when first we practice to deceive." Walter Scott might well have said this about the Sham ID "Aadhaar" Scheme, had he been alive now.

In explaining the deception and the hoax that is being played on the people of India it is difficult to decide where to begin and how to move towards the end.

Well it – the deception – is right at the very beginning. It commences with the choice of the person to drive this initiative – the hoax of the Sham ID/"Aadhaar". A book published recently outlines how a certain bureaucrat put in a word at the right places, and lo and behold, the crown prince of the grand old party of India called him to come over to Delhi. And thereby hangs a tale. An early morning call, so the story goes, leads to a meeting between the then PM, Mr. Manmohan Singh and the author and architect of the scheme, Mr. Nilekani. The result – Mr. Nilekani is appointed head of an entity labeled, Unique Identification Authority of India. The corporate honcho bids for cabinet rank and is granted that, as if such privileges could be dished out at the will of the PM in democratic India. Article 74 of the Constitution be blown. There was not a whimper of protest or question on the grant of cabinet status. Having lived for centuries under sultans and rajas, we docilely accept every whim of the king, even a democratic king. The recipient, rather than politely declining to accept, if it – cabinet rank – was offered, had worked for it. He too did not think that transgressing the Constitutional provision is wrong.

When the scheme was announced in Jan 2009, I was astounded. The first thought that occurred to me was, "How can this work? People's lives have a dynamism not seen in any material world. People are born, grow up, study, work, marry, have children, travel, fall sick, migrate, change places of work and living. How can there be a unique, unchanging ID for all purposes for all time? After all, an ID would, of necessity, have elements other than some biometrics tagged to a number."

So, I wrote to the PM and Mr. Nilekani. I asked them how they propose to make this work. What is the purpose? I set down some misgivings in the letter. Neither did I expect a reply, nor did I get one from either of them.

ENROLMENT IS VOLUNTARY, BUT SHAM ID "AADHAAR" IS COMPULSORY FOR LIVING!

The deceit was planned right from the start. Mr. Nilekani was reported in media on many occasions as saying, "It (the Sham ID/"Aadhaar") is voluntary, but service providers may ask for it." Here's one government entity, UIDAI, saying it is voluntary, while, tongue in cheek, also saying, other government organs would ask for it. If this were not deception, then what is? Even today, the Targeted Deliveries Act (also called, "Aadhaar" Act) talks of enrolment as an "entitlement"! As the readers know, the government has made it compulsory for several government services to which people have undeniable rights, such as, the right to food.

Those were the heydays of the hare-brained scheme. The euphoria generated by the corporate honcho with his media created charisma had intoxicated the ignorant, presstitute media, who were unabashedly singing paeans.

BRAND NAME – "AADHAAR", A PRIVATE TRUST

The brand name, "Aadhaar", is another hoax. Mr. Nilekani has/had a private Trust of the same name. By some mysterious happenstance, serendipity, the name of the government program coincided with the name of his Trust. Ostensibly, the logo and name were chosen through a public competition. There is no information on how the brand name came to be. It baffles imagination how Mr. Nilekani never once reacted to the choice of the brand name of the scheme, which is also the name of his private Trust. A news story in 'Business Today' datelined 17-08-2003 reported it. The URL of the report is in the Appendix.

Brand names are marketing tools. Why such trade/commercial devices are needed for a program meant to provide either IDs for those who do not possess these or for government to provide rights of citizens, confounds one.

I decided to probe the details of the scheme. RTI came in handy. Hundreds of RTI applications were filed. A pattern of avoidance of straight answers to queries emerged. RTI had to be used as if a hostile witness was being cross-examined in a criminal trial. This spoke volumes about the charade of transparency propagated by those behind the Sham ID/"Aadhaar" Scheme.

DECEIT REVEALED IN PASSING THE RTI BUCK

UIDAI played the game of passing the buck with all my RTI applications. This speaks volumes for its pretensions of transparency. There will more on the transparency façade later. If I queried the head office in Delhi, the application would be passed on to the Bengaluru regional office and vice-versa. Often it would then be sent to the "Technology Center". The merry-go-round of RTI applications suggested either that no one knew where the information was available, or alternatively there was indeed a deliberate attempt to frustrate and obfuscate.

Let me elaborate using a typical example. I would leave it to the reader to judge whether the illustration reveals and proves deceit or not.

In 2011, an RTI applicant (Mr. Veeresh Malik) had sought to know the country of origin of the contractors of UIDAI. The CPIO did not provide the answer and so the matter went to the appellate authority. Mr. Davinder Kumar, Deputy Director General and Appellate Authority of UIDAI replied in July 2011 stating, "There are no means to verify whether the said companies/organizations are of US origin or not."[3] The reply is in **Appendix 'List of Documents' Serial No. 2** at the end

---

[3] RTI Reply of UIDAI to Mr. Veeresh Malik – "No means to verify country of origin—"

of the book. Meanwhile, I had applied for copies of the contracts between UIDAI and the firms providing biometric technology services. How I obtained copies of these contracts is a story in itself, to which I shall come shortly. For now, the reader should know that the first page of the contract gives the country of origin of the contractor. It is inconceivable that the appellate authority would either be unaware of the country of origin of his organization's vendors, or that if he did not know, he would not have asked his colleagues to find out the same. The scanned copy of the first page of the contract between M/s. L 1 Identity Solutions Operating Company Pvt. Ltd. and UIDAI[4] is in **Appendix 'List of Documents' Serial No. 3** of the book. It shows that the company is a US firm located in Delaware. Could there be any doubt that the appellate authority was practicing willful deceit? But then, is not all deceit always willful? The question is not whether he was deceitful, but what were his motives in acting so? Could he have acted alone? Were his superiors and colleagues having copies of the contract aware of the reply he gave?

Let me now come to the story of how I obtained a copy of the contract. When I applied under RTI for a copy of the contract, I received the reply from the CPIO of UIDAI that it cannot be furnished. He took shelter under Section 8.1 (d) RTI Act 2005, which provides for exemption from disclosure of information of commercial nature which, if given, could compromise the competitive position of the concerned organization. I appealed stating that since the contract has already been awarded, there could be no adverse effect on the competitive position. The appellate authority stuck to the position taken by the CPIO. I then appealed to the Central Information Commission (CIC). As part of the opaqueness in its functioning, while carrying on the pretense of transparency, UIDAI sent junior officers who pleaded ignorance of the matter before the IC. At the hearing in Aug 2012, Information Commissioner (IC), Ms. Sushma Singh, ordered UIDAI to send senior officials who had access to the information sought and asked them to justify the application of Section 8.1 (d) RTI Act. The next hearing was on 10 Sep 2012. The UIDAI officials now came with a letter addressed to the Commission and copy to me stating, "The contractual obligations are finished and as such they have no objection in furnishing me a copy of the contract." I had to pay a sum of ₹ 900 or so, and having paid the amount, received the copy. My friend and co-activist, Dr. Gopal Krishna, assisted me by appearing before the Commission and

---

[4] Scanned copy of the first page of the contract between M/s. L 1 Identity Solutions Operating Company Pvt. Ltd. and UIDAI

by collecting the contract copies. Copies of contracts with L 1 Identity Solutions Operating Company Pvt. Ltd. and M/s. Accenture were thus obtained.

It was then that I noticed that not only were the two contracts identically worded, but the same pages, Appendices I, J and K had been removed from them. This was a fraud not only on me but also on the CIC. I then wrote to the Commission informing it of the duplicity of UIDAI in pretending to furnish the contract while withholding certain appendices. By then Ms. Sushma Singh had retired and a new Information Commissioner, Mr. Sharat Sabharwal had taken over. Next, I received a letter from one Vijay Bhalla, Registrar CIC, informing me that the Information Commissioner had asked that compliance of the order be verified.[5]

After this I received another letter from the same person, Vijay Bhalla, Registrar, stating that the Information Commissioner is not issuing any fresh order, but that he has directed that "limited financial information may be furnished".[6] Finding the letter ridiculous, I filed a writ petition in the Delhi High Court which is pending since 2014. It is numbered 9143 of 2014. UIDAI has not filed a reply as yet. The case has been adjourned 4 times. Notices have been issued to both L 1 Identity Solutions Operating Company Pvt. Ltd. and Accenture. The latter has filed appearance. Neither company has filed any reply.

Summarizing the episode, one finds UIDAI first claiming there is no way to verify the country of origin of its contractors. This is a lie, since the first page of the contract has the names and addresses of the contractors. Then, refusing to furnish copies of the contracts sought under RTI using Section 8 (1) (d) of the RTI Act. Next, when asked to justify application of the said section, informs the CIC that it has no objection to give contract copies since the contractual obligations are finished. After this, UIDAI hands over contract copies with pages (annexures) removed. Again, when asked for the pages which were removed, once more takes the plea of confidentiality under RTI Act.

Clearly, the attempt to hide the contract is anything but unintentional.

I made a search of the UIDAI website today (06-11-2017) for its contractors. A screen shot of the webpage of the search results is placed in **Appendix 'List of Documents' Serial No. 6**.[7] Why does UIDAI want to hide even the names

---

[5] Item 4 in Appendix 'A' Letter from one Vijay Bhalla, Registrar, CIC informing me that the Information Commissioner had asked that compliance of the order be verified

[6] Letter from Registrar, CIC stating that IC has said that "Limited financial information may be provided."

[7] Screen shot of UIDAI webpage search results for its contractors.

of its contractors? Interestingly, in 2010, UIDAI website did contain not only the names of its contractors, but also the amounts paid to them. Why have these details been removed now? Who ordered their deletion?

ENROLLING AGENCY FRAUDS AND INACTION

Earlier, in 2010, UIDAI website had names and addresses of 209 Enrolling Agencies (EAs). A year or so later, the number had dwindled down to about 153. No explanation was ever given as to why the number reduced. Now, the UIDAI website does not have any details of EAs.[8] This is yet another crucial factor in the hoax I refer to as Sham ID/"Aadhaar". EAs were, it appears, empaneled indiscriminately. Thus, all and sundry were in the list. There were stock brokers, a printing press, a tea estate, an education society, small IT firms and so on. The empanelment and the biometric and demographic data collection process are unbelievably silly. UIDAI listed this motley group, many riff-raff firms as empaneled EAs. UIDAI then entered into Memoranda of Understanding (MOU) with government departments and organizations like banks, civil supplies departments, etc. The entities with which UIDAI entered into MOU are labeled "Registrars". The registrars are supposed to choose firms from the empaneled list and appoint them as EAs. Thus, UIDAI is not responsible for any frauds (and there are numerous such crimes) that the EAs indulge in. A neat arrangement, one could say. The EAs were not to sub-contract their work to other firms. Yet, many did exactly that. Three firms of a group of family-owned firms that go by the name of "Alankit" were empaneled. All of them had the same address in Jhandewalabagh or Jhandewalan, Delhi. One of these was the EA for Bengaluru. The firm subcontracted the work to another called Global ID Solutions. This firm in turn further subcontracted the enrolling work to other sub-sub-contractors. The firm took sums of ₹ 2 Lakhs or so for granting the sub-subcontract jobs. A firm which approached Global ID Solutions was asked to pay ₹ 5 Lakhs. This firm then complained to UIDAI. Mr. Stalin, an official of UIDAI at Bengaluru filed a complaint with the High Grounds Police Station. The police raided the firm and seized incriminating documents of fraud using UIDAI letter head and issuing the Sham ID numbers to many people. Even so, the original EA which subcontracted the work to Global ID remains an EA. Nothing is known about the results of the police investigations. This is true of all such enrollment frauds.

---

[8] EA name search of UIDAI website – Screen shot

'HEADLINES TODAY' TV AND COBRA POST STING OPERATIONS

Sting operations by 'Headlines Today' TV and Cobra Post have revealed numerous cases of rampant fake enrolments. UIDAI is strangely silent on all these.

In 2014, 'Headlines Today' telecast a panel discussion in which Shri Ravi Shankar Prasad participated. He said that the Sham ID/"Aadhaar" Scheme is a danger to national security and that illegal immigrants are getting the "Aadhaar number". He now has found new virtues in the Scheme! Significantly, he recently admitted in a press statement that 34,000 enrolling centers have been shut down for irregularities or defaults. In fact, what many EAs have been indulging in are criminal activities. They are known to take bribes, as revealed in the sting operations, to provide illegal immigrants and others with the Sham ID "Aadhaar" number. Common sense would suggest that it would be impossible to accurately and safely collect data – biometric and demographic – of over a billion people spread across a nation as large and diverse as India. Why anyone in his/her right sense would persist in this foolhardy exercise boggles sane minds.

LARGEST JUNK DATABASE IN THE WORLD

And this, despite an admission in Clause 4.1.1 of Annexure 'E' to the contracts of UIDAI with its BSPs[9] which says that demographic data is inaccurate. A scanned copy of the clause is in the Appendix of List of Documentary Evidence. The Clause states, *"While certain demographical information is also provided, UIDAI provides no assurance of its accuracy. Demographic information shall not be used for filtering, during de-duplication process, but this capability shall be preserved for potential implementation in later phases of the UID program."* The words show how defective the entire project is. The deceit in the constant refrain of foolproof identity, of use of the Sham ID "Aadhaar" number as KYC norm is shocking. The word, *"also"* in the Clause is proof of the casual approach to collection of demographic data. It is as if this were an incidental, insignificant activity. It demonstrates the ignorance of both the capability of Information Technology as well as biometric science. "Garbage in – garbage out" is basic to IT systems. If data cannot be gathered accurately and input without corruption, IT systems are worthless.

The marketing gimmick of the brand name, "Aadhaar" has befuddled not only the gullible and those not acquainted with biometrics, but also the higher echelons

---

[9] Scanned copy of Clause 4.1.1 of Annexure 'E' to the contracts of UIDAI with its BSPs

of society, into imagining that a sophisticated technological breakthrough has been achieved in setting up the giant database, which in reality, contains garbled data that cannot be put to any use.

Like the proverbial crow strutting with borrowed peacock feathers, UIDAI shamelessly carries on the façade of having set up the most sophisticated biometric database in the world. UIDAI does not have biometric technology. It uses licensed foreign software and hardware. As will be shown later, UIDAI cannot even use the licensed technology. The licensor has given UIDAI a "Black box". The Black box is under the control of the Biometric Solution Providers – foreign contractors of UIDAI. The phrase, "black box" is not mine but, is in UIDAI's contracts. UIDAI merely sends biometric and demographic data to the black box, which sends back the result of de-duplication. The claim that UIDAI has set up the largest database of its kind in the world is silly, but it is enough to fool even the judiciary. One Supreme Court justice observed in a case, (I think it is in the case of linking the Sham ID "Aadhaar" to PAN), "It is a sophisticated database" or words to such effect. There were earlier observations by Supreme Court justices, for example, in a case where the question was regarding wastage of food grains. When told about the difficulties in distributing to the poor, the judge remarked, "Why don't you use 'Aadhaar'?" In yet another case, the one on school scholarships scam in Kerala, the judge asked the state government to use 'Aadhaar'.

The marketing fraud using the brand name employs various labels. Thus, UIDAI officials talk of "Aadhaar" enabled, leveraging "Aadhaar", "Aadhaar" linked and so on. It is as if "Aadhaar" is something that can enable many things or that it can be used to advantage in many situations. No one cares to ask, "What is 'Aadhaar'?" So, the pantomime can go on. The three-judge bench hearing the case before reference to a five-judge bench, had allowed the use of the Sham ID "Aadhaar" for two welfare schemes, namely, PDS and LPG subsidy. The bench sent the case to a five-judge bench to determine whether the issue of privacy should be referred to a larger bench. After the reference was made to the larger bench, UIDAI approached the five-judge bench to allow the government to use it for more schemes. UIDAI played a trick on the five-judge bench. As said earlier, the Court is of the view that some sophisticated technology is used for preventing corruption. The duplicity is in appearing to be using biometrics, which is supposedly foolproof. When UIDAI approached the Court for using "it," UIDAI made it look as if biometrics was being used in both PDS and LPG, whereas biometrics was never used in LPG for point-of-delivery authentication.

The phrase, "use it" refers to using 'Aadhaar', and by this is meant the allegedly foolproof technology that eliminates corruption. This is the make-believe world UIDAI has created using the brand name. However, the idea of point-of-delivery authentication was given up after the pilot trials at Mysore and Tumkur. The trials showed that point-of-delivery authentication just cannot work. The Court was not told of this fact. In PDS, the state governments which attempted to use point-of-delivery authentication at ration shops were yet to experience the impossibility using of it. The presiding judge, the then CJI, asked the petitioner counsels, "If it can be used for two schemes, why not for four more or even more?" The simple answer/counter could have been, "Biometrics is not being used, since it does not work. UIDAI is using biometrics only for issuing numbers to people and claiming that these numbers are unique because biometrics uniquely identifies persons, which is not true." The petitioners' counsels could also have used the opportunity to alert the Court to the fact of the data being given to foreign firms. Unfortunately, the petitioners' counsels did not do so. The result was that the Court granted the government permission to "use it" ("it" means – Sham ID "Aadhaar") in a few more schemes. This was not a sanction to make it compulsory. Yet, not only did the government proceed to mandate linking of the Sham ID "Aadhaar" in those areas where it had sought the Court's permission for use, but it proceeded to extend the compulsion to many other areas. The compulsory linking of the Sham ID "Aadhaar" to file income tax returns, PAN and mobile phone numbers are examples of government going beyond the brief it had asked for.

The discussion which I shall take up later on biometrics will make it clearer as to why biometric identification is fallible for uses and areas where the present Indian government is attempting to employ it, and hence, it is a misapplication of technology. This is not a sophisticated marvel of technology as courts and public (barring exceptions) have come to believe, but sheer ignorance on the part of some and stupidity on the part of others, compounded by the dishonesty of yet others. It is inconceivable that the persons driving the project are not aware of the pitfalls of biometric identification for such large and diverse populations, as that of India. In fact, being aware of the limitations, UIDAI set up a Unique Biometric Competency Center. Nothing is known of the Center now. RTI queries are returned quoting Clause 7 of the Aadhaar (Data Security) Regulations.

The only claim to sophistication UIDAI may assert is the sophistry it uses to hide the truth from the courts and public. The case wherein UIDAI came before the Apex Court in an SLP against the order of a court in Goa which had ordered

UIDAI to grant access to its biometric database to the CBI for investigating a criminal case, is typical of its chicanery. In its SLP (Crl.) 2524/2014, UIDAI argued that biometric data is confidential and granting access to CBI would violate privacy rights of people. UIDAI has no qualms about giving access to foreign firms while simultaneously denying the privilege to the premier investigating agency of the government. The contractual grant of access to all data to foreign firms is described below. I have brought this to the notice of all major media channels, including TV Channel editors, like Mr. Arnab Goswami, who wears his patriotism on his sleeve. I have given them the documentary evidence of the contracts, yet not one has raised the issue at all, let alone, with any seriousness.

ACCESS TO ALL DATA PROVIDED TO FOREIGN PRIVATE COMPANIES

As the reader may have noticed, there was (and even now exists) a deliberate attempt to hide UIDAI's contracts, especially with Biometric Solution Providers (BSPs). UIDAI played a fraud on the CIC and me, by pretending to deliver copies of the contracts, but while doing so, surreptitiously withholding crucial appendices to the contracts. This has been described above as well as the fact that the matter is now before the Delhi High Court.

Unfortunately for UIDAI, even the portion of the contract which was given to me contains information that exposes the fraud UIDAI is playing on the people of this country. People have been repeatedly assured that the data is safe, only "yes/no" answers are provided and so on. Clauses 15.1 and 15.3 of Annexure 'A' of contract between UIDAI & L 1 Identity Solutions Operating Company Pvt. Ltd. read thus: Clause 15.1 – "By virtue of this contract M/s. L 1 Identity Solutions Operating Company Pvt. Ltd., the team of M/s. L 1 Identity Solutions Operating Company Pvt. Ltd. may have access to personal information of the Purchaser (UIDAI) and/or a third party or any resident of India, any other person covered within ambit of any legislation as may be applicable."

Clause 15.3 – "The data shall be retained by M/s. L 1 Identity Solutions Operating Company not more than a period of 7 years as per Retention Policy of Government of India or any other policy UIDAI may adopt in future."[10]

---

[10] Scanned copy of Clause 15.1 and 15.3 of Annexure 'A' of Contract between UIDAI and M/s. L 1 Identity Solutions Operating Compay Pvt. Ltd. is in the Appendix.

So, Clause 15.1 gives the foreign firm access to all data of all residents. Clause 15.1 is interesting in that UIDAI seems to imagine that it has the authority to adopt policies different from the Government of India! "Imagining India" is here taken to new levels, not even mentioned in the book by that name.

Not content to permit foreign firms to have access to all our data, UIDAI in the Contract goes on to ensure that they are allowed much more than mere access. Clause 3.1 of Annexure 'B' of the contract between UIDAI and L 1 Identity Solutions Operating Company Pvt. Ltd. is a case in point. The Clause reads thus: "In the course of the Agreement, the Biometric Solution Provider may *collect, use, transfer, store, or otherwise process (collectively, "process") information that pertains to specific individuals and can be linked to them ("personal data").* Biometric Solution Provider warrants that it shall process all personal data in accordance with *applicable law and regulation.* (Emphasis mine). Biometric Solution Provider further warrants that it shall process such personal information only for the purposes of this Agreement, and shall not use or disclose such information, otherwise pursuant to purposes of the Agreement."[11]

Several questions arise here. Read with Clauses 15.1 and 15.3 of Annexure 'A' of the contract between UIDAI and L1 ID Solutions, what was the necessity for Clause 3.1 of Annexure 'B' of the contract? Clause 3.1 allows the foreign firm to do anything it wants with the data. It allows the firm to collect. Collect what? Data? From where? India? The foreign firm does not need a contract with UIDAI to collect data from other countries, does it? Have the foreign firms, BSP Contractors of UIDAI, been collecting data in India? What data and whose data have they been collecting? How have they been collecting the data? What are the data sources to which they have access? Who gave them access to these sources? For what will they use the data? For purposes of the Agreement? The "purposes of the Agreement" could be construed as for providing "Biometric Matching Services". This is mentioned on page 8 of Annexure 'A'. The purposes are elaborated in Annexure 'E'. If the clause were only for Biometric Matching Services, then what are they allowed to use it for? Why is this clause needed at all, since the Contract would enable them to do all that is required to match biometrics? Where are they to transfer the data to? How would UIDAI know if the data is put to use by these foreign firms for any other purpose? The qualifying

---

[11] Scanned copy of Clause 3.1 of Annexure 'B' of Contract between UIDAI and M/s. L 1 Identity Solutions Operating Company Pvt. Ltd. is in the Appendix.

phrase, "applicable law and regulation" does not specify the country whose laws and regulations are applicable. After all, these are foreign firms subject to laws of their own countries, even if UIDAI tried to hide the countries to which they belong. The US Patriot Act enjoins these firms to provide the intelligence agencies of USA access to information the agencies require. The clause allows the foreign vendors to store the data. The other clause, 15.3 states that they are to store the data for 7 years. Are we to assume, if one were to go by repeated assurances of UIDAI and various government spokespersons, even ministers, that data is not shared, that the firms who store the data would not look at it? Clause 3.1 also allows the BSP Contractors to process and link the data to specific individuals. Who are these "specific individuals?" Who chooses the "specific individuals" for so linking data?

While all this would show that the data is systematically given to foreign firms for unrestricted use, UIDAI has been lying to the people of this Nation whose personal data it has collected, that the data is safe and not shared with anyone. The questions here are, "Does the action of giving all the data to foreign firms constitute a crime under Indian law? And if so, what provisions of the IPC have been transgressed?" Has the Government any right, if so under what law or provision of the Constitution, to collect data of the people of the country and hand over the same to foreign entities?

The CEO of UIDAI was asked by a journalist of the "Times of India" about these clauses. He gave the incredible reply, "Contract clauses are not always exercised"! This is reported in the 'Times of India' Bengaluru edition of 01 Sep 2017.[12]

One wonders at the cavalier reply from a person who is the custodian of the entire biometric and demographic data of the country. Does he take all Indians to be fools to buy his bluff? Who decided to incorporate these clauses? Who decided not to implement them? When and why was that the decision not to do so, taken?

The deception continues into the Targeted Deliveries Act. The Act has as its objectives, "Good governance, efficient and transparent delivery of subsidies, benefits and services." Yet, UIDAI and every facet of it have been taken out of the ambit of RTI by Clause 7 of the Aadhaar (Data Security) Regulations. Clause 7 reads, "All procedures, orders, processes, standards and protocols related to security, which are designated as confidential by the Authority, shall be treated as

---

[12] 'Times of India' news report quoting CEO of UIDAI, Shri. Ajay Bhushan Pandey.

confidential by all its personnel and shall be disclosed to concerned parties only to the extent required for giving effect to the security measures. The nature of information that cannot be shared outside the Authority unless mandated under the Act includes, but not limited to, Information in CIDR, Technology details, Network Architecture, Information security policy and processes, software codes, internal reports, audit and assessment reports, applications details, asset details, contractual agreements, present and future planned infrastructure details, protection services and capabilities of the system." The system is to be totally opaque to the people of India.

Is it not ironical that an authority of the country, set up under an Act of Parliament (which should reflect the will of the people), collects all people's data and hands it over to foreign firms, while laying down regulations to prevent any information at all about the process from being accessed by the very people it is supposedly serving? And this, while claiming the objective is transparency?

The irony is also in the contract with BSPs. Clause 3.1 of Annexure 'B' of the contract between UIDAI and L 1 Identity Solutions Operating Company Pvt. Ltd. which provides for access and use of all data by foreign firms, has the paragraph title, "Privacy of Data".

UIDAI seems to have had misgivings about the access clauses of 15.1 to 15.3 of Annexure 'A' and 3.1 of Annexure 'B' of its contracts. An escape clause appears to have been incorporated in the contract in Clause 4 of Annexure 'E', which deals with Automated Biometric Identification Subsystem (ABIS). This is the heart of the Sham ID "Aadhaar" Scheme. It is where the foreign private companies de-duplicate "biometric templates".[13] These templates of persons who enrol are stored by the BSP companies for de-duplication. When another person enrolls, the process is repeated, and that person's template is also sent to the BSP. The ABIS of the BSP then compares the two templates and responds to accept the second enrollment as a new one or rejects it as a duplicate of the first person.

A precaution to avoid the BSP from knowing whose biometrics it is examining appears to have been incorporated in the contract. This is baffling, since the earlier clauses provided for not only access but also allow all kinds of use of the data. However, an elaborate process is prescribed in Clause 4.1.1 of Annexure

---

[13] The jargon needs little explanation. When you put your fingerprints on a biometric scanner, it records an image of your fingerprints. Fingerprints are curves which have ridges (high points) and valleys (depressions). Eight to twelve points on these curves are taken and converted by patented algorithm of biometric technology companies into a digital binary string of zeros and ones.

'E' of the contracts. It says that "Each de-duplication request will contain an indexing number (Reference ID) in addition to the multi-modal biometric and demographic data." A footnote adds, "ABIS will not be aware of the UID #, nor will it be aware of UID # maps to reference ID." If the intention were to prevent the foreign private companies from knowing the person whose biometric data is being sent, it does not make sense to give them demographic data. Hence, the mystery remains.

Here is a picture of an illustration explaining how the biometric image is converted to a digital template. It is obtained through Yahoo search.

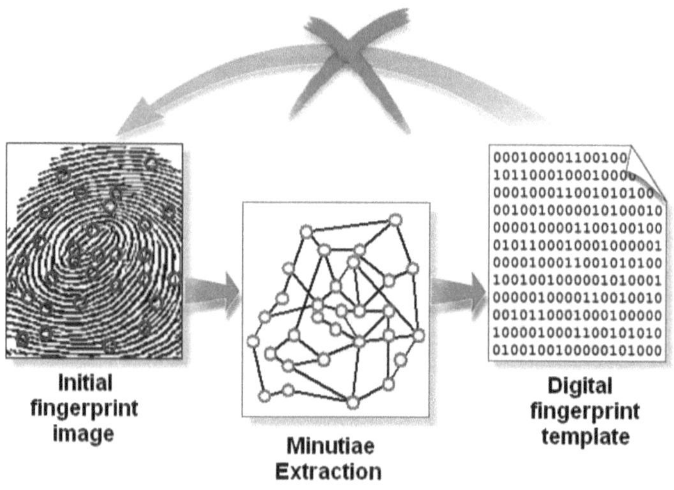

Fig 9: Biometric Template - Explained

Another intriguing and unnoticed feature of the Sham ID "Aadhaar" is that there is a Pakistan connection to the story. We in India seem to be following Pakistan in the game. Pakistan started an identical program well before India fell into it (the trap – set by whom?). They called it NADRA (National Database Registration Authority). Pakistan was trapped first. After all, it's long been a vassal state of Uncle Sam. We have or are just about to become one. So, Pakistan launched NADRA in 2008 or so, a year before we did. In 2009, the Pak chief of NADRA received the ID World International Congress Award at the event in Milan, Italy. The very next year, 2010, Nilekani, UIDAI boss, was given the award. He did not go to Italy, but his private secretary received it on his behalf. The hesitation is palpable, and so are the reasons for it. There is a proverb in Malayalam. It goes thus, "On the head of the chicken thief, the feathers will be." It is very appropriate to the context of Nilekani's dithering and the discomfort he would have felt in participating in the ID Congress and accepting the award.

I had saved the URL links to the news reports of ID World awards.

This is the copy of the saved page.

Tariq Malik, Deputy Chairman NADRA receives ID Outstanding Achievement Award 2009

www.**nadra**.gov.pk

ID

NADRA

NN

ID-World-award

NADRA website -

ID World International Congress 2009: Dated 3rd November, 2009

The international biometrics lobby has now taken the pages out of their website. UIDAI too does the same. UIDAI is proud of its achievement in Guinness Book of World records, but fights shy of the ID-World-award. Why? The AG mentioned the Guinness Book achievement in his arguments in the SC

ID World has also taken out the story of Nilekani's award at Milan in 2010, a year after Pakistan's Malik got it. However, the news of the award to him is in another website, 'Toxic Watch'. The URL to the news is in the appendix.[14] Nilekani's private secretary spoke at the Congress.

UIDAI is closely following NADRA. Thus, NADRA was faster on the draw in linking its biometrics and data with both bank accounts and mobile phones. The news about these is also available in a website called 'Planet Biometrics'. NADRA linked biometrics to bank accounts in 2014 and to mobiles in 2015. The links to these too are in Appendix.[15]

---

[14] Why Nilekani gave contacts to Safran Group & took awards from it | ToxicsWatch Allian http://www. toxicswatch.org/2013/09/why-nilekani-gave-contacts-to-safran.html

[15] Pakistan turns to biometrics for banking

<http://www.planetbiometrics.com/article-details/i/2409/>

Pakistan completes biometric re-verification of 72 million SIMs

<http://www.planetbiometrics.com/article-details/i/2752/>

Delusional Ignis Fatuus of UIDAI's Hope in Biometrics and Information Technology

The Merriam-Webster dictionary gives two meanings to the phrase, "ignis fatuus":

1. a light that sometimes appears in the night over marshy ground and is often attributable to the combustion of gas from decomposed organic matter
2. a deceptive goal or hope

For our purpose, the second meaning is relevant, since the Sham ID "Aadhaar" is not a light over marshy ground. It's not light at all. It is as dark and opaque as a black hole. Everything about it is shrouded in secrecy and double talk. Ironically, its proponents are never tired of shouting from the roof tops that it stands for transparency. For example, no one knows why the BJP which so vociferously opposed it for 5 years, suddenly found unknown virtues in it after April 2014 – the moment it became the ruling party. The PM, Mr. Modi, had personally campaigned against it during the 2014 elections.[16] He said that it is corruption and a danger to the nation. He said that he, as CM of Gujarat, had written to the then prime minister, Mr. Manmohan Singh. He has not told the nation why he changed his mind/stance. In this, he is totally unlike his counterpart in Britain, Cameron, who too campaigned against its equivalent in that country during the 2009 elections, and scrapped U.K.'s National ID Card Act as his first action upon forming the government in Jun 2009. Nothing can so starkly demonstrate the difference between honesty in politics than this. Here, when asked about certain electoral promises, the chief of the party laughed it off as, "*Chunauvi Joomla*" (meaning a spin or charade). There is not even an understanding that telling lies to the electorate is unethical. Here, it is smartness to deceive the electorate. People are fools to believe that political promises would be fulfilled.

---

[16] The link to the video of Modi's election speech at Bangalore in 2014 is in the appendix.

A charitable explanation could be that the PM fell prey to the "Extraordinary Indian Delusion" regarding the magical properties of biometric identification and of assigning numbers to each and every person and putting them all into a database. It is said that the one identified as the author of the scheme met him for a few minutes and he (the PM) was convinced. Strangely, the PM campaigned against this person. Twenty minutes or so is all it takes for the holder of the highest office in the country to change his view on a policy that affects the entire population. It is as cavalier as cavalier can be.

Even judges of the Supreme Court have been taken in by the lie and propaganda. Some judges have observed, while hearing petitions on distribution of food and pilferages, "Why don't you *use* 'Aadhaar'?" As if "using" 'Aadhaar', whatever that means, will prevent theft.

Later, I will have a lot to say on the deception in the pretension of "using" 'Aadhaar'.

The Sham ID "Aadhaar" Scheme is anchored in the false, unscientific belief that biometric identification is foolproof.

Section 5 of The Targeted Delivery Act [The Aadhaar (Targeted Delivery of Financial and other Subsidies Benefits and Services) Act, 2016] states,

"Special measures for issuance of Aadhaar number to certain categories of persons

The Authority shall take special measures to issue Aadhaar number to women, children, senior citizens and persons with disability, unskilled and unorganized workers, and nomadic tribes or to such other categories of individuals as may be specified by regulations."

The population in the categories mentioned would easily amount to over 80% of the country's population! Why does the overwhelming majority of the population require special measures? Evidently biometric recognition has serious difficulties among these categories. This is an admission of the awareness within the government that it is impossible to use biometric identification for large sections of people in this country. Then, why is the government bent upon wasting public funds and persisting in this exercise in futility? The compulsion comes from outside, perhaps?

These facts were known long ago even when the project started in 2010. So, UIDAI cannot plead ignorance. Knowing the difficulties, UIDAI even set up Unique Biometric Competency Center (UBCC). However, that too, like everything else has fallen into the black hole of UIDAI. It has been taken off the UIDAI website.

Let me quote an article which appeared in the Technology section of 'The Economist' on 1 Oct 2010. It is titled, "The Difference Engine: Dubious Security". One could find it in the Technology section of the journal with the heading, "Babbage" and sub-heading, "Biometrics". It explains the origins of the delusion.

It begins with the following statements.

"THANKS to gangster movies, cop shows and spy thrillers, people have come to think of fingerprints and other biometric means of identifying evildoers as being completely foolproof. In reality, they are not and never have been, and few engineers who design such screening tools have ever claimed them to be so. Yet the myth has persisted among the public at large and officialdom in particular. In the process, it has led—especially since the terrorist attacks of September 11th 2001—to a great deal of public money being squandered and, worse, to the fostering of a sense of security that is largely misplaced."

Obviously, many decision-makers in India have been taken in by beguiling imagery of these concocted pieces of fictional entertainment. It is somewhat comforting to know that other nations too fall prey to such erroneous ideas.

The idea that biometric identification provides uniqueness of identity is a fabricated myth created by the biometric business lobbies. The scientific and mathematical proof of this truth is set out next. However, before going into such proofs to help those unfamiliar with science and mathematics understand why biometric identification does not work in large populations, here is an analogy.

Let's take the photo of one of your friends, and mix it with say, ten other photos. Then try to identify the photo of your friend. You would probably do it in about 2 or 3 minutes. Now, mix your friend's photo with a thousand other photos and repeat the exercise. It might take you 30 or 40 minutes. If your friend's photo is mixed with a million other photos, you may never find your friend's photo, especially if the bunch of mixed photos contains people resembling her/him. This exercise is one of comparing images and human decision-making. In biometric identification/de-duplication, a computer compares biometric templates (the biometric measure – fingerprints, etc. – converted to machine-readable binary strings are compared by the computer). When the computer is used to match millions of such templates, it would make errors. To compound the problem, the biometric template is not a 100% foolproof representation of the individual from whose biometric characteristics the template was generated.

Now, let's look at the scientific evidence.

REPORT NATIONAL ACADEMIES OF USA, 2010

Four National Academies of USA, The National Academy of Sciences, The National Academy of Engineering, The Institute of Medicine and The National Research Council published a joint research report in September 2010. The report titled, "Biometric Recognition: Challenges and Opportunities" may be downloaded from the Internet.[17]

The Executive Summary on page 1 of the Report has the principal conclusions. The first few of these conclusions state as follows,

> ➢ ***"Human recognition systems are inherently probabilistic, and hence inherently fallible.*** (Emphasis is mine) The chance of error can be made small but not eliminated. System designers and operators should anticipate and plan for the occurrence of errors, even if errors are expected to be infrequent."
>
> ➢ The scientific basis of biometrics – from understanding the distribution of biometric traits within given populations to how humans interact with biometric systems – needs strengthening particularly as biometric technologies and systems are deployed in systems of national importance.
>
> ➢ Biometric systems incorporate complex definitional, technological, and operational choices, which are themselves embedded in large technological and social contexts. Thus system-level considerations are critical to the success of biometric systems. Analyses of biometric systems performance, effectiveness, trustworthiness, and suitability should take a broad systems perspective.
>
> ➢ Biometric systems should be designed and evaluated relative to their specific intended purposes and contexts rather than generically. (Emphasis mine). Their effectiveness depends as much on the social context as it does on the underlying technology, operational environment, systems engineering and testing regimes.

---

[17] URL of the report is below
http://sites.nationalacademies.org/cs/groups/cstbsite/documents/webpage/cstb_059722.pdf

UIDAI and its main proponent never considered any of these even when they knew about them. He would not also have informed the political decision-makers about the difficulties likely in implementing the project across the population of India. What motivated him to proceed in the face of scientific evidence to the contrary would only be known if and when the project is investigated as it should be, if nothing else, for the dangers it poses to national security, criminal assault on the poor who are denied food and mendacious wastage of public money.

Biometric systems, as the research reveals, may be used only for specific purposes and contexts, and they are to be evaluated relative to these. They cannot be implemented generically across large, diverse populations for all and sundry purposes. Ignoring this basic principle, the borrowed biometric technology is sought to be deployed for the entire population of India for all government activities and even applied for private commercial purposes. How silly can one get?

The Report adds, "There are numerous sources of uncertainty and variation in biometric systems, including the following:

> **Variation within persons**. *Biometric characteristics and information captured by biometric systems may be affected by changes in age, environment, disease, stress, occupational factors, training and prompting, intentional alterations, sociocultural aspects of the situation in which the presentation occurs*, changes in human interface with the systems and so on.

> **Sensors.** Sensors age and calibration —— play a role. (Imagine the difficulty, nay, impossibility, of maintenance and calibration of millions of scanners when the system is ubiquitous and used by every service provider and private entity).

> **Feature extraction and matching algorithms.** Biometric characteristics cannot be directly compared but require stable and distinctive "features" to first to be extracted from sensor outputs. Differences in feature extraction algorithms affect performance, with effects sometimes aggravated by requirements for achieving interoperability among proprietary systems. Differences between matching algorithms and comparison scoring mechanisms and how these interact with preceding sources of variability of information acquired and features extracted, also contribute to variation in performance of different systems.

> **Data integrity.** *Information may de degraded* through legitimate data manipulation or transformation or degraded and/*or corrupted owing to security breaches, mismanagement,* inappropriate compression or some other means. *It may also be inappropriately applied to a context other than the one for which it was originally created, owing to mission creep* (for example using data collected in a domain purely for the sake of convenience in a domain that demands high data integrity) or inappropriate re-use of information (for instance, captured biometric information might be incorrectly assumed to be of greater fidelity when transferred to a system where higher fidelity is the norm).

In the Sham ID "Aadhaar" Scheme the above aspects of uncertainty and variation in biometric systems have been completely ignored. This could be due to either genuine ignorance of the capabilities of the technology and requirements of the system, or a deliberate attempt to rush headlong despite the knowledge that it will lead to severe problems. The latter seems be more probable, although this could also be due to foolhardiness caused by ignorance.

From the pilot trials conducted halfway through the project, the factum of effect of age, environment, disease, stress and occupational factors have come to be known. There is an acknowledgement of this truth as evidenced by the provision in Section 5 of the Aadhaar (Targeted Delivery of Financial and other Subsidies, Benefits and Services Act). Here is an acknowledged need for special measure for women, children, senior citizens, persons with disability, unskilled and unorganized workers, nomadic tribes, etc. For these people, biometric identification simply does not work, does not result in unique IDs due to the poor quality of their biometrics. UIDAI set up Unique Biometric Competency Center (UBCC). Nothing is known about it now. In fact, it has been removed from the UIDAI website. This is yet another illustration of how UIDAI refuses to accept the reality but obstinately persists in stupidity.

The other aspect is the complete failure to understand the adverse effects of mission creep leading to inappropriate application to many diverse areas with totally different requirements and context. The Sham ID "Aadhaar" Scheme began with the justification of providing an ID to the poor on the false assumption that lack of ID prevents them from accessing welfare benefits. UIDAI is not just guilty of mission creep but, of a mad mission rush where angels fear to tread.

The Sham ID "Aadhaar" Project was originally created for ensuring that rations are properly distributed under PDS, albeit, this too was based on the mistaken notion that there are fake ration cards. The hope was that biometrics would eliminate fake ration cards. From that context, the scheme has now been extended to over 60 other areas. It is now applied to bank accounts, income tax, pensions, provident fund, stock broking, scholarships and so forth. The unbelievable stupidity of inappropriately applying to several other contexts other than the one for which it was originally designed (assuming that some thought went into the design of the system for PDS), and the ignorance of its effect on data integrity, is inexplicable.

The US Academies Report comes to a telling conclusion. It states, "**Principle:** *Users and developers of biometric systems should recognize and take into account the limitations and constraints of biometric systems – especially the probabilistic nature of the underlying science, the current limits of knowledge regarding human individual distinctiveness, and the numerous sources of uncertainty in biometric systems.*"

MATHEMATICAL PROOF OF FALSE POSITIVE MATCHES

Dr. Hans Mathews published three mathematical papers on the False Positive Matches that would occur as more and more people are enrolled in the UIDAI database. The website of the Center for Internet and Society published some of these. An article in the Economic and Political Weekly is one of them.[18] Dr. Mathews has by mathematical probability theory proved using UIDAI's own published error rate for its biometric system, that False Positive Matches could be 1 in 100 when the last 100 million of the billion Indian population is enrolled. UIDAI's error rate is under laboratory conditions. He concludes by saying that under field conditions False Positive Matches could increase by a factor of 10. His mathematical prediction has been proved uncannily right by UIDAI's inadvertent claim, but ignorant admission, on page 171 of its counter affidavit to my petition, that 80 million fake and duplicate enrollments were detected. This was in 2015 when about 800 million people had been enrolled. That makes 1 in 10 people having False Positive Matches. How in heaven's name can such a defective system be used for finding fakes and ghosts in databases from PAN to PDS to LPG?

---

[18] "UID Summary" - https://cis-india.org/internet-governance/uid-summary-of-findings.pdf/view

THE ULTIMATE ID THEFT

In the Mar 7, 2008 edition of 'Times Online' LSE Professor, Ian Angell wrote an article titled, "ID cards are the ultimate identity theft." It had the subtitle, "Computer systems always fail - and the national database will do so big time." Both the title and the subtitle would equally apply to our Sham ID "Aadhaar" Project. Prof. Angell was Professor of Information Systems in the Department of Management of the London School of Economics (LSE). He is now Professor Emeritus. He, as well as LSE, ran an objective campaign which had active civil society also separately, perhaps, campaigning, against the U.K. National ID Card Act. The campaign succeeded and the Act was scrapped in 2009. It was a major election issue. Conservatives leader, Cameron's first action on taking over the reins of office in June 2009 was to have a Bill moved to scrap it. I have mentioned above the contrast between him and Modi and between U.K. and India in political styles and ethics. When one reads his article, and examines the Sham ID "Aadhaar" Project, the ignorance of IT systems in India is revealed in all its true colours. We pride ourselves on being an IT super power. Yet, we do not seem to have basic understanding of the capabilities and limitations of IT systems. When a project is launched and managed by the leading media-created IT icon, Mr. Nilekani, the exposed ignorance is even more galling.

I must quote the professor in some detail, as there are valuable lessons for us in his article. After having said that the U.K. ID card project will fail big time, he says, "The ID project is one of the biggest computer systems envisaged - far more complex than the failing NHS system. And it's another disaster waiting to happen. Still the politicians naively claim there will be no problems: it will be totally secure because of biometrics. (Haven't our politicians and bureaucrats too made such silly claims?) Apparently iris scans, fingerprints, face-recognition software will all work perfectly, be amazingly cheap to implement - and all foolproof. It must be true, as they've been told this by those selling the technology. Baroness Anelay of St Johns, with a group of parliamentarians, was once given a demonstration of a facial recognition system. It failed; indeed the system subsequently crashed, twice. The reason? The baroness was told her face was "too bland".

Note what he says, is about a project one tenth the size of our disaster. Ours is not a disaster waiting to happen. It is one which has happened, and yet, not recognized or acknowledged.

Our politicians too, with equal naivety, claim that there will be no problems. Shri Ravi Shankar Prasad is one such example. Bureaucrats are no less stupid.

The CEO, Mr. Pandey, writes and wrote quite recently eulogising the wonders of the Sham ID "Aadhaar". The article is titled, "Getting rid of ghosts: 'Aadhaar' is a foundation for new clean India, not a surveillance state." He imagines or for other reasons wants to promote Sham ID "Aadhaar" as an anti-corruption tool.[19] He and his predecessors harp on the theme that the Sham ID "Aadhaar" is similar to US – SSN. It is not, as explained in Wikipedia. [20] In his article, Mr. Pandey states, "Similarly, in the U.K., every important service requires NIN." Would Mr. Pandey care to explain, if this were so, why did the U.K. come up with the National ID Card Act and why was it scrapped? Why did the present U.K. PM call it (the National ID Card Act) an assault on personal liberties and term it intrusive bullying. Of course, the Sham ID "Aadhaar" protagonists here have been saying that the U.K. ID Card project is different from ours. The U.K. card was for combating illegal immigration and terrorism. Our 'Aadhaar' is voluntary! As per our Act, it is an entitlement. How wonderful! Nobody can deny us the right to be tagged, fingerprinted and numbered.

Next, see what Prof. Angell warned his country's citizens about. He told them – "But the ID project will be different, we are told. According to the rhetoric, an ID card, one central point of reference, will be so much more efficient and beneficial than you having to prove your identity daily, by producing driving licences, gas bills and so on. Its proponents fail to see that if any of these documents is erroneous, then we don't use the one with, say, a mistake in the address to prove

---

[19] Article by CEO, UIDAI – "Getting rid of ghost: Aadhaar is a foundation for new clean India, not a surveillance state." The URL is <https://www.pressreader.com/india/the-times-of-india-mumbai-edition/20171111/282411284599613>

[20] https://en.wikipedia.org/wiki/Social_Security_number Social Security was originally a universal tax, but when Medicare was passed in 1965, objecting religious groups in existence prior to 1951 were allowed to opt out of the system.[15] Because of this, not every American is part of the Social Security program, and not everyone has a number. However, a social security number is required for parents to claim their children as dependents for federal income tax purposes,[12] and the Internal Revenue Service requires all corporations to obtain SSNs (or alternative identifying numbers) from their employees, as described below. The Old Order Amish have fought to prevent universal Social Security by overturning rules such as a requirement to provide a Social Security number for a hunting license.[16]

Social Security cards printed from January 1946 until January 1972 expressly stated that people should not use the number and card for identification.[17] Since nearly everyone in the United States now has an SSN, it became convenient to use it anyway and the message was removed.[18]

Since then, Social Security numbers have become de facto national identification numbers.[2] Although some people do not have an SSN assigned to them, it is becoming increasingly difficult to engage in legitimate financial activities such as applying for a loan or a bank account without one.[19] While the government cannot require an individual to disclose their SSN without a legal basis, companies may refuse to provide service to an individual who does not provide an SSN.[20][21] The card on which an SSN is issued is still not suitable for primary identification as it has no photograph, no physical description and no birth date. All it does is confirm that a particular number has been issued to a particular name. Instead, a driver's license or state ID card is used as identification for adults.

our identity. With the ID card, we won't have the choice. Even if the card is not compulsory, all financial systems will converge on it, and anyone without a card faces great cost and inconvenience."

Are we not being told the same things over and over and over – "more efficient" (this is stated as the objective of our Act), "You don't have to prove your ID daily." "It is a portable ID. A person can draw BPL rations from any shop." And have all systems converged on it here, as Prof. Angell predicted would happen in his country had the U.K. ID card been implemented? Of course, we will be told that our IT stalwarts are superior to the guys in U.K. We are the IT Super Power. What our experts would fail to mention is that the Iris Biometric algorithm UIDAI's vendors use, was developed and patented by a Cambridge professor.

Another bit of information the torch-bearers of the Sham ID "Aadhaar" Project would never mention is the LSE research report on the U.K. ID Cards Project. They would, as Mr. Nilekani did, dismiss the U.K. project as different. It is worth looking at how U.K. went about the ID card project, and compare it with what our architects did. The difference is the gap between maturity and knowledge on one side and immaturity and ignorance on the other. For example, the U.K. study was done over a 6-month period guided by a steering committee of 14 professors. Extensive consultations were done with over 100 industry representatives, experts and researchers in U.K. and around the world. The study was commenced as soon as the Bill was announced. According to David Moss who has extensively studied our Sham ID Scheme, *"First UIDAI assumed that today's mass consumer biometrics technology is reliable enough to deliver unique identification and adequate verification. They made all their plans accordingly. They hired staff. They contracted with registrars and enrolment agencies and introducers and authenticators (as per the UIDAI Model). They paraded the most senior politicians in the land to give the project their backing. They briefed the press and they ran a nationwide publicity campaign. Global, even. All the while, they were making promises, raising expectations, committing themselves. A lot of hope, wishful thinking, the best of intentions, sackloads of public money, and the benefits would be monumental. Then, and only then, they conducted a trial to test the feasibility of Aadhaar. That's the wrong way round."*

UIDAI put the cart before the horse.

Moss continues, "How reliable are the biometrics Aadhaar depends on?"

"Earlier reviews of the chaotic mass consumer biometrics market suggest that UIDAI have taken on an impossible task."

"But now UIDAI have conducted their own, up-to-date, proof of concept trial and, in the *Conclusion* section of their report, they say: *"The biometric accuracy levels necessary for de-duplication of all residents of India are achievable."* This follows the claim in the *Results* section of the report that *"we can be confident that biometric matching can be used on a wider scale to realize the goal of creating unique identities."* (Emphasis in original.)

"In fact, those conclusions do not follow from the evidence reported. Nothing in UIDAI's surprisingly low quality report suggests that it would be feasible to prove that each electronic identity on the CIDR is unique. Not with a billion+ people on the database. Far from it, **India can be confident, from the figures quoted in UIDAI's proof of concept trial report, that de-duplication could never be achieved."** (Emphasis mine.)

How do UIDAI and Moss come to diametrically opposite conclusions? Wishful thinking on the part of UIDAI?

Moss has used UIDAI's error rates to do simple school level arithmetic, unlike Dr. Hans Mathews who got his results from sophisticated probability theory (which too, for an ordinary mathematician should not be difficult).

David Moss talks in his paper on the "Sea of false positives" – that is, one person's biometrics being mistaken by the computer's automatic system to be that of another.

Here is how he calculated that it would be impossible for UIDAI to de-duplicate. **"The sea of false positives"** "It just takes a simple two-step argument to prove the point. Nowhere does the maths involved rise above schoolboy level.

Step 1 – Uniqueness

UIDAI must create one electronic identity on the CIDR corresponding to each real person in India. Each electronic identity will include a copy of the person's fingerprints and irisprints. If UIDAI are to prove that each electronic identity is unique, then each set of biometrics must be compared to, and shown to be different from, every other set of biometrics.

UIDAI know that. As they say in the *Results* section: *"the matching analysis was done on two sets of 20,000 biometrics, for a total of 40,000. However, the number of comparisons was several orders of magnitude more than 40,000, since each set of fingerprints would be matched against every other set of fingerprints in the data set."*

How many unique pairs of biometrics can be chosen from 40,000? Answer: 40,000 x 39,999/2 = 799,980,000. UIDAI are right. 40,000 is a number of the order of 10^4, whereas the number of comparisons which have to be made to prove uniqueness is of the order of 10^8.

The population of India is of course not 40,000. More like 1.2 billion or 1.2×10^9. So that the number of comparisons between pairs of biometrics that would need to be made to prove uniqueness is 7.2×10^{17}.

Step 2 – False Positives

It would take a very long time, but, in a perfect world, those 7.2×10^{17} comparisons could be performed by computer and it could be proved automatically that there are no duplicates, i.e. each electronic identity is unique.

In the real world, problems arise. UIDAI say quite rightly that they must expect the odd false positive. In other words, on occasion, it will look as though two people have the same biometrics."

Moss states correctly. "When a false positive arises, it has to be investigated by a team of human beings. It can't be resolved by computer."

"How many false positives should India expect? In the *Results* section of their report, UIDAI define FPIR, the false positive identification rate, and they say *"we will look at the point where the FPIR (i.e. the possibility that a person is mistaken to be a different person) is 0.0025%. "* At that point, UIDAI would get 2½ false positives on average for every 100,000 comparisons.

Given that UIDAI have to make 7.2×10^{17} comparisons, how many false positives should they expect? Answer: $(7.2 \times 10^{17}) \times (2.5 \times 10^{-5}) = 1.8 \times 10^{13}$. That's 18,000,000,000,000 false positives for people to investigate and resolve.

It's just not going to happen, is it? India has got better things to do with its time than to clean up the mess left behind by today's unreliable mass consumer biometrics.

And that's the end of the argument."

Bismarck said, "Fools learn by experience. I prefer to learn from other's experience." Some of those pushing and praising the Sham ID "Aadhaar" Project are doing so out of ignorance. If so, they are to be pitied. Or they are fools who refuse to learn from their own experience. As mentioned earlier, by its admission in the counter affidavit, UIDAI noted that there were 80 million False Positive Matches, which it mistakenly bragged as detection of duplicates. If its claim of finding duplicates were accepted, it would mean that every one of the 80 million people enrolled twice.

Moss concludes, "*The proper conclusion from UIDAI's proof of concept trial seems to be that the concept is not proven, the system design is a failure, its hypothesis is wrong, unique identification is not achievable. Ask any 16 year-old studying science (any logical 16 year-old, come to think of it, not just science students), that should be the signal to halt Aadhaar and think again.*"

LONDON SCHOOL OF ECONOMICS: RESEARCH ONLINE PRESS RELEASE 27 JUNE 2005

Thus far we have seen quite a few proofs that the Sham ID "Aadhaar" does not provide unique IDs. That's why I chose to call it "Sham ID" and always add the prefix, "Sham ID" – for indeed that is exactly what it is. The brand-name masquerade may fool all the people some of the time, some people all the time, but it can never fool all the people all the time.

LSE published its research in 2005. Surely, before lobbying for biometric IDs and launching the Sham ID "Aadhaar" Project, Nilekani and anyone who gave him the idea should have done some study. If so, how did they miss the LSE research? Could the biometric ID scheme have been his idea? Certainly not, since, he could not have known anything about biometrics.

The LSE research study was conducted over a six-month period. Fourteen (14) professors guided the research. Extensive consultations were held with nearly 100 industry representative, experts and researchers from The U.K. and across the world. The Department of Information systems of LSE coordinated the research project. The LSE research report concludes highlighting 6 areas of concern. These are:

Multiple purposes – The report states, "Evidence for other national identity systems shows that the systems perform best when established for clear and focused purposes." [Contrast this with our omnibus Sham ID/"Aadhaar" Project, which is applied across the board to any and all purposes. There are 63 applications as of now. Not content with this mad mission rush into several areas, for reasons unknown, UIDAI has even gone about inviting private players to develop applications on what is termed 'Aadhaar' platform. There are no limits to stupidity. As a wisecrack put it, there are two things which are infinite, God and human stupidity.]

Will the technology work – On this, the report concludes, "No scheme on this scale has been undertaken anywhere in the world. Smaller and less ambitious schemes have encountered substantial technological and operational problems that are likely to be amplified in large-scale national systems. The use of biometrics creates particular concerns because this technology has never been used at such a large scale."

Is it legal – The report says, "In its current form, the Identity Cards Bill appears to be unsafe in law. (The validity of our Targeted Deliveries Act is under question at the time of this writing. Its legality is seriously in doubt.) A number of elements potentially compromise Article 8 (Privacy) and Article 14 (discrimination) of the European convention on human rights." [The European convention is drawn from the Universal Declaration of Human Rights, to which India is a signatory. The Sham ID "Aadhaar" Scheme as well as the Targeted Deliveries Act is in violation of most of the 30 Articles of the Universal Declaration of Human Rights (UDHR).]

Security – LSE Report states, "The National Data Registry will create a very large pool of data in one place that could be an enhanced risk in case of unauthorized accesses, hacking or malfunction." [Already there are reports of large-scale data leaks and endemic malfunction. Data of 130 million people were unintentionally put in public domain. For this, the NGO which brought the leak to public notice was harassed and threatened with dire consequences. Quite a few other leaks have also been reported. Authentication failures have resulted in starvation deaths and denial of food to the poor.]

Citizens' acceptance – LSE concludes, "An identity system that is well accepted by citizens is likely to be far more successful than one which is controversial and raises privacy concerns." [The government has been ambivalent on privacy rights. The matter was referred to a bench of 9 justices in 2015. It took two years for the bench to give its orders. It concluded that privacy is a fundamental right under the Indian Constitution. Meanwhile, taking advantage of the delay, the government rushed the Targeted Delivery Act through one house of Parliament, the lower one. Also, in the interregnum, the government coerced and frightened millions of people to enroll in the Sham ID "Aadhaar" Scheme.]

Will the ID cards benefit business? – LSE holds, "Compliance with the terms of the ID Cards Bill will mean even small firms will have to pay £ 250 for smart card readers and other requirements will add to the administrative burdens firms face." [Indian businesses, large ones, hope to gain a bonanza. These include mobile phone service providers, IT firms, authentication agencies and so on. Small firms like ration shops will find it impossible to continue business.]

The LSE report then raises ten key concerns all of which are applicable to our Sham ID "Aadhaar" Scheme in greater measure.

I have dealt at length with the ignorance and foolhardiness with which UIDAI, and to an extent, the government, taken in by biometric business lobbies or by their own wishful thinking, have been rushing with the Sham ID "Aadhaar" Project. Let me close this with an observation. UIDAI, as well as some equally ignorant high persona, have publicly echoed the claim that the world's largest and most sophisticated database of its kind has been set up by it.

The ignorance on the other element of the project, Information Technology, is equally appalling. To this let us now turn our attention.

IGNORANCE OF INFORMATION TECHNOLOGY (IT) AND ITS IMPACT

Many in India like to proudly claim that we are an IT superpower. A few years ago, I remember reading a news report of someone in USA calling our IT businesses as "Chop shops." There is an element of truth in it, much as it may hurt our national pride. And we dislike such uncomfortable truths, more so in the post truth world of today, where feelings and emotions take over the ability to reason.

I have often wondered why our "IT giants" have not come up with anything like Facebook, Oracle, Adobe, Twitter, Google, Microsoft, Apple or Linux. We have not even produced an email client. In the hardware world of IT, we have nothing to show. Wipro existed in the hardware business for a time but, is no longer heard of today. The Chinese have been able to buy IBM's hardware business. Why did not any in India think of it?

It therefore does not surprise me to see the ignorance displayed by UIDAI which was headed by the media-created Indian IT icon making the basic error of ignoring the fundamentals of data input for IT systems… "Garbage in – garbage out" (GIGO), is a popular IT phrase about what happens in the industry if one is unable to collect and input accurate data.

In the case of UIDAI, the technology team seems to be ignorant of the basics of IT or have deliberately ignored it. UIDAI have not given a thought to how demographic data would be accurately collected or how misuse or theft of the data by those collecting it could be prevented. There are about 30,000 enrolment centers. Initially, there were 209 Enrolling Agencies. Many of these indulged in fraud, enrolling people for a price. The Government admitted that 50,000 enrolment centers were shut down. Surely, these centers would have input data of several million fake enrolments. How could such data be detected and removed? Any fool would know that it is well neigh impossible to do so, but not the fools who run this show. This was explained earlier. The UIDAI contracts with BSPs admit the fact. Yet, no one whose attention was drawn to it seems to take any serious note of it.

IDENTITY, IDENTIFICATION, ID CARDS, ID NUMBERS – AN AUTHORITY AND THE ACTS

Another significant facet of the Sham ID called "Aadhaar" Scheme, and the Act that seeks to give this the cover of legitimacy, is in the way in which they differ from initiatives in other major democracies to provide IDs to people. Two major countries attempted this. One is the USA and the other the U.K. Notice that in both these countries, they passed the law first. Both laws referred to "ID Cards". The U.K. aimed to have a national ID Card; the US, a Real ID. In India, we are not provided IDs or ID cards but, *identification numbers.* The Aadhaar Act is not one which provides IDs or ID cards, but numbers for identification of people. The Indian Act creates an *"Authority for Identification."* From Authority to authoritarianism it is but a short step. We were moving rapidly in that direction when the Supreme Court cases slowed down the process.

Then, to pretend that we too have ID cards, UIDAI encourages the use of the phrase, "Aadhaar card". UIDAI does not issue ID cards. It asks people who enroll to laminate the acknowledgement letter with the Aadhaar number and use it (as an ID card?). The acknowledgement letter has no signature and no security feature, like a hologram, for example. It can be easily cloned.

Two nations have "Authorities" for the purpose, Pakistan and India. Pakistan has the National Database Registration *Authority* (NADRA); and India, its very own, Unique Identification *Authority* of India (UIDAI).

When a person has an ID card, he/she may identify herself/himself with the ID card. Pakistan is more forthright. It talks of setting up a database. India deviously creates an "Authority" to identify people through an allegedly unique number and pretends to be providing IDs, mislabeling them as "Aadhaar cards", and creating a number of databases – a central database with UIDAI, allowing foreign firms to have databases with the same data to which they are also authorized to add information, and state databases called State Resident Data Hubs (SRDH).

The Indian Sham ID "Aadhaar" number is neither proof of citizenship nor proof of address, although, through sheer propaganda, people and organizations have been led to believe that it may be accepted for both purposes. The Act and the UIDAI website mention the fact that the Sham ID, called "Aadhaar" is not proof of citizenship; yet, government notifications and banking rules allow its use for purposes for which only citizens are eligible, for example, to open bank accounts, obtain PAN cards etc. That the Sham ID, called "Aadhaar" addresses given to UIDAI's BSP Contractors are inaccurate is admitted in UIDAI's contracts with them.

Let us now look at how the Act was dragged through the judicial processes in the country and how this enabled UIDAI to force enrolments into the scheme.

Dragging the Issue through the Courts

DENIAL OF JUSTICE BY DELAY

Everyone decries delayed justice. "Justice delayed is justice denied," is a favorite and hackneyed, clichéd quote. Yet, for those who experience it–the denial of justice through delays in the judicial process—it is very real.

That the government who is to administer justice would be a willing participant in the denial of justice and/or an active player in it, is a sickening thought.

Our Constitution begins with the lofty words, "We the people of India, having solemnly resolved to… secure to all its citizens: Justice… " The first thing we gave ourselves on that momentous night when we had our tryst with destiny has been brought to nought.

The deceit does not end with various kinds of deception planned, orchestrated and practiced by the government and UIDAI, which was described earlier. There appears to have been a systematic effort to prolong judicial scrutiny of the Sham ID "Aadhaar" Scheme. When I first realised that there was something fishy about the Sham ID "Aadhaar" Project, I thought that the best way to expose the racket was to test it in a court of law. At that time (2009) there was no law for UIDAI which was then an entity set up through an order. Some of us joined in a campaign, which would later come to be called, "Say No to UID", met in Bangalore to brainstorm on how we could tackle what then seemed to us a menace. I had started discussions with an advocate, Mr. B. T. Venkatesh. He had advised me that a civil suit could be filed under Order 1 Rule 8 Code of Civil Procedure.

Many disagreed with his advice, but I chose to go with it. The civil suit was filed on November 19, 2011. It was numbered OS 8181 of 2011. My reasoning was simple. A civil suit would give me a chance to put the protagonists of the Sham ID, called "Aadhaar" Scheme, in the witness box to cross-examine them to bring out the truth. This was not to be, as things would turn out, both due to the ignorance and gullibility of activists opposed to it and the ignorance of the people of this country as a whole, and also due to the manipulations of our opponents and complete lack of knowledge of such matters and complacency among the judicial establishment.

The first hearing was in December 2011. The respondents were UIDAI and the Union of India. Mr. Somasekhar, V. K. joined me in the plaint. The defendants did not file any written statement as required under Order VIII Rule 1 of CPC. Instead, they merely filed an IA for dismissal of the suit under Order VII Rule 11. We filed objections to their application. The court recorded the fact of the written statement not being filed and proceeded with the trial. Under the civil procedure code, failure to file written statements by respondents is to be taken by the court as admission of the facts in the complaint.

Thereafter, every month UIDAI took adjournments at each hearing.

I then filed an application for urgent hearing. At the hearing on Apr 16, 2012, the judge accepted my application. He looked round the court hall and observed, "This is a serious matter. Thousands of crores of rupees are being spent." He then pointed to the persons in the hall and said, "It affects you." He turned to his clerk and said, "It affects you." He continued, "I will have day-to-day hearings." He posted the case to May 22, 2012.

On May 22, 2012, the UIDAI counsel again sought adjournment stating the Solicitor General would like to appear. The case was adjourned to June 3, 2012.

On June 3, 2012, the advocates went on a strike. The case was postponed to July 3, 2012.

On July 3, 2012, the judge read out his order, dismissing the suit, stating that it is waste of time of the court. He proceeded to impose penalties on both complainants, my friend Somasekhar and me, of ₹ 25,000.00 on each of us.

What happened between Apr 16, 2012 when the judge ordered day-to-day hearings and July 3, 2012 when he not only dismissed the suit, but went on to impose penalties on the complainants?

NOTHING! Nothing legitimate that should normally cause such a reversal in the court occurred in the intervening period.

One is left wondering as to what could be the reason for the judge's sudden volte face. Your guess is as good as mine, but we lose faith in the judicial system when such inexplicable events happen.

Next, we—my co-petitioner and I—appealed to the Karnataka High Court. The court insisted that we deposit the penalty in the court before the appeal is heard. I am told that this is the tradition or practice. Perhaps, it came into being as a measure to prevent unscrupulous persons using the judicial process to delay justice. Yet, here is a case where justice is denied by the very process that seeks to ensure justice. Such an example of irony, shall we call it judicial irony, (like dramatic irony?), is rare.

So, we were left with no alternative but to approach the Supreme Court. Thanks to my friend and co-petitioner, Mr. Somasekhar and through his friend, Mr. Ananth Kumar, then a Member of Parliament and now minister, we were helped by BJP's legal cell. Mr. Bharat Kumar of the legal cell helped me to obtain the services of Ms. Aishwarya Bhati as my counsel. She is a wonderful person, absolutely reliable, sincere, with high standards of dedication and integrity unmatched in all professions. I am singularly lucky in having her as my counsel; and her father, Gp. Capt. Bhati (Retd.) is as fine a gentleman as one could ever see in the Defence Forces. I have an excellent relationship with the family. Jaideep, Aishwarya's husband, another fine gentleman, has become a good friend. He has left a great corporate career for taking up legal practice.

Aishwarya filed my appeal in the Supreme Court in 2013, as an impleading petition.

Later, Dr. Usha Ramanathan, another good friend and co-activist against the Sham ID, called "Aadhaar", introduced me to Mr. Gopal Subramanium. This was fortuitous. He suggested that a regular writ be filed, as otherwise, we may not get adequate time for arguments. So, my writ was filed and numbered 37 of 2015.

I had the good fortune of meeting Mr. Subramanium quite a few times. It was a pleasure. I spent many hours explaining the facts of the case. He was keen to know the technical details and had resources to check these aspects. On one such occasion, he desired to meet a technical person who had worked in UIDAI. Gopal Krishna, an anti-sham-ID activist and friend, helped me locate such a person. My memory fails me when I try to recall his name. He came readily. It was about 8.30 PM when he came to Mr. Subramanium's office. Mr. Subramanium had a number of questions for him, especially about seeding. He left after a good three hours of a very useful conversation. If he happens to read this, I hope he would get in touch with me so that I may be able to thank him.

Most of what I describe about the hearings is from memory. They may contain some errors in sequence or dates, but nothing that would materially affect the facts.

The Supreme Court bench hearing the case was headed by B. S. Chauhan, J. Jasti Chelameswar and Sharad Arvind Bobde J. Shyam Divan argued for 4 days or so. He painted a picture of surveillance and intrusion into privacy. In 2013, this bench had issued orders that the Sham ID, called "Aadhaar" should be voluntary.

During the hearing in April 2014, just before the summer vacation, Advocate Aishwarya raised the issue of my contempt petition (No. 144 of 2014) which she had filed. Chauhan, J. refused to hear the petition. I could not make any sense of his decision. He posted the case to a date after the vacation. He retired soon after and went on to become the Chairman of the Law Commission.

(Here is an aside which has little to do with the story of the Sham ID, but nonetheless is relevant as the judgement of the Supreme Court is awaited. I confess to be opinionated, as many humans are. Here is an opinion on insulating the judiciary from the executive. We have two choices. One, to make the tenure of judges of the Supreme Court lifelong… second, to let the judiciary decide on all post-retirement judicial appointments. For this, reserve certain posts, like the Chair of Human Rights Commission, as posts reserved for retired Supreme Court judges. Let a collegium of judges decide on these appointments. The executive should have no role in it; after all, the government is the biggest litigant before the court.)

Justice H. L. Dattu became CJI on Sep 28, 2014. In Aug 2015 he referred the Sham ID case to a larger bench (of 9 justices) for opinion as to whether privacy is a fundamental right under our Constitution. This reference was due to the cardinal tactical error on the part of the activists who insisted on arguing the point that since the Sham ID, called "Aadhaar" scheme violated privacy rights, it must be declared illegal.

They were barking up the wrong tree. Despite being told that privacy rights, while extremely important as a human right, are little understood and even less appreciated in India, and that it would be easily countered by the counter argument that it is to be balanced against public good, some prominent activists, notably Dr. Usha Ramanathan, continued to labor the point.

Strangely, the contempt petitions too were clubbed with the main case in the reference. The reference is under the proviso to Art. 145 (3) of the Constitution of India. The proviso to the Article states, "Provided that where the Court hearing an appeal under any of the provisions of this Chapter other than Art. 132 consists of less than 5 judges and in the course of the hearing of the appeal the Court is satisfied that the appeal involves a substantial question of law as to the interpretation of this Constitution the determination of which is necessary for the disposal of the appeal, such Court shall refer the question for opinion to a Court constituted as required by this clause for the purpose of deciding any case involving such a question and shall on receipt of the opinion dispose of the appeal in conformity with such opinion."

Several points are noteworthy and indicative of how justice is dispensed in India. Firstly, the contempt petitions had nothing to do with the issue of whether privacy is a fundamental right or not. Why then were these clubbed with the reference of the main case? One can only believe that there is a reluctance to adjudicate on the acts of contempt.

Secondly, the proviso is applicable only when the Court hearing the case consists of less than 5 judges. The Court of Dattu, J. had 5 judges. The Court need not have referred the question of privacy to a bench larger than 5 judges. I am told that there is a convention that if a judgement were pronounced by a court with a certain number of judges, then to overrule it, a bench with a larger number of judges is required. A very good convention, indeed, but should convention take precedence over speedy and effective delivery of justice? "There is safety in numbers," is that the reason for the convention or tradition?

However, the wording of the proviso clearly indicates that the framers of the Constitution did not think so. They visualised a quick reference and that only if there were less than 5 judges hearing the case.

The Article says that the court hearing the case "[S]hall on receipt of the opinion dispose of the appeal in conformity with such opinion."

It is obvious that the Constitution was certain that the opinion would be received soon and that the court hearing the case would be able to use the opinion to dispose of the case.

The Constitution did not conceive of the procrastination in Indian courts where cases drag on for decades.

When convention supersedes the basic requirement of justice–that is justice without delay–then justice no longer exists.

Since some of the judgements quoted by the Attorney General (AG) were pronounced by courts with 7 judges, Dattu's court thought that 9 judges would be required to hear the reference. This suited the AG and the government and UIDAI. They were now free to coerce and intimidate the hapless population into rushing to enrol. And this, despite the fact that even while referring the matter for opinion, the court reiterated the earlier orders making it clear that enrolment is voluntary.

As I was coming out of the court, I heard the AG, who was also walking out, remark to someone beside him, "Aur kya chaiye? PDS, LPG, Jan Dhan sabkuch hogya." (What else do you want? Sham ID can be linked to all these.)

What inference could one draw from the remark?

Thakur, T. S, J. took over as CJI in Jan 2017. He did nothing to constitute the larger bench. He even refused to hear mentions pleading for constitution of the reference bench. Does this not say a lot about the absolute lack of appreciation in the highest levels of the judiciary on the importance of the case? How could one not understand the importance of an act of government which impacts everyone in the country?

It was reported in the media that Thakur, J. wept in a public meeting in the presence of the Prime Minister, at which he (Thakur, J.) was pleading for filling vacancies of judges in courts. This was indeed a rare, if not an exceptional spectacle, in this and any other country of the world. Public display of emotions by the highest judicial and Constitutional functionary of the Nation says a lot about the psychological make-up of our people. We could pride ourselves on being all too human. Our emotional approach to many issues which face us as a Nation, is more a bane than a boon.

Next, Khehar, J. took over as CJI in Jan 2016. In July 2017, he constituted the 9-judge bench to hear the privacy reference. The bench pronounced its verdict in Nov 2017. It held privacy to be a fundamental right.

What was gained by this judgment is debatable. Privacy enthusiasts were thrilled. To me, it was time wasted and leeway given to government to pressure and push people into enrolling in the Sham ID, called "Aadhaar" Scheme.

Over 100 notifications were issued in the interregnum making the Sham ID compulsory for everything from mobile phones to bank accounts to filing of income tax returns. So much for the success of the privacy verdict.

By this time, the bench which had heard the case had disappeared with retirements and the judges being shuffled to other benches. So, a new 5-judge bench had to be constituted. The least that could have been done was to reconstitute a new bench only replacing those who had retired from the earlier bench. Chelameswar, J. and Bobde, J. of the previous bench were still available. However, they were not in the new bench. Where does that leave Article 145 (3), which states that the bench which made the reference shall upon receipt of the opinion (from the reference bench) dispose of the appeal based on the opinion expressed by that bench? It appears as if the Supreme Court could ignore the Constitution or dilute its provisions to the detriment of dispensing justice as the Constitution mandates.

Dipak Misra, J. took over as CJI in Aug 2017. He constituted a 5-judge bench to hear the main case. Apart from himself, Justices, Sikri, Bhushan, Chandrachud and Khanwilkar constituted the bench.

It is neither possible nor necessary to set out the details of the arguments on both sides in a narrative such as this. I shall not therefore make such an attempt. However, I would very briefly outline the basic points made by the advocates, as best as I understood them from information made available to me. I was not present in the court, but was in touch with the happenings daily, through Twitter posts of Prasanna and Bhatia and other sources of information. I thank them for it. These are very useful.

As was the previous practice, Shyam Divan opened the arguments for the petitioners. He continued his theme of privacy rights and surveillance. He dwelt on the changed relationship between state and citizen, and whether the Aadhaar Law remain in the statutes. This did not find much purchase with the judges. They probed him with questions on how the balance between public good and private rights could be attained. His answers did not seem to convince the bench.

Next were Kapil Sibal and P Chidambaram. While Sibal told the court that this case would be the most important case ever, he did not elaborate on how this would be so.

Chidambaram spoke on the legality of passing the Act as a Money Bill, and so did Arvind Datar who followed him, later. The latter also dealt with the linkage to PAN and the amendment to the Income Tax Act to make it compulsory to do so.

Gopal Subramanium, who kindly agreed to argue my case, *pro bono*, also dealt with right to privacy. Subramanium had spent considerable time understanding varied aspects of the case through discussions wherein Usha Ramanathan, Prasanna, and I were present. His staff of 5 or 6 young advocates was invariably present. When I brought the contract clauses of UIDAI's contracts with Biometric Solution Providers (BSPs), his reaction was to term it, "Surrender of Sovereignty." Yet, it appears that he did not say so in court. He, as well as Divan mentioned the data being shared with foreign private companies. However, the seriousness of this seems to have been lost upon their Lordships.

Subramanium was at his eloquent best. I had an uneasy feeling that much of what he said was simply too heavy for the judges.

I had drafted my petition (No. 37 of 2015) and sent this to my advocate, Aishwarya Bhati and to Subramanium. Talha, one of Subramanium's junior counsels, used to make changes, some of which I did not like, but was helpless to prevent. For example, while I would have preferred to urge the irrationality of the Sham ID Aadhaar Scheme and the dangers of handing over all data to foreign entities, he felt that proportionality should be the main thrust of the arguments.

Then, Anand Grover, who too had kindly agreed to represent me, *pro bono*, argued my case. I had several discussions with him and he was gracious enough to spare his precious time. I had also prepared the petition (1058 of 2017) on the same lines as my previous petition. I had approached Grover since I felt that Subramanium would not press the argument of scientific and mathematical impossibility of uniqueness of biometric identification, which was the fulcrum on which the government's case could be demolished.

Arvind Datar, K V Vishwanath and Meenakshi Arora followed with arguments for various petitioners.

Most of the arguments were based on illegality of sections of the Aadhaar Act, like Section 59, inequality under Article 14 of the Constitution, project being beyond stated objectives of the Act, failure of security of the State Resident Data Hubs (SRDH), the existence of many types of frauds in PDS such as eligibility fraud, quantity fraud and identity fraud, etc. This last was from a research–survey report of Reetika Khera and John Drèze.

Khera and Drèze have done a great service by their surveys and publications in print media of the hardships faced by the poor who are denied rations for various reasons since the introduction of the Aadhaar Scheme for PDS.

In all these arguments, the fact that biometrics does not provide unique identity and that Section 5 of the Aadhaar Act is an admission of failure of biometric identification does not seem to have been effectively brought out.

The court was told that the contract with L 1 Identity Solutions Operating Company Pvt. Ltd. provides access to all data and that hence the Aadhaar was *ab initio* insecure.

It appears to me that the court has not yet grasped either the significance of the access to data provided to foreign private companies through the contracts or the impossibility of using biometric identification for targeting subsidies, benefits and services.

I would request the senior advocate arguing for me (Anand Grover) to find ways of bringing this home to the judges hearing the case, should an occasion arise in future. In my view, it is possible to do so. God willing, I hope to meet him on May 7, 2018 since he informed me that he would get about 30 minutes on 8th May to rebut the AG's arguments. (The dates here pertain to the time of writing this book. Subsequently, I did meet him and spent quite some time laboring these points. However, his emphasis was different.)

As I write this (May 3, 2018) the arguments are continuing. The Attorney General is arguing now. His first point is the money spent (₹ 9000 crores, which he calls an investment).

Next, he said that official identification is a basic human right! I wonder wherefrom these people get such ideas. He said that privacy rights must give way to distributive justice, whatever that may mean. Perhaps, this is the difference between understanding of human rights in the developed Western world and by us.

The CEO, UIDAI was allowed to make a Power Point Presentation (PPT) in the court. Contrast this with the court ignoring two CDs[21] containing sting operations exposing rampant corruption and fraud in the enrolment process for Aadhaar. These were filed with my petitions. I don't know whether these were brought to their notice or whether the judges saw them.

What could be the reasons for this?

Could it be that the judges do not read the petitions? It appears that they do not read them. I find it strange that the judges do not read the affidavits and petitions and if they do, choose to ignore such crucial pieces of evidence.

While the court permitted the PPT of the CEO, UIDAI, similar facility was not provided to the petitioners. Evidently, there is a bias or deference to the Government. Does this augur well for justice and judiciary? Only time will tell.

I requested my advocates to plead with the court to permit me too to make a PPT presentation. I was told that the court allowed the petitioners to ask questions of the CEO, UIDAI.

---

[21] Here are the links to the videos
Cobra Post - https://drive.google.com/file/d/0ByFVGYRcgU7MVl9CaGNHVHFTWXc/view?usp=sharing
UID fraud exposed in Delhi - https://drive.google.com/file/d/0ByFVGYRcgU7MYzI1WXlMYVJKMHM/view?usp=sharing

Accordingly, I sent a list of questions after careful study of the slides in his PPT. Then I found that these questions were not submitted to the court, but instead, some other questions of other petitioners, or those questions which certain advocates imagined were relevant, were submitted to the court.

These were put to the CEO, UIDAI. The questions did not address issues such as the clauses in the contracts granting access to foreign entities. The questions did not dwell on the impossibility of biometric identification leading to unique IDs.

Nothing in the questions brought out the junk data in the UIDAI database.

The CEO, UIDAI was thus allowed to get away with pulling wool over everyone's eyes.

Whoever decided not to submit my questions to the court did not have the courtesy to inform me that they were not being submitted. Even now, I have not been given any reason for not doing so.

I don't even know who took the decision not to submit my questions. I can only surmise that someone misguided the advocates to do so for reasons best known to them.

The case seems to be proceeding like events in Lewis Carroll's "Alice in Wonderland".

It is incredible that the AG and others like Rakesh Dwivedi, argue on data being safe and UIDAI having robust security. The AG was quoted as saying that the UIDAI servers are housed in a building with 13-foot high walls and guarded by Government security personnel. He also mentioned that the foreign private company personnel are escorted in and out of the UIDAI server facility when they come for carrying out work (of de-duplication?).

Dwivedi said that the UIDAI's license agreement with BSPs is like the court clerk using Windows OS! And the court seemed to buy this argument. There was no comment or question from the bench.

Earlier, I am told that when Shyam Divan informed the court that UIDAI does not have the source code of de-duplication software of the BSPs, Justice Chandrachud had an astonished look. That's all!

Yet, all advocates and their Lordships deliberate on data protection and privacy. Does it not occur to these gentlemen that it is ridiculous to talk about data protection when ALL data is being handed over to foreign private companies?

Why is it that they don't seem to appreciate that talk of privacy is meaningless when the foreign private companies are permitted under the contract to collect (more data? What else? From where? How?), use (for what?), transfer (where to?), store (where?) process (what does this mean?) If the BSPs are to do de-duplication, they would obviously have to process the data. Why a specific mention permitting them to process data? and link to specific individuals (Who are these? And who decides those chosen for linking?).

Apart from the apparent inability on the part of the court as well as the advocates to realize the seriousness of handing over all data of people of the country to foreign entities, the court also, like the government, does not appear to have a sense of priority. It took years for the larger bench to be constituted. The court did not hear the case continuously, as would have been done, had it understood priorities of national and people's security.

During the final arguments in rebuttal, I am told that while Mr. Subramanium was presenting the case, Chandrachud, J. observed that his mother, the wife of the former Chief Justice of India, had to get her bankers to her house every month to have her fingerprints scanned for her to receive her pension, as the wife of the former CJI. His lordship was not amused; but there are several questions that rise here. Do her fingerprints prove that she is the wife of the former CJI? Is pension a right as held in many judgments or is it a subsidy, benefit or service provided by the government? Why do we have this ridiculous spectacle which makes us the laughing stock of the world? Can you believe it, the AG, in his arguments proudly informed the court that UIDAI has been mentioned in the Guinness Book of World Records!

He made another ludicrously absurd statement. Striving to convince the court on how secure the UIDAI data is, as mentioned earlier, he said that the UIDAI servers are housed in buildings with 13-feet-high walls!

One of the cunning things which UIDAI did was to enroll judges in the initial days. Supreme Court judges too were enrolled when not much information was available to them on what the scheme was really about. Thus, judges became unwitting and unsuspecting accomplices in the UIDAI hoax. The judges did not have to go to enrolment centers. Instead, enrolments were done in court premises, as per information available to me.

INDIAN ATTITUDE

Sadly, the complacency and lack of appreciation of the seriousness of handing over the data of the entire population to foreign entities is not confined to the Supreme Court or the advocates or even to the activists. Why do I club activists among those who do not take this with the seriousness it deserves? Well, they continue to harp on surveillance, privacy, exclusion and everything else. One activist even attributed malice to me for asking, "Who decided not to submit my questions to the court?"

Most people do not think or realize that handing over data of the nation is treason. I have met and spoken to politicians in government and opposition, and media persons and given them documentary evidence of the contracts, the attempt to hide the contract and so on.

Thus, I first talked to Arnab Goswami, when he was with Times Now. I had travelled all the way to Mumbai from Bangalore, after seeking an appointment with him. He asked me to meet Kenneth Hector and Megha Prasad, on the Times staff. I met them both, showed them the contracts and the court documents of Accenture having been found guilty under three US Laws: the Truth in Negotiations Act, the False Claims Act and the Anti-Kickbacks Act. Times Now did nothing with the information provided. The Channel chose to ignore the information I had given them.

Next, I met Bhupendra Chaubey and Madhav Gopal Krishna. Nothing came of these meetings. Somasekhar spoke to Rahul Kanwal. He is the person who anchored the 'Headlines Today' expose on UIDAI enrolment frauds. Yet, he did not take the evidence any further.

I met several politicians from across the political spectrum, and personalities such as Swami Agnivesh. Among those whom I met and gave copies of the evidence were Members of Parliament from JD (U) and CPI (M) or CPM, as they are sometimes called.

Among the CPM functionaries to whom the evidence was given were the party's top leadership. This included Prakash Karat, Brinda Karat and Nilotpal Basu. Through them, I obtained appointments with the Kerala CM, Pinarayi Vijayan and Thomas Isaac, the finance minister. Vijayan asked me to meet his Political Secretary, Dineshan Puthalath. After spending about an hour with Puthalath, he summarized my elaboration of the Sham ID called "Aadhaar" Scheme saying, "In short, the entire data is being given to US (Intelligence Agencies)."

Thomas Isaac did not have time, as he had to attend a function. So, after a brief 10-minute meeting in his office, he suggested that I travel with him in his car to the venue of his function. I could thus spend about 30 minutes with him in the car as we were driving down. After my explanation of the Sham ID called "Aadhaar" Scheme and the fact of the data being handed over to foreign private companies, I asked him why he was linking the Sham ID, called "Aadhaar" with

BPL ration cards. To this, he gave a strange reply. He said, "I need some number; and this (Aadhaar number) is available." He also mentioned that if the linking of ration card numbers with the Sham ID "Aadhaar" numbers is not done, the Center might deny the Central Government contribution of PDS subsidies.

My purpose in meeting the CM and FM of Kerala was to request them to ask for copies of the UIDAI-BSP Contracts and then hold a press conference to make public the fact of all data of people being handed over to foreign private companies; and then state that the Government of Kerala is rescinding the Memorandum of Understanding with UIDAI on the ground that all data of people is being handed over to foreign private companies.

I am sorry to say that the CM and FM did nothing of the sort. Instead, they went about even more vigorously linking Sham ID, called "Aadhaar" with many state schemes, such as pensions.

This is one of the most perplexing aspects of the approach of Indians to the Sham ID, called "Aadhaar" Scheme. Not much thought is given to anything. It is, as we say, a *"chaltha hai"* attitude. It's a Hindi phrase which means, "Anything goes (is acceptable)." It doesn't bother us too much if decisions are delayed, if people in government or others utter lies, if projects are poorly implemented, if hygiene is poor, so be it. We accept shoddy service from hospitals or hotels or government.

Secondly, there is an acceptance of opinions of the rich and famous without question. The very appointment of Nilekani to head UIDAI, his being given a cabinet rank–with perks and privileges of the position–as if it were the Prime Minister's to bestow, is just one relevant example.

Another book about the "Aadhaar" Scheme describes in juicy detail the circumstances that led to the appointment. It was his contact with Rahul Gandhi and Manmohan Singh that settled the appointment. These gentlemen evidently believed that he could do some wonders. Their objective seems to have been to use IT for streamlining India's welfare system. Laudable indeed, but they did not have the knowledge, or if they did, left it to their chosen corporate honcho to deliver.

No public deliberations on the project, as in Britain or USA, were ever done. Instead, there was just an announcement by the PM of the setting up of UIDAI and Nilekani to head it.

No one in media or politics questioned the appointment, the grant of cabinet status or what the scheme was all about. The only explanation is that all were equally ignorant and did not open their mouths lest their ignorance be revealed. Even the scientific establishments, the management and research institutions and public bodies engaged in policy research or studies did not ask questions or comment about it. There was docile and silent acceptance.

CURRENT STATUS OF THE CASE IN THE SUPREME COURT

As of date, and I am writing this today, the 5th of May 2018, the AG has rounded up his arguments and the petitioners would have the opportunity to rebut the government arguments next week.

Given the all-round ignorance, I wonder what the advocates for the petitioners, who are themselves not comfortable getting into details of biometric or information technology, could do to prove to the court the irrationality of the project and the whimsicality of decision-making in contravention of the Rule of Law, as I have been pleading.

I am on my way tomorrow to make one more attempt with my advocates to egg them on to find arguments persuasive enough to make the court realize the futility of the project and its dangers to the people and the nation, so that it may order the destruction of all data and additional steps to protect people whose data escapes destruction.

By the time this book is printed, the orders would have been issued and readers would know whether my efforts succeeded or not.

I anticipate that the court would strike down certain sections of the Aadhaar Act, like Section 57.

I just received a text message from Mr. Grover giving me an appointment at 4 PM today. I hope to discuss with him how he proposes to convince the court that the Sham ID, called "Aadhaar" Scheme is useless for any purpose and to convince the court regarding the data being handed over to foreign entities while pretending that data is safe and secure, behind "13-feet-high walls", as the AG told the court.

There is an intriguing aspect of senior advocates appearing for litigants and arguing cases on their behalf. My experience is as follows. We meet the senior advocates, request them to take up the case and explain the facts of the case to them. Unlike advocates "on record", litigants don't sign Vakalatnama, recording the fact of the seniors' representing the litigant. These seniors have a number of juniors clerking for them. Usually, meetings are held by the seniors with the juniors and with the litigants. The task of drafting the petitions, affidavits and applications are assigned to the juniors. In my case, Subramanium allocated the task to Talha and later to Pawan Bhushan. Many others in his office used to attend the team meetings and take notes/contribute to the discussions. Grover gave the job first to Vijayanth Singh, then to Suraj Snap, Srinidhi Rao and later to Varun Mathew. Priyam Cherian, Nehmat Kaur and Upasna were others working on the case.

I am ever grateful to the seniors who provided such huge resources without a penny in payment. All worked *pro bono.*

All of them were keen, sincere and very capable advocates from highly reputed law schools. However, being inexperienced and not well conversant with technology and facts of the case, they approached it from varied perspectives. My impression is that both the seniors and their staff of junior advocates did not fully grasp the scientific impossibility of implementing such a scheme. They also seemed to believe that the court would not understand or accept the irrationality of unscientific decision-making. Perhaps they could be right. I am not sure. However, I am of the view that this – irrationality - should have been our main focus.

Thus, for instance, Talha's draft which was largely the one finally filed with certain additions that I insisted upon, had proportionality and privacy rights as its theme.

It was difficult for me to convince the juniors working on the case in the offices of both seniors that the main points I wished to urge were the irrationality of using biometric identification, the impossibility of applying IT in the manner envisaged for solving problems like theft of subsidies, and most importantly, not only the data was being handed over to foreign entities but also, their being authorized to do whatever they wished to with the data.

My repeated suggestions that both the law which legitimizes the use of biometric identification and the executive actions implementing the law are in violation of the Rule of Law, and hence against the basic structure of our Constitution which is democratic, were not accepted and did not find any or adequate place in the petitions. I think that this was because the young, inexperienced advocates working for these seniors did not comprehend the facts and their implications. This was true of the offices of both seniors.

My advocates on record were Aishwarya Bhati for the first petition, 37 of 2015, argued by Subramanium, and Anando Mukherjee for the second petition, 1058 of 2017, handled by Grover.

I had the uneasy feeling that the seniors relied more on the juniors than on the litigants, at least in my case.

It was difficult for me to obtain appointments with Subramanium. Grover always responded to my requests for meeting him. Both of them rarely spoke on the phone with me.

Once, in 2018, I had a long Skype conference call with Subramanium and his staff. It was very useful and kind of him to do so when I expressed my difficulty in traveling to Delhi at short notice.

In 2016, I travelled to Chennai to meet Subramanium. I met him in the Taj where he was staying. It was kind of him to agree to meet me despite personal commitments for which he had gone there. We met for over two hours. I was delighted with the time he gave me and the promise to be in touch. He was wary of conversing on the phone and suggested that I get a Blackberry phone which he said was secure. I did purchase one, a Blackberry Passport, for ₹ 50,000/-. However, he never spoke to me on phone. We had a few exchanges of text messages for appointments, but that was all. I can very well understand this, as I know how hard pressed advocates are for time.

The advocates on record hardly had any say in the drafting of the petitions. This I find rather odd. Most petitioners too, rarely, if ever, met or discussed with the seniors, as far as I know. Perhaps, I am the only petitioner who interacted with the seniors frequently both for drafting petitions and for preparing arguments.

Usha Ramanathan and Prasanna were two persons who coordinated between the advocates. Usha was convinced that privacy rights and surveillance were the most important points that would succeed with the court. Only very late in the case, after Shyam Divan's pitch on these two points did not seem to get through with the court, did she realize that a change in strategy was needed. She emailed me seeking suggestions. I replied proposing changes in the order in which the senior advocates argue the case. She did not agree and said that it is not possible. She also did not seem to agree to my suggestions that irrationality and Rule of Law should be one of our main planks.

Another strange practice in the Supreme Court, and perhaps in some other courts as well, is for the court to restrict the time for arguments. It is strange because the judges must realize that they are to hear all that both sides wish to present and restricting the time for arguments would lead to missing out on crucial points and miscarriage of justice.

I have reasons to believe that in PILs, like the Sham ID, called "Aadhaar" case, where there are number of petitioners and advocates, those in Delhi coordinating between the advocates have a lot of say in how the case for the petitioners is presented.

As a result of this, the questions I had painstakingly compiled on the PPT of the CEO, UIDAI were not even submitted to the court. No one told me as to who took the decision not to do so not to submit my questions. Courtesy demanded that whoever took the decision at least inform me of the decision, if not the reasons for it.

There is a cartoon that best illustrates the attitude of some courts to PILs. Here is one I received from a friend.

Fig 10: Justice?

I am mentioning all this in some detail to point out that this is a serious lacuna in our system of dispensation of justice.

The way in which this case progressed, if it may be termed progress, gave me insights into how our judicial system operates. The system does not seem to be for litigants. It is some kind of a club composed of members of the judiciary and members of the bar. Both have political affiliations or biases. The judiciary does not exhibit this to the untrained or unobservant eye. However, the biases, affiliations and ideological inclinations of judges are whispered among the bar members. In the instant case, I was told that two are predisposed towards the government. One is neutral and that is perhaps good. Yet another has no views at all but follows the majority.

Litigants are viewed as a necessary evil. At least that is what one may discern from the manner in which they are looked upon by those who guard the courts. For example, a petitioner in the Supreme Court has to obtain a letter from her/his advocate to enter the court, even to attend the hearing of her/his case. He/she has to deposit his/her mobile phone. For depositing the phone, he/she has to produce copies of his/her ID and the letter given by the advocate. Advocates, on the other hand, are allowed to carry their phones into the court hall. The client does not sit near her/his advocate but has to take a place beyond a barricade where visitors crowd around. He/she can hardly hear what is being said either by the advocates or the judges. Government officials, especially the privileged ones, are allowed inside where the advocates sit. In the Sham ID, called 'Aadhaar' case, the CEO, UIDAI was sitting next to the AG. As mentioned earlier, he was also permitted to make a Power Point Presentation (PPT). Contrast this with the shabby treatment given to petitioners. I requested for equal treatment and to be allowed to make a presentation. This was not granted. I don't even know whether my advocates sought permission for this or not. I was told that we may submit questions, which as mentioned earlier, were, in my case, not submitted to the court. I am not aware who decided not to submit my questions. In a conversation, Prasanna mentioned, "We cannot ask hundreds of questions." I had always understood that questions to witnesses are allowed or disallowed by courts based solely on relevance and not on their number.

The evidence of the sting operations by 'Headlines Today' and Cobra Post, were not played in the court. My request to my advocates to seek permission from the court to play these fell on deaf ears.

If this is what happens to educated, well-off litigants who are articulate and can afford the luxury of travel expenses to attend court hearings, imagine the plight of the poor who have no clue on what is going on. Most of them do not even know the language of the higher courts, which is English. Death sentences too are awarded through this process wherein the hapless victim is unaware of the basis on which he/she is condemned (or acquitted).

Most people do not know on what basis dates are fixed for hearings. Many advocates maintain relationships with court clerks and registry officials. Usually, in the court, the court clerk calls out the date. Sometimes the advocates request changes, and the court allows advocates on either side to come to an understanding for the date of the next hearing.

My case in Delhi High Court (9143 of 2014) is typical. Four years have passed, and it is yet to be heard. It was listed for hearing on May 4, 2018, but was postponed to November 19, 2018 since some other case took precedence.

Yesterday (May 7, 2018), I met my advocate, Mr. Grover. We discussed the written submissions in rebuttal. Earlier the same morning, I had received a draft of this from Priyam. She had perhaps not read my draft sent to her and others a few days back. This is usual among the advocates. They tend to ignore the clients' views. That is understandable for normal cases, wherein the client is only expected to know some facts but not the law.

Even so, it does not make sense to ignore clients. After all, they know the facts better than advocates. They are the ones seeking justice and they know their grievance, whereas the advocates could only link the facts and the inferences therefrom to the law that is transgressed.

Priyam's draft missed out almost all the vital points. It did not mention that under the contracts data is being continuously handed over to the foreign entities. Strangely, she included a number of media reports of data leaks. I had to explain to her that talking of data leaks is absurd when the entire data is contractually made accessible to foreign entities. I would not fault her for this. All other advocates and anti-aadhaar activists do so. One has to only read the emails in groups like, Say-no-2-UID or Re-think Aadhaar, or look at the number of tweets whenever a data leak is reported.

I suggested changes and additions and emailed these to Mr. Grover and the team.

Just now, at 10 PM on May 8, 2018, I received a text message from him informing me that he has read, edited and approved it.

The case was not heard today (May 9), even though it was scheduled. Grover informed me that it would be heard on Thursday, May 10, 2018. Probably, the CJI was busy with the appeal against the Rajya Sabha Speaker's ruling disallowing the motion to impeach him. I read a Twitter post stating that the CJI has constituted a 5-judge bench to hear the appeal. One wonders how he could constitute the bench when he has a personal stake in the appeal. Well that is how the Indian judiciary functions.

The hearings are over. The Supreme Court has reserved its orders. Probably the orders may be issued by the end of the month (May 2018).

As one waits the outcome, two of Murphy's laws seem relevant. He calls them "Bachman's Inevitability Theorem". The theorem is, "The greater the cost of putting a plan into operation, the less chance there is of abandoning the plan—even if it subsequently becomes irrelevant."

Its corollary goes thus: "The higher the level of prestige accorded the people behind the plan, the less the chance of abandoning it." Both are indeed true. And I have an uneasy feeling that the Supreme Court orders when they come out will be one more proof of the theorem and its corollary.

The chance of continuing the Sham ID, called "Aadhaar" Scheme is buttressed by editorials like the one in 'Deccan Herald' of May 3, 2018. Its headline reads, "Enable, Don't Disable." The subtitle is "Aadhaar use should be reasonable, making it non-binding for phones is welcome."

This typifies the ignorance of people, even editors (who do not stop to reflect or examine facts, but rush to opine based on convenient reasoning–mostly driven by the instinct of self-preservation), and the power of brand names to obfuscate reality. Note how the subtitle starts with the phrase, "Aadhaar use," What does this mean? Does the editor know what "Aadhaar" is or what it means to use "Aadhaar"?

It is worth examining the phrase. Even the Supreme Court used the phrase. In its orders, it permitted the use of "Aadhaar". The AG pleaded for the government to be allowed to use "Aadhaar".

Firstly, "Aadhaar" is the brand name of the scheme which I prefer to call Sham ID, called "Aadhaar", since, as explained earlier, it is a sham ID. How could it be used? Common sense which is an oxymoron, since it is indeed rare, tells us that an ID has limited uses and a Sham ID has none whatsoever. "Aadhaar" is a Sham ID since biometric identification has been scientifically and mathematically proven to be not unique across large, diverse populations and when applied for a variety of applications. UIDAI inadvertently confesses that it deleted 80 million enrolments, it cannot distinguish between citizens and non-citizens; UIDAI admits that its demographic data is inaccurate; sting operations revealed rampant fraud and corruption in enrolments, and Pak spies and illegal immigrants have been found in possession of Aadhaar numbers. How anyone may place reliance on such an ID is inexplicable.

If, as the editor of Deccan Herald has done, anyone uses the brand name "Aadhaar", he/she has his/her own conception of what it means. After all, brand names are about capturing share of mind. So, the person who uses the word "Aadhaar", may be under the mistaken notion that it is fool proof identification and such identification is essential for certain purposes. Admittedly, identification is necessary for very many purposes. However, one needs to look at the immediate purpose the person who uses the phrase has in mind. In the example here, the editor imagines that this worthless ID and identification using it, has applications in "elimination of duplicate PANs or enable direct benefit transfers of welfare monies to marginalized sections of society." The editor, like many others, has fallen prey to the bluff of the alleged wonders of Sham ID, called "Aadhaar".

On May 10, 2018, Gopal Subramanium concluded his arguments. As usual, he was at his eloquent best. I was not present in court. Prasanna, Gautam Bhatia and others summarized his case against the Sham ID, called "Aadhaar" in several Tweets. It is from these that I have been able to garner the gist of presentation of the case. He said that there were 144 notifications making the Sham ID Aadhaar number compulsory for various government services. He said that the aim of the law may be laudable, maybe there is no malafide, but no purpose of the law has been attained or is attainable by law. Sikri, J. asked him about de-duplication enabling targeted delivery reaching the correct beneficiary. To this, Subramanium agreed that it is indeed affirmative action law, but this too is subject to scrutiny. I wish he had explained to the judge that targeting is impossible since biometric identification is fallible, that knowing this, UIDAI does not use biometrics except for generation of Aadhaar numbers. Once the number is assigned to persons, biometrics is hardly, almost never, used during the so-called targeting. It is this kind of belief systems, even among judges of the highest court, which results in hoaxes like the Sham ID, called "Aadhaar" getting away with its charade.

He pointed out that the state has adduced no evidence that "seamless delivery has changed the landscape." He referred to the tragic event where a woman in Jharkhand was denied rations despite having a ration card.

Next, he spoke about the progression of rights through the Apex court rulings. He specifically mentioned how pension has been included in Part 3 rights. He said that Section 7 reinforces the asymmetry between state and citizen. He contended that claim to proper purpose is not the same as purpose. He stated that the law lacks purpose. Perhaps he could have elaborated on this. The ostensible purpose of the law appears dubious. It has the objective of good governance and transparency. Yet it makes all activities of UIDAI opaque. Section 7 of the Aadhaar (Data Security) Reg., 2016 specifically shields UIDAI from any public scrutiny.

It takes UIDAI out of the ambit of RTI. UIDAI's responses to my RTI queries culminating in my appeal to the Delhi High Court are proof of this.

He drew the attention of the court to the report of the amicus curiae proving that POS machines do not work in ration shops in Delhi.

He told the court that while authentication (of IDs) is at the heart of the Act, authentication simply does not work. Reading Section 57 of the Act, he stated that there is no effective oversight. Chandrachud, J. agreed and observed that there is a need for a hierarchy of regulators. The newspapers promptly picked this up for obvious reasons. The aim is to somehow or other keep the farce of unique biometric identification going, and if setting up regulators is the way to do it, then why not?

I wish Subramanium had told the court that regulators cannot overcome scientific and mathematical impossibilities.

On Section 7, he said the wording of the section is one of condescension, and asked whether all affirmative actions under Articles 14, 16, 17 and 21 are subject to conditions now.

He quoted Justice Black, "This is a government of and for the people, not over the people."

Chandrachud, J. asked, "Are subsidies largesse or a matter of right?" To this, Subramanium responded by pointing to the judgment in "Bandhua Mukti Morcha" (Bonded Labor Rehabilitation) and said that the issue (which, the judge raised) was settled in 1982. He added, "It too is now subject to "Aadhaar"."

He said that under Section 7 a beneficiary should be made aware that he is such a beneficiary to preserve his dignity. Chandrachud, J. observed that Section 7 is only an "enabling" provision. I am at a loss to understand why the Learned Justice came to this understanding of the law. Its wording is plain enough. It empowers the governments make the establishing of identity as a condition for receipt of subsidy, and that condition further requires the beneficiary undergo authentication or furnish proof of possession of "Aadhaar". I can only infer that his Lordship has a priori decided that Section 7 is legitimate.

He, Gopal Subramanium, said that Section 7 is not a legitimate aim and that the true aim is different from the stated one.

He countered the AG's contention of balancing rights. The AG had tried to pit the poor against the petitioners, who he termed elitists. He said that balance cannot emasculate any of the conflated rights.

He drew the attention of the court to documents (studies) on fakes/ghosts that the AG had referred to. The last study was in 2007 and that relied on the previous one which, was in 1997.

I wish he had used my argument that there are no fakes/ghosts, as per RTI replies I received. I think Anand Grover would bring this out. I had suggested that in written submissions, we add the fact that if at all there were fakes/ghosts, then why is it that there has been no investigation into the crime of preparation of these fake/ghost IDs. I had also suggested that it is not sufficient to claim that there are fakes/ghosts, but that it must be shown that fakes/ghosts received subsidies. Further, mere preparation of fake/ghost ration cards would not enable drawal of subsidized rations. It is necessary to enter the details of such ration cards into government databases and then allocate them to specific ration shops. The data input can only be done by government employees.

The repeated assertion of fakes/ghosts is a frivolous, if not diabolical, argument to justify the Sham ID, called "Aadhaar" Scheme.

He said that the doctrine of mere possibility of abuse does not apply here, since denial has actually taken place.

He pointed to the previous day's judgment holding that Parliamentary Committee reports could be accepted as evidence. The Parliamentary Committee on Finance had questioned the legality and utility of the Sham ID, called "Aadhaar" Scheme.

He summed up the reliefs sought:

1. Act to be struck down
2. Data to be destroyed and structures to be dismantled
3. In cases of deprivation leading to death, compensation should be given to families of the deceased

Prasanna's Tweet had only the following paragraph on Anand Grover's arguments.

"Anand Grover (my other advocate) finishes his brief submission after handing over his written submissions. He points out how safeguards and contracts have not been rebutted and how 139AA is specifically challenged in his petition."

Grover was given only 30 minutes to present his arguments. I am not clear as to who decides the sequences of arguments or the time allowed to each advocate. This is a strange practice of the Indian Supreme Court.

I don't know whether Prasanna missed it or whether none of the advocates pointed out to the Supreme Court Section 5 of the Aadhaar Act. As explained earlier, it is an admission of failure of biometric identification.

An intriguing facet of the Supreme Court hearings of the case is the manner in which the bench hustled the advocates. The court allotted very little time for the petitioners' counsels. The counsels had then to decide how the allocated time would be divided among them. They did not meet, discuss and decide, as one would expect. Instead, a few activists who were "coordinating" between the advocates told them how much time each of them would get. This was quite mystifying to me. Firstly, I am astounded at the Supreme Court stipulating the time allowed for arguments to petitioners' advocates on so momentous a case.

Kapil Sibal told the court that this would be the most important case of the century, or words to that effect. Obviously, the court was not impressed. It is an indication of the lack of appreciation on the part of the learned judges of the implications, consequences and import of the case – how it would impact the lives of all Indians, including themselves. Contrast this with cases involving financial effect, the Reliance gas pricing case went on for 3 months or so. A reason for this could be the lack of knowledge of technology and its applications, in this case biometric and information technology. UIDAI succeeded in creating the illusion of foolproof biometric identification and its utility in eliminating duplicates and fakes and thus preventing theft of welfare funds. It did not occur to their Lordships to question these claims. My assessment of the unbelievably little time allocated to the petitioners is due to the preconceived idea they might have harbored that the Sham ID Scheme is good, it is useful for preventing "leakages" of subsidies and they only need to address issues of protecting privacy, data security and the element of compulsion and some minor irritations such as linking to bank accounts and phone numbers. The court's attitude is then understandable. It is one of, "We know what you are driving at, so don't waste time." From this one may even anticipate the nature and content of the order the court is likely to pass. The lack of awareness, among the public, the political class, the judiciary, the bureaucracy, the press and the academia, and the ability of some of the rich and famous to befuddle even the highest levels of enlightened, educated society in this country, in sharp contrast to the developed West, is starkly brought out in the way our Supreme Court has handled the case.

Now we await the judgment with bated breath. It reminds me of Shakespeare's Julius Caesar.

> *Between the acting of a dreadful thing*
> *And the first motion, all the interim is*
> *Like a phantasma or a hideous dream.*
> Shakespeare: Julius Caesar: Act 2, Scene 1, Page 4

As we await the judgment, let me share with the readers of this book research findings of irrationality among human beings. Dan Ariely, in his book with the title, "Summary of Predictably Irrational" quotes research data on judges thus: "In the judicial system, judges often hold their esteemed position because they are believed to be impartial, fair, and capable of bringing reason and rationality to bear on cases of grievance. However, even these supposedly paragons of rationality are capable of behaving irrationally. A German study of junior judges asked them each to roll a dice before ruling on the next sentencing. The study found that judges who had rolled a dice and received a higher number were more likely to give a longer sentence. (My comment – He is talking about sentencing. These must be criminal trials. The research claim is that the length of the sentence depends of the roll of a dice!) Similarly, judges who rolled a dice that received a lower number were more likely to give a shorter sentence.[22] These irrational decisions were guided by chance and the roll of a dice. The rational behavior of these judges was no match for the suggestion of a number. In another example, an Israeli study found that judges were more likely to grant parole to prisoners appearing in their court rooms earlier in the day – the difference could be as much as 70 percent parole rate by the end of the day.[23] The researchers chalked up this irrational behavior to decision fatigue, meaning human judgment becomes less rational over time as people engage in mentally strenuous work. However, the irrational decision-making held true: Regardless of the prisoners' cases, they were subject to random dangers of coming before the courtroom at the wrong time of day.

I only hope that the right dice is rolled by their Lordships in our Supreme Court. I had mentioned that I have never lost a case. I hope too that this will not be the first one.

---

[22] Playing Dice With Criminal Sentences: The Influence of Irrelevant Anchors on Experts' Judicial Decision Making **http://journals.sagepub.com/doi/abs/10.1177/0146167205282152**
[23] Extraneous factors in judicial decisions <http://www.pnas.org/content/108/17/6889.full>

The Campaign

LESSONS IN HOW NOT TO CONDUCT A SOCIAL ISSUE CAMPAIGN

The campaign against the Sham ID, called "Aadhaar" too has many lessons for the campaigners. Again, we have not learned from our erstwhile British masters. The contrast between their campaign against the U.K. National ID Card Act and the campaign here is revealing. In the U.K. they had only one body, the "NO2ID". Here is a picture from Wikipedia of a U.K. campaign event.

Fig 11: Meeting in London against ID cards, 2005. Left to right, the speakers are Tony Benn, Shami Chakrabarti, Mark Littlewood and George Galloway.

When in January 2009 the then Prime Minister, Manmohan Singh announced the intent to set up the Unique Identification Authority of India, I wrote to him and Nilekani. To me, who am not computer illiterate, this was an impossible project, one against the basic principles of IT systems. Neither of them replied or even acknowledged my letter. In my letter, I had pointed out the immense difficulties with such a project. The very collection of data and keeping it up-to-date would be impossible. I had worked in an NGO where we had seen first-hand the unacceptably high error-rate in voter lists. My experience in developing a computerized production, planning and control system for manufacture of missiles was the reason for grave misgivings about any chance of success with such a venture. Subsequent events would prove me right. The CEO, UIDAI has admitted to the Supreme Court that 50,000 enrolment Centers were shut down due to fraud. Many years earlier, in 2014, two sting operations, one by 'Headlines Today' and the other by 'Cobra Post' had revealed the rampant corruption and fraudulent enrolments.

In 2009 itself I decided to launch a campaign against this hare-brained scheme (with apologies to the swift and loveable animal).

I suggested the contours of the campaign to my friends and associates Bangalore. There is an e-group, Citizens Action Forum. I posted my views and requested people to join it. The response was lukewarm. Some voices of sympathy and nothing substantial. This is understandable. In our country ignorance about such matters is considerable. One member of the Forum proudly announced that he had enrolled. He even wrote to the local head of UIDAI! He is one of those who hero-worships the rich and famous and would like to be seen rubbing shoulders with them. He likes to bask in reflected glory. The then president of the CAF society, gravely pontificated that there were serious issues concerning the Sham ID, called "Aadhaar". (As mentioned right at the beginning of this book, I shall always prefix the words, "Sham ID" to "Aadhaar". The brand name is part of the elaborate and quite successful strategy of hoaxing the entire nation. The CAF president did not use my prefix but, merely referred to it as, "Aadhaar".)

Another member, one who had worked for some time in Singapore, was of the view that it will be useful and also said that Singapore had similar systems. In any case, a small city state, however "Developed" it might be, with a single-party democracy, is hardly an example worth emulating.

He also remarked in a post that the opposition to the scheme appears to be more due to animosity to Nilekani rather than any real concerns. This is another peculiarly Indian trait. We are quick to attribute motives.

Another group, most, or all, of whose members were in favor of Open Source, sprung up to oppose Sham ID, called "Aadhaar", on the grounds that it uses proprietary software, meaning the MS Windows Operating System. This is yet another example of jumping to conclusions without any analysis or investigation.

They, it seemed, would be happy with the scheme if it were using open source desktops. Clearly, they had no clue of the algorithms and the proprietary nature of the biometric de-duplication software or hardware used. Not only this, but they also had no idea of how biometric identification works.

This group was interesting in more ways. They were a "closed" group, wary of the ideological leanings of those participating. The membership was strictly controlled. Postings to the group's blog/e-group were monitored by moderators and those of different persuasions were denied entry. They used some proprietary open source software which blocked any email to the group which had a BCC address. The open source guys did not mind proprietary software as long as it was labeled 'open source', irrespective of conditions imposed. I did not know this at the time. Later, I found that my emails to the group were held up for moderation. Interestingly, even today, my comments are posted in many national newspapers and TV websites without moderation. Very soon after I started posting comments in these, they realized that I never employ intemperate language, and they posted my comments immediately.

I joined the group since my purpose was to take as many people into the campaign as possible.

The group did not take their campaign forward but were only exchanging emails among themselves! They continue to do so to this day, 8 years on.

A friend of mine, a Rashtriya Sevak Sangh (RSS) member, who was opposed to the Sham ID project, was invited by me to join the group. The group refused to admit him. I resigned from the group on this issue. However, if I post any mail to the group, they do allow it.

Contrast this with the U.K. campaign. Wikipedia says that "NO2ID" is a broad based group including political parties. The Conservative party which opposed the U.K. National ID Card Act was part of the group's campaign. Imagine allowing BJP to join the "Say NO2UID" group.

I was willing to work with BJP since they were opposed to the Sham ID while they were in the opposition. Their *volte face* later is another story.

The BJP connect was fortuitous.

Before I come to that story, let me describe how the anti-Sham ID campaign progressed or rather floundered. What lessons could be learned on how not to conduct a social campaign.

To begin with, one of the activists organized a talk in Bangalore. Usha Ramanathan and Ramkumar, a professor from TATA Institute of Social Sciences,

Mumbai, spoke at the meeting. It was attended by Prof. Trilochan Sastry of IIM (B) and Dr. Rajeev Gowda, now Congress MP. I too spoke at this meeting.

A NGO, INSAF – Indian Social Action Forum, based at Delhi, conducted a seminar in 2011. It was held in the Constitution Club at Delhi. A few Members of Parliament attended it. I think there were only two or three. All were from Bengal. I gave a short presentation, in which I could bring out some of the difficulties in implementing the scheme. After the seminar, I met the MPs from Bengal. One was from CPI and the other from CPM. I did write to them for support for the campaign, but nothing noteworthy came of it. One the MPs, Moinul Hassan, also from Bengal, to whom I was introduced by the MPs I met, corresponded with me on email. He did evince interest in the initial stages, but thereafter this also led nowhere.

I had suggested, in the seminar, that all those who are opposed to the scheme should come together and follow the U.K. campaign model. It appeared to me that there were not many takers for the proposal.

Reetika Khera was one of the speakers at the seminar in Delhi. If memory serves me right Kalyani Menon Sen too spoke.

Khera, then a researcher, I think, was working with Prof. John Drèze. As far as I recall, she dealt with exclusions of the poor and its possibility. Both Drèze and Khera continued their good work and produced many papers. They did prove exclusion.

None of the activists thought of joining together.

While in Delhi, I met Gopal Krishna, then a student doing his doctoral work. He is now a Ph. D.

Usha Ramanathan was a prolific writer against the scheme. From 2013 or so up to 2017 she wrote a number of articles in various newspapers, notably, the Statesman, for which, I think she penned 16 articles. Her articles were published in Economic and Political Weekly (EPW). She once told me that she knew the editor of this magazine and asked me to write an article. It was not published. When I enquired of her, she informed me that my style of writing did not find favor with EPW. There the matter ended.

In 2012, an article of mine was published in the 'Deccan Herald'. This, I am told caught the attention of Ram Krishnaswamy. He is settled in Australia. He started a blog, "Aadhaar Articles". It seems to have received numerous hits. The blog carried a lot of information about the Sham ID, called "Aadhaar" Scheme. Almost every article and news report about it was in the blog. It was well curated except that he did not comment or present his views on the articles or news most of the time. Nevertheless, his blog provided a lot of useful information.

The campaign meandered on but took on a life of its own when two events triggered a sense of anger and frustration among the middle class. One was the compulsory linkage to LPG. The Government and UIDAI had used the pretext of the Supreme Court allowing use of the Sham ID, called "Aadhaar" in LPG, to misconstrue the order as license to make it mandatory. This was in 2013.

In 2015, after the reference to the privacy bench and the permission to use the Sham ID, called "Aadhaar" for Jan Dhan and a few other government programs, the UIDAI began pushing enrolments with a vehemence bordering on some kind of desperation. The intention seems to have been to face the court with a *fait accompli*, if and when, the final hearing comes about. The Sham ID number was being insisted upon for school admissions, entry to exams and scholarships.

Then came Reliance Jio. They took the Sham ID number and biometrics for issuing new connections. Banks and phone companies started to threaten people with denial of services if the linking was not done.

I received a couple of text messages from the bank or phone company every day.

This triggered a wave of frustration among the youth and the middle class. The real face of the Sham ID and its protagonists was being revealed.

Let me go back to 2012. In December of that year, a few friends helped me organize a seminar on the scheme. B K Chandrasekhar, a former minister and member of the Legislative council, helped us hold an event in the IAS officers' Association premises. J T D'Souza, an IT security expert, came from Mumbai. He demonstrated how easily fingerprints could be captured and used in a scanner.

I was intrigued by one person in the audience, a CAF member, gesturing to me with his hand, as if to say, "What is going on?" Evidently, since he has a preconceived notion that fingerprints are foolproof identification, he could not understand that it may be faked even when demonstrated before his very eyes.

This is a significant aspect about the concept and implementation of the scheme that I noticed during the campaign as well as during the hearings in various courts.

The architects of the scheme are so sure of the colossal ignorance about both IT applications and biometric technology, and this, coupled with governmental support at the highest levels (which is itself born out of ignorance and misplaced faith in personalities), they are confident of fooling all the people all the time.

They have almost gotten away with their deception.

Thanks to Pramod Biligiri who published it on Facebook, the details of one of the earliest (20-04-2010) seminars against the Sham ID, wherein, along with Usha Ramanathan and Ramakumar, I participated, are still available. The page may be accessed from the URL available in the appendix.

Fig 12 (a): Photo of UID Seminar 20-04-2010.

My friends from CAF, Mukunda, Vidyadhar, Anil Kumar and Sivasankaran may be seen here.

Fig 12 (b): The author at an early seminar on the Sham ID

This is a photo of the same seminar. I am seen raising some "Common Sense Questions".

I set up a page in my website for the anti-Sham ID campaign. It is still available. My logo for the campaign is pictured below.

Fig 13: 'The Fifth Estate World' website campaign logo

The by-line of the logo captures the malintent of the scheme.

There is every reason to infer that the Sham ID 'Aadhaar' Project was conceived as an experiment by evil minds. I am equally convinced that these minds exist outside India. Indians are incapable of such pure evil. The holocaust did not happen in India. Guantanamo bay was/is not in India nor is it Indian.

However, Indians suffer from cultural predilection for Western ideas and inducements. We are easily divided. 'Divide and Rule' is not something which we invented, but which the British found could be used to manipulate us. They did it quite successfully, for two centuries.

Some people here have adopted the tactic with significant success.

Even the AG, when he pitted the alleged privacy elites against the marginalized poor, was playing the game our erstwhile white masters taught us, by example.

Why is the Sham ID 'Aadhaar' Project evil?

The central idea behind it is that people could be numbered, and since numbers are easy to manipulate in computer systems, people who are assigned numbers could also be manipulated to do the bidding of those in authority. This is known as "Database State Control". Everyone when in government would like to have it, and when out of government would oppose it. Governments are not inanimate entities. They are human beings. To most, control is always better than the need to convince to have their way. What better tool can one have for this than the ability to switch off or on a person and her/his daily needs for living?

Is it any wonder then, that the present PM, in all of 15 minutes that he is reported to have met Nilekani, after the 2014 elections, decided to implement the Sham ID, called "Aadhaar" Scheme? The very scheme that he had opposed both as CM of Gujarat and during the election campaign, he determines is very useful in a 15-minute talk with Nilekani. Such is the power of the need to control, that it makes people take irrational decisions.

So, the idea to use a system of assigning numbers to people took hold of the government and its minions. The question was how to sell the plan to the people without creating suspicion/distrust and consequent opposition?

Now, if someone says that we will all be given unique numbers, we would say, "What nonsense?" So, it was necessary to invent a way in which numbers could be assigned to all people without attracting opposition. The simple solution was to pretend that sophisticated technology is used to provide people with unique IDs. Here is a benevolent government giving the poor something they do not have.

Therefore the pretense of biometric identification arose. That's what the vision and mission of UIDAI say in its website. The vision is to provide unique IDs. And how is this to be done? By "*delivering Aadhaar numbers* universally to residents in India." UIDAI also has the vision of providing a "*digital platform* to authenticate anytime anywhere."

Who has and owns the "digital platform"? UIDAI, of course. This is the concept of the evil genius behind the plan–assign numbers to everyone, put all the numbers on a digital platform, and use it to control all the numbers.

In the selling of any product or idea, brand names are vital. Brand names have the advantage that they are perceived differently by customers and recipients of advertising. Thus, some may look upon say, IBM, as an ethical company, while others may carry the impression that it is technologically superior. The brand name IBM means different things to different people.

Similarly, the brand name, "Aadhaar" conveys different perceptions to different people. Supreme Court judges may think of it as useful technology to prevent theft of subsidies. Finance ministers, like the one Kerala, who I met, may imagine it to be necessary for creating databases of welfare recipients.

Incidentally, the brand name "Aadhaar" is the name of a private Trust of Nilekani. UIDAI publicizes that there was a public competition for its logo and was thus chosen through a transparent process. Like most of its public postures, given to deception, here too is a sleight of hand. While the public competition was for the logo, the choice of the brand name is left unsaid, and people associate that too with the transparently open competition. To tell lies, it is not necessary to utter them. Silence too could be a lie, as many an investigator who interrogates criminals and their accomplices would know.

Does this sound similar to what the former PM, Narasimha Rao said, "The decision not to decide is also a decision."?

Apart from the brand name, slogans were used to push the project. One such was, and perhaps is, the slogan, "One India, One ID". "Mera Aadhaar, Meri Pechan" Many were thrilled at the prospect of getting rid of all other IDs and having just one ID. Putting all your eggs in one basket? Those who thought that this was a wonderful idea did not care to think a little more and hence could not see beyond their nose.

I must say categorically that not everyone who supported or supports the Sham ID, called "Aadhaar" Scheme does so with ulterior motives.

Many genuinely think that it is useful. For example, the Supreme Court when hearing a PIL by PUCL on wasted food damaged in storages due to not being distributed to the needy, observed, "Why don't you use "Aadhaar"? This was, I think in response to the Government's stand pointing to the difficulties in ensuring that the distribution reaches the intended beneficiaries. One would think, why is it that the Government does not set up the system of fool proof distribution first before going in for procurement? Well that's how governments work. They usually act and then think, unlike many normal humans; not to deny that many humans too are predisposed to government's ways of doing things.

Many are motivated by personal loyalties to the personalities involved, be they politicians or others. Many who hero worship an IT honcho would be inclined to support his plans blindly. Still others may see in it a business opportunity. I came across many politicians who told me that their party workers are into the enrolment business and hence they cannot oppose the program as it would hurt them.

There are of course, those who knew the dangers of the scheme to both the people and the nation, and the impossibility of using it for any purpose, and yet continued to implement it. These are not innocent. An investigation would reveal who they were or how they were led to do what they did.

It is up to the reader to decide who falls into which of the categories of the votaries mentioned above—the innocent, the gullible, the villains, the sycophants, camp-followers, the complacent and the genuinely misled.

We may digress now, to briefly look at how some promote the Sham ID "Aadhaar" Project. This is seen in one of the two books published on the Project.

Of the two books that have been published on the Sham ID, called "Aadhaar" scheme, one is titled, "Aadhaar" – A 'Biometric History of India's 12-digit Revolution.' Shankkar Aiyar is its author. The blurb says that he is a famous columnist who has analyzed budgets and covered elections. I notice that his first name is spelt with a double "K" which is unusual. Perhaps someone involved in his naming believed in numerology. This is quite common in India. The late Tamil Nadu CM, I am told, added an additional "a" after her name on the advice of numerologists.

This book is revealing on how Nilekani went about the task of getting into government. It also reveals how Indian governments take decisions. Rationality takes a back seat. The decision depends on the whims and fancies of persons in authority, and that too, not necessarily in government. There could be, and are, extra-constitutional and extra-governmental authorities who take decisions, and the bureaucrats (derisively referred to as "Babus") implement them based on their loyalties or ideological slant.

Aiyar does not bat an eyelid when describing the stratagems that were needed and were adopted for (shall I say, to "maneuver" oneself into government?) Nilekani to be appointed to head UIDAI. There was the experience of an outfit called Bangalore Agenda Task Force, BATF for short, which, was set up in 1999 and lasted until 2004 or so. It was ostensibly to ensure planned development of Bangalore. The results are there for all to see. (A recent Karnataka High Court judgment has ruled that government participation with such private organizations for developing public plans and schemes is illegal.) BATF was set up during the S M Krishna – Congress regime. He is now with the BJP. Not to be outdone, the BJP Government that followed his, set up Agenda for Bangalore Infrastructure Development, abbreviated as ABIDe. These are both replicas of the US "Revolving doors" between corporate sector and government. We follow the white man, closely.

The latest avatar is called Bangalore Political Action Committee (B.PAC). The same old wine in new bottles. The same corporate personae keep coming back under different names and banners.

The reader may wonder why I am mentioning these here. What is their relevance to the Sham ID, called "Aadhaar" Scheme?

Firstly, the fact that decisions which, impact the livelihoods of over a billion people and affect the very existence of one of the largest nations of the world, are taken with such flippancy, is bewildering.

Secondly, this chapter is on the Campaign. Described here is also one part of the other side–the pro-side of the campaign. Aiyar's book mentioned here is an element of it. Its hero, Nilekani, was part of BATF.

Aiyar is privy to intimate details of the goings on within government leading to Nilekani's appointment. (As for how Aiyar got all these details, your guess is as good as mine.) As we all know, there was no advertisement, no job description or search committee–nothing at all. His appointment was simply announced by the then PM. It was like the sultanates of old. The emperor chose his vazir. The King was the Law, as Louis the XIV is reported to have said, "L'État, c'est moi" (The State? I am the State– Carlyle's rendering into English).

This is how Aiyar describes (in pages 16 to 21 of his book) the events leading to the appointment and the decision to launch the Sham ID, called "Aadhaar" Scheme. It reads like a spy thriller. He says, "The text message was terse: Can you be in Delhi by 5 PM this evening? It was Friday, 22 May 2009. — The message was from Rahul Gandhi". (Aiyar does not say whether Nilekani went to Delhi or not and if he did, who he met or what transpired, if he met anyone. Later, he appears to say that Nilekani did not make the trip.) Aiyar continues, "It was not an entirely unexpected message. Nilekani had received a call on May 16, a few hours after the 2009 results were out. The political air was thick with ambition and optimism. It was not clear if the young scion of the Gandhi family would join the government. What was clear was that he had a major say in who would be inducted.

Like his father, Rahul Gandhi is invested in pet peeves and pet projects. He had come to believe that the system needed, to put it in millennial speak, a 'person from another planet".

"While Rahul was keen, the core team of the Congress–essentially, Sonia Gandhi, Pranab Mukherjee, A K Antony and Ahmed Patel–was not confident about defending the lateral induction.

Nilekani had known Rahul Gandhi since 2004, when he had visited Bengaluru during the S M Krishna regime, and expressed an interest in knowing more about technology solutions for e-governance. Nilekani had also known Manmohan Singh for some time....

The induction through UIDAI got a positive response from Sonia Gandhi, Pranab Mukherjee and Rahul Gandhi. 'The logic', as Rahul Gandhi points out (was this the source of insider information?) is simple." "I believe that there are certain projects which when handed over to an insider within government, can die on arrival. I knew Nandan, I knew what drove Nandan. I knew he was the guy that could pull it off."

(Notice the first name basis of the RG-NN relationship. It is of such things that momentous decisions that affect us all are made by those who we elect to represent us. Notice too the difference between a mature democracy–the U.K.– and our politicians' method of decision-making. In the U.K. there was informed debate within and outside Parliament. The U.K. government passed a law. Even after the passage of the law, the opposition continued to pick holes in it, not because they were the opposition, but because they found it anathema to freedom and democracy. The London School of Economics carried out a detailed study and showed how the project of biometric identification of just about 66 million people is not worth the effort, and that setting up such a database *is* fraught with insurmountable difficulties and beset with dangers.)

Aiyar says in his book, "He (Nilekani) then sought an appointment and met with the prime minister on June 15 (2009) — They met for around thirty minutes that Monday morning *to finalize the terms of engagement.* (Emphasis mine.) He asked for cabinet rank. He ensured he would report to the prime minister and that the announcement of his induction would be in his words–it was critical that he be 'invited' to join the government. He asked for a special cabinet committee on UIDAI so decisions could be empowered and *insulated. (Again the emphasis is mine. The wish/intent to insulate decisions is intriguing. It reveals a streak of mind wherein he does not want anyone to scrutinize his decisions. Is this how one opts for public service?)* He got an assurance that the law bestowing statutory authority to the autonomous body would be prioritized. Manmohan agreed on all counts. (My comments: Did Manmohan have a choice? What a pathetic state our politicians have reduced the office of the prime minister to!) Even as he was raring to get started, Nilekani learnt his first lesson before joining government; lie low. (My question: *Was he sneaking into government?*). Say nothing, speak to no one, tell no one anything of any announcement until the announcement actually happens. This after all, was the Government of India. What was about to happen as lateral induction was disruption, for politicos, for bureaucrats and for status quo-ists. He waited (*My comment: The spy thriller syndrome?*). On 25 June, the Government of India announced, "The cabinet today approved (*My comment: Should the announcement have said, "The cabinet rubber-stamped"*) the creation of the position of Chairperson, Unique Identification Authority of India (UIDAI). The Prime Minister has invited Shri Nandan Nilekani, currently co-chairman, Infosys, to join as UIDAI Chairperson in the rank of Cabinet Minister."

Aiyar almost appears gleeful in narrating this spy thriller version of entry into government of a corporate honcho and to head a body with no legal sanction or

Parliamentary approval or discussion. I wonder why it does not cross their minds that doing something patently illegal and that too surreptitiously, is not a matter to be proud of.

Many of us have heard the infamous "Radia Tapes". Those who heard them would have realized how cabinet appointments are "fixed" in this country (as perhaps, in many others too). One top corporate figure in the tapes talks of the party which was forming the government as his shop! Another corporate chieftain wrote a hand-written letter to a party chief for his choice of person to be made the Telecom Minister–the same minister who was jailed when the scam broke out and is now acquitted by the trial court.

Given such shenanigans in cabinet formation, it shouldn't be a surprise that Nilekani was granted cabinet rank without being elected to Parliament and hence without the necessity of being answerable to Parliament.

One other intriguing point needs to be said about the episode as described in Aiyar's book. This is about the "terse" text message from Rahul Gandhi to Nilekani. The intriguing question is, "How did Aiyar come to know of the message?" Common sense tells us that text messages on mobile phones are known only to the sender and the receiver. Who gave the message to Aiyar–the sender or the receiver? Your guess is as good as mine. The answer to the question will reveal how such a book in praise of the Sham ID, called "Aadhaar" came to be written.

Nothing could bring out the stark contrast between those who respect the sanctity of law and Rule of Law and those who have scant regard for it, than a look at the process adopted by the U.K. for its U.K. National ID Card and the way in which our country's leaders went about setting up UIDAI and appointing its first chairperson. The U.K. process is described in Wikipedia.[24]

Aiyar says, "Between his meeting with Manmohan Singh and the announcement, Nilekani spent time consulting friends like Srikant Nardhamuni — and Sriram Raghavan of Comat Technologies, all of whom knew the challenges of inducting technology to improve the delivery of government services."

I need to mention the last named friend of Nilekani, Sriram Raghavan. His company, Comat Technologies, was selected as a partner in March 2006, under the Build, Operate and Transfer (BOT) model of Public-Private-Partnership (PPP) for a project to computerize issue of ration cards to eligible families in

---

[24] The Wikipedia URL is available in the appendix.

the State of Karnataka. The Comptroller and Auditor General (CAG)[25] was highly critical of the selection, contract and implementation. It was meant to be a computerized *biometric* system of ration cards. The CAG commented, *"The oversight over implementation of computerisation was so defective that the partner persistently bypassed the contracted procedures and carried on with the work in a totally uncontrolled environment. This resulted in an abnormal increase in the number of ration cards including to those for the families below poverty line. The Department failed to enforce various provisions in the agreement resulting in several inadmissible payments to the partner."* (Sriram Raghavan's Comat Technologies.)

The CAG added, *"Although the partner was to complete the project set-up phase by October 2006, it remained incomplete even after five years after the scheduled date of completion. After receiving a payment of ₹ 54.23 Crore, the partner (Sriram Raghavan's Comat Technologies) closed the operations permanently in November 2010 without transferring any of the assets except the database of ration cards. An evaluation of the database by a third party showed that it was incomplete in many respects and suffered from many deficiencies and was not capable of preventing duplication of ration cards."*

The CAG concluded, *"The PPP project ended up as an example of doubtful value for money in a crucial area of governance."*

Is it possible to believe that Nilekani was not aware of what Comat Technologies and its officer, Sriram Raghavan, did in the contract with the Food and Civil Supplies Department of Karnataka Government?

Granting that he was unaware of it, he must be a poor judge of people and organizations.

In 2010, Comat Technologies was empanelled as an Enrolling Agency of UIDAI. It was given the task of enrolment at Mysore. How could a firm that was castigated by the CAG for what amounts to fraud be empanelled for such a sensitive work as biometric and demographic capture of people for assigning of (allegedly) unique numbers?

In keeping with its standards of ethics, the enrolment Center of Comat Technologies was involved in fraudulent enrolments. This was reported in a sting operation in Jan 2010, aired by a news channel, TV 9. I took up the matter with the then Principal Secretary in the Food and Civil Supplies Department,

---

[25] The Executive Summary of the CAG report No. 2 (Civil) for year ended Mar 31, 2011, obtained through RTI is in the appendix.

Shri Vidyashankar. After continuous follow up for over 7 months, finally, in July 2010, I was given a copy of an FIR filed with the Narasimha Raja Police Station regarding the fraud in COMAT's enrolment center…The FIR is numbered 01 of 05-01-2010. It was astonishing to find that the FIR did not name Comat Technologies, the Enrolling Agency. The FIR was against an auto-rickshaw driver and a few others.

Even after the CAG report and the FIR, Comat Technologies continued as an Enrolling Agency of UIDAI.

My purpose in this detailed description of Comat Technologies' activities is to show how the entire system of enrolments is so defective that no reliance may be placed on the data being input to the UIDAI servers. The sting operations referred to earlier, are evidence of the flawed Sham ID, called "Aadhaar" enrolment process. The reason for this is an astounding callousness in the approach to data collection. That the head of UIDAI came from one of the most respected IT companies and yet he allowed the data input to be done in this cavalier fashion is inexplicable.

Another reason for detailing the Comat Technologies episode is because, while its Managing Director is said to be a friend of Nilekani's, his company, as per a CAG audit report has indulged in a serious financial offense. Now, Infosys, Nilekani's company, prides itself on ethics, whether true or not. If the old adage, "Birds of a feather, flock together," is based on normal human experience, then the ethics of UIDAI would itself be questionable.

Then again, how could Aiyar know about Nilekani consulting someone, and whom he consulted, "between his meeting with Manmohan and the announcement"?

UIDAI's attitude to RTI and the desire to insulate decisions, (whatever that may mean) is not particularly flattering for those who trumpet transparency and good governance, whether in government or in the corporate world. Given his need for insulation, it is understandable why UIDAI has been taken to staggering levels in the Aadhaar Act. Under Section 7 of the Aadhaar (Data Security) Regulations, all activities of UIDAI have been taken out of the ambit of the RTI Act.

Having described in some detail about the only book that came out in support of the Sham ID "Aadhaar" scheme, let us turn our attention back to the campaign against it.

A facet of the campaign was the engagement of activists with Government. Usha Ramanathan met the Parliamentary Standing Committee on Finance to which the UIDAI Bill had been referred. I wrote to the Committee. Nilekani, I am told, made a presentation to the Committee. I have also been told that when the Committee put questions to him, he was not very forthcoming and left rather quickly. In December of 2011, the Parliamentary Standing Committee on Finance published its report on the Aadhaar Scheme. The Committee trashed the scheme as, "Directionless," "Conceptually flawed" and a threat to national security.

I had written to the Committee and was gratified to note that my point that corruption in PDS is not due to lack of ID or fake IDs, but that the discretion to decide eligibility was the cause, was included in the report. Yashwant Sinha, BJP MP chaired the Committee.

Four times in four consecutive reports the Committee repeated its stand. The report was not even debated in Parliament. While the Congress-led UPA's reluctance to discuss the report is understandable, it is inexplicable why neither BJP nor any other party pressed for a discussion.

Unfortunately, the dialogues by activists with government, political parties and bureaucrats were very few and minimal.

THE SERENDIPITOUS BJP CONNECTION IN THE CAMPAIGN

In the meantime, the Parliament elections were looming large. Nilekani was the Congress candidate from Bangalore South constituency, held by BJP's Ananth Kumar. As luck would have it, V K Somasekhar, a former St. Josephs, Bangalore student, who was jailed during the emergency as a protestor along with BJP politicians, became involved in the anti-sham ID campaign. He was close to Ananth Kumar. He called me one day in 2014 and said that Ananth Kumar would like to meet me. Somasekhar told me that Ananth Kumar would like me to make a presentation about the Sham ID, called "Aadhaar" to him. I rigged up a quick PPT and rushed to Jayanagar, Bengaluru, to the residence of Ananth Kumar. He gave me a patient hearing. I found him to be a very intelligent person, quick to grasp. He got the essentials of my pitch against the Sham ID, called "Aadhaar" in just a few minutes. He told me that he would fix meetings for me to dialogue with BJP MPs.

Meanwhile, the "Say NO2UID" Group had prevented Somasekhar from joining the group due to his RSS background and known pro-BJP ideological stand.

Ananth Kumar, true to his word, fixed meetings with BJP MPs in double quick time. This showed his clout within the party. Then came the logistics.

Initially, his office funded our (Somasekhar's and mine) travel to Delhi and stay there. Later, Rajya Sabha MP, Rajeev Chandrasekhar paid for my travel and stay, while Somasekhar's expenses were taken care of by Ananth Kumar's office. We made trips almost every week. (Rajeev Chandrasekhar is also a petitioner against the Sham ID "Aadhaar" in the Supreme Court. Soon after the 2014 elections, he withdrew his support to me for travels to Delhi.)

Earlier, in 2012, our (Somasekhar's and mine) case against the Sham ID, called "Aadhaar" was dismissed by the lower court and we had decided to appeal to the Karnataka High Court. Somasekhar told me that former justice, Rama Jois wished to meet us, as he also desired to campaign against the Sham ID, called "Aadhaar". So, Somasekhar and I met him in his residence in Bengaluru. He said that he was planning to file a case in the Supreme Court. I tried to dissuade from doing so. Instead, I suggested that he join in the appeal to the Karnataka High Court and later in the suit in the lower court. I explained the advantages of doing so by suggesting that it would give us a chance to put the people behind the project in the witness box and examine or cross-examine them. He did not buy the argument. He was bent upon approaching the Apex court and questioning the validity of the executive actions in setting up UIDAI under Article 73 of the Constitution. Although he was quite upset by my suggestion, he said he would help us get an advocate to represent us in the Supreme Court. He then spoke to Ram Jethmalani. We agreed that one of the activists could meet Jethmalani. I requested Usha Ramanathan to do so, but I think she was not inclined to meet him.

Later however, during one of our trips to Delhi, Somasekhar took me to meet some Akhil Bharatiya Vidyarthi Parishad (ABVP) office-bearers. Somasekhar requested them to introduce us to an advocate who could represent us in the Supreme Court, if need be.

At this stage, we were still inclined to pursue the appeal in the Karnataka High Court. This was not to be, as the High Court insisted that we deposit the penalty of ₹ 25,000.00 each imposed on us by the lower court before the appeal is heard. We did not want to do so. Hence we were left with no alternative but to approach the Supreme Court.

The ABVP members called Bharat Kumar, who was secretary of the BJP advocates association – Akhil Bharatiya Adhivakta Parishad (ABAP). He is a cheerful, helpful, fine gentleman. He readily agreed to help us. He set up a meeting with BJP advocates. Aishwarya Bhati, who was then secretary of the

Supreme Court Bar Association (SCBA), kindly agreed to represent me, at the suggestion of Bharat Kumar. Amit Sharma was to represent Somasekhar.

After the 2014 elections, when BJP assumed office and Modi became PM, there was a notable slackening of enthusiasm on the part of BJP friends to continue opposing the Sham ID with the same vigor as before.

I met Bharat Kumar in Delhi and asked him about the views of the BJP. He was non-committal. It was interesting to watch the slow but steady change in the PM's attitude. Initially (in 2014), he hardly made any reference to the Sham ID, called "Aadhaar", although there was a passing mention in his Independence Day Red Fort address to the nation. Newspapers started putting out reports that the PM/PMO were for the Sham ID, called "Aadhaar" and would implement it. Slowly, the PM became associated more closely with the Sham ID, called "Aadhaar". It was included in the budget for 2015-16. Then there were news reports of officials from the PMO calling secretaries in state governments pushing for speedy implementation of the scheme.

The final act of perfidy was the passage of the Aadhaar (Targeted Delivery of Subsidies, Benefits, and Services) Act, 2016, as a Money Bill. This was to avoid discussion in the Rajya Sabha, where the BJP did not have a majority.

Two unanswered questions remain. What made the PM support the Sham ID? Obviously, his hesitation shows that he was feeling uneasy at going back on his election campaign against it. He had to wait until people forget his speeches. Probably, he hoped that the scheme would be welcomed by the people and his change in stance could be justified. That has not happened. The scheme was *ab initio* unworkable, being both scientifically and mathematically impossible. Added to this was the unbelievably flawed enrolment process.

The second question is, why did the MPs and ministers, who too had met me, and used me in their election campaign, not oppose the PM or advise him against it? Subservience is part of our culture. Perhaps, it is a legacy of the past, a habit cultivated during the British rule which is difficult to shake off. Many an Indian politician would not hesitate to utter lies. Even those in high positions and media-created personalities speak falsehood without so much as a by your leave. Thus we find Nilekani, depicted in the media as a paragon of virtue from the "ethical" corporate, Infosys, saying tongue in cheek, "Aadhaar is voluntary, but service providers may ask for it."

Others in government, like the former DG, UIDAI, R. S. Sharma, and the current CEO, UIDAI often write in newspapers articles extolling the wonders of the Sham ID, called "Aadhaar" Scheme. Are they ignorant of the failure of biometrics? Are they unconcerned or equally ignorant of the dangers of Pak spies, illegal immigrants, etc. obtaining Aadhaar numbers?

Don't they see the results of the sting operations that expose rampant corruption and fraud in enrolments? Are they not aware that subsidies of rations or LPG are not stolen by the poor through fake/ghost ration cards or connections? Why don't they ask the thefts to be investigated? Could they be unaware of the LSE report on the U.K. National ID Card Act and its scrapping? There were attempts to differentiate between the U.K. ID Card and the Indian Sham ID, called "Aadhaar". One point made by these people is that the U.K. ID card contained details of the person. Another was that the U.K. ID card was meant for preventing illegal immigration. So what? Haven't they read Prof. Ian Angell's article which showed that it is impossible to secure an ID database such as the U.K.'s national ID card database. Prof. Angell also explained that it would be impossible to input accurate data or keep the data updated.

If they haven't read it, they should read the US National Academies Report titled, "Biometrics: Challenges and Opportunities".[26] The report is available for free download and also as an e-book or print edition.

I can understand ignorant people Tweeting support for the Sham ID, called "Aadhaar" out of party or personality or ideological loyalties; but these (the former DG and present CEO, UIDAI) are persons who should know.

The progress or transition of the case through the Supreme Court has been described earlier and is not repeated here.

There were a number of seminars organized by the anti-sham ID campaigners. Others like Citizens Voluntary Initiative for the City (CIVIC) organized one such seminar. This was in 2012. At my request, CIVIC invited the local head of UIDAI, Ashok Dalwai, and the e-governance director of Karnataka Government, Dr. Ravindra (?) to the panel discussion. I must thank Ms. Kathyayini, Executive Director of CIVIC for accepting my request to host the event. She did this despite her view that the Sham ID, called "Aadhaar" Scheme would do good to the poor. She is one of those innocent, perhaps, ignorant (of biometrics and information technology) supporters of the project. The campaigners were given barely 5 to 10 minutes to state our case. The UIDAI person was given almost half

---

[26] Biometrics: Challenges and Opportunities – US National Academies Report 2010. The URL is available in the appendix

hour. Midway through the UIDAI presentation, the audience started pestering the speaker, Dalwai, with questions and finally shouted him down. This is sad. Unfortunately, it is also a typical Indian attitude towards debates and discussions, where rationality takes a back seat and emotions rule.

Another event was organized in the JNU (Jawaharlal Nehru University) campus. Here Prof. Ramakumar from TISS and others spoke. At this event, I requested Ramakumar, who is a member of the State Planning Commission of Kerala to help me obtain an appointment with the State leaders, the CM and FM, with whom he had a fairly good rapport. After the event, I made several attempts to follow up with Ramakumar. These were futile. Finally, I did succeed in getting appointments with both the CM and FM of Kerala through the good offices of Nilotpal Basu, CPI (M) MP. I thank him for his help.

The meetings with the Kerala leaders were also without any positive outcome, as I have mentioned in detail earlier. None of the persons who I met responded to follow up emails or phone calls. I have often wondered what causes such apathy and indifference to so important an issue. Could it be ignorance or are there other reasons?

Sucheta Dalal, founder of 'Money Life' Foundation was another ardent campaigner and supporter of the anti-sham ID campaign. She is the one who, as a young journalist, at great risk to her life, exposed one of the biggest scams in Indian history, the "Harshad Mehta" scam. She organized many events on the Sham ID and invited speakers to these programs. I was one of the speakers at perhaps the first of her programs. During that event, a person from the audience, whose name I remember as Ashok Kalbag, was arguing in support of the Sham ID, called "Aadhaar" Scheme. Later I learnt that he was working for some outfit with connections to Nilekani. When I queried him on his source of income and job/business, he clamped up and did not respond.

Money Life also organized programs at which Usha Ramanathan and Anupam Saraph spoke. Anupam Saraph holds a doctorate degree from Netherlands and is a professor at the Symbiosis Institute of Computer Studies. He has been a vigorous campaigner and a great help. He compiled a list of frauds using the Sham ID Aadhaar numbers.[27] These, 101 in number, are in an Excel sheet in the appendix. They are newspaper and media reports of the crimes. One of the characteristics of these and many other crimes, like seizure of cash in elections,

---

[27] Aadhaar Enabled Frauds – Compiled by Anupam Saraph

is that they are soon forgotten. My RTI queries to both UIDAI and Election Commission (for cases of seizure of cash during elections) elicited replies stating that once the FIR is filed, they have no information on the outcomes. That is strange. The FIR is a First Information Report to the police. A statutory authority of the government is reporting a crime to the police and then the authority forgets about it. Something is certainly wrong with the thinking behind such irresponsible conduct.

Worse, UIDAI takes no action to prevent the frauds. This is not surprising. UIDAI can do nothing to thwart such crimes since the system of enrolment is so flawed that it facilitates crime. Further, by promoting the Sham ID, called "Aadhaar" as, a requirement for every conceivable government service, UIDAI has created a premium on the Sham ID.

In my view, the campaign is not a success since the campaign objective of withdrawing the Act and destroying data has not been achieved. One of the lessons we need to learn from the failure of the campaign is that unless political parties are involved, the chance of success is low. I note a hesitation on the part of activists to engage with political parties.

Contrast this with what the campaigners in anti-U.K. National ID Card Act did. Here's the history of that campaign quoted from Wikipedia. "NO2ID arose initially from various campaigning groups to become an entity in its own right. Its initial form was to act as an umbrella group including staff and officers of Liberty, Charter 88 (now Unlock Democracy), Privacy International, the Foundation for Information Policy Research, the 1990 Trust and Stand.org.uk.[1] NO2ID-branded material first appeared in 2002, published and paid for by Liberty and Charter 88.

NO2ID's support is broad based including political parties on the political left (such as Respect and the Greens), in the centre (such as the Liberal Democrats) and on the right (such as the United Kingdom Independence Party and Conservative Future, though the Conservative Party has pledged to scrap the ID scheme), as well as civil liberties groups such as Liberty, Privacy International, Action on Rights for Children, the Open Rights Group and Genewatch UK, other organisations including trades unions (e.g. UNISON, the National Union of Journalists & the University and College Union) and public bodies including District, City and Borough Councils,[2] the Scottish Parliament, the National Assembly for Wales and the London Assembly and individuals such as Neil Tennant, Philip Pullman, and Conservative Mayor of London Boris Johnson have affiliated to or made public declarations of support for the NO2ID campaign."

The campaign was a broad coalition of diverse groups and political parties with one aim–that of repealing the U.K. National ID Card Act.

In sharp contrast, in India the campaigners did not come together into a single forum or group. As noted earlier, one of the first campaign bodies, the 'Say No 2 UID' did not accept Somasekhar because he was a rightist/ RSS member.

In the U.K., the opposition political parties, Conservatives and Liberals had the abolition of the Act in their 2009 election manifestos.

I made the mistake of not requesting BJP to include the scrapping of the UIDAI in its manifesto.

Ananth Kumar arranged for Somasekhar and me to meet many top BJP leaders and MPs. Thus we had individual meetings with Sushma Swaraj, Ravi Shankar Prasad, S S Ahluwalia, Arun Jaitley, Piyush Goyal, and L K Advani.

The efforts of Ananth Kumar resulted in granting me an opportunity to address the BJP Parliamentary party in the Annex of the Parliament building. I thank him for this.

About 200 BJP MPs from both houses of Parliament were present. I was given 5 minutes time but, took about 10 minutes. Advani presided over the meeting. Rajnath Singh and Arun Jaitley were on the dais with him. During my Power Point Presentation (PPT), Jaitley asked me to give him the material on which I was basing my case against the Sham ID. This was strange, as only the previous day, when Somasekhar and I met him in his office in Parliament, we had given him all material, including documentary evidence, such as data being handed over to foreign entities. We then had another set of documents given to him from Ananth Kumar's office in Delhi.

Immediately after my presentation of the case against the Sham ID, Advani held up a monograph which was jointly written by some of us activists, titled "UID is NOT Yours" and showed it to the audience of MPs. I had earlier sent this to many MPs from all major parties. I had sent it to about a 100 MPs. Advani was the only MP to acknowledge its receipt and he was also the only one who had read it. Showing it to the BJP MPs he said, "Read this. Don't use the word, 'Aadhaar'. It is the name of a private Trust of Nilekani."

After the meeting, Ananth Kumar and Ravi Shankar Prasad took us to the TV journalists present outside and Prasad addressed them. Not one of the media channels carried the news of this.

As part of the anti-sham ID campaign, I have spoken on camera a number of times explaining the futility and dangers of the Sham ID, called "Aadhaar" Scheme. Many of these are available as You Tube videos.[28]

Here's a picture of Kshitij interviewing me on one of the You Tube videos.

Fig 14: Kshitij Urs who interviewed me for a You Tube video

The link to this video is <https://www.youtube.com/watch?v=J8YtkVf2cjY&t=10s>

One of the videos in the appendix is Modi's election campaign speech at Bengaluru in 2014. He roundly criticizes the Sham ID, called "Aadhaar" and calls it a corrupt scheme. In another video two years later in 2016, he praises the same Sham ID, called "Aadhaar" as very useful. Why do our leaders, politicians of all hues, activists, people in general – the so-called 'aam aadmi', authors, intellectuals, business persons, and media personalities exhibit this behavior?

I have often wondered about this peculiarly Indian phenomenon. Then one day, I recalled reading an excellent book which answered the question quite well, though in part, a substantial part.

This book has the arresting title, *"Games Indians Play"* (that is apart from IPL cricket and Kabaddi). V Raghunathan is its author. It follows a similar title of another book, one on a branch of psychology, "transactional analysis", by Eric Berne, *"Games People Play."*

---

[28] List of You Tube Videos and other URLs mentioned in this book are in the appendix.

Fig 15: Eric Berne

This is Berne's photo available from Wikipedia.

The games Indians play have nothing, well almost nothing, to do with transactional analysis. Our ego states (to use Berne's terminology) are derived largely from our cultural surroundings. Parenting has a big say in our subsequent behavior. It has been said that when a child walks to school for the first time, it carries with it 25,000 hours of taped messages in its brain. Everything it experiences is then interpreted in the light of the recordings of the experiences of the first five years of the child.

If we are merely an evolved primate species, then, "Monkey see, monkey do" is applicable to us. We see people discarding garbage on to streets or people spiting at stairway corners and imitate them.

According to Berne, people transact (interact with others) from what he calls, "Ego states". These are psychological positions or mental states. He postulates three ego states, namely, Parent, Adult and child. The Parent state is one wherein the person transacts with authority in relation to the person addressed; much like parents do when talking to their children. The Adult state is one in which rational transactions (communications, discussions) could take place between adults. It is the one that is largely productive. The Child ego state is one wherein the person seeks attention, just as children do when wanting something from parents.

My observation of Indian behavior is that we mostly transact from either the Parent or Child ego states. One has to only watch the Arnab Goswami show on Republic TV to appreciate what I am saying here. Contrast this with a panel discussion by Tim Sebastian on BBC TV and the difference is glaring.

Raghunathan gives twelve 'canons' of Indianness in the book "Games Indians Play.

1. Low trustworthiness
2. Being privately smart and publicly dumb
3. Fatalistic outlook
4. Being too intelligent for our own good
5. Abysmal sense of *public* hygiene (I have seen how cleanly we keep even our huts in deep rural India.)
6. Lack of self-regulation and sense of fairness
7. Reluctance to penalize wrong conduct in others
8. Mistaking talk for action (Is it any wonder many believe the rhetoric of the PM?)
9. Deep-rooted corruption and flair for free riding
10. Inability to follow or implement systems
11. A sense of self-worth massaged only if we have authority to break rules
12. Propensity to look for loopholes in laws. (Does this explain the Aadhaar Act as a "Money Bill"?)

The first canon–Low trustworthiness–is so true; we even take pride in it. What else would justify the chief of a victorious party saying after the elections that the major election promises of the one who became PM were false, and that the people were fools to believe him?

The truth of this stark reality is even more apparent when we see that the loyalists of these worthies admire the cleverness of the one who made the promise and the debating skills of the other who justified it.

The reason perhaps, for the failure of activists to get together to form one body to jointly take the anti-sham ID campaign, is lack of trustworthiness. We don't trust each other. We also mistake talk for action. Many activists talk (and write) a lot. These are misunderstood as useful substitutes for action.

The shenanigans in government formation in Karnataka, as I write this, are typical of the propensity to look for loopholes in the law. Anything, however immoral or illegal or unethical is justified in the race to the bottom of good governance ranking, as long as "our guy" is in power.

There were many "silent" contributors to the anti-sham ID campaign. Anand Venkatnarayanan, a young techie is a very good example. He thoroughly exposed the false claims of UIDAI regarding savings in welfare funds as the result of use of the Sham ID, called "Aadhaar". He posted his excellent analysis on Twitter.

In this context, it is interesting to note the fervent support to the Sham ID by those who are enamored of the use of technology, but have very little knowledge of it. The PM and Andhra CM, Chandra Babu Naidu are two such. They have a religious faith in technology coupled with little or no understanding, knowledge or experience in the use of IT, in particular. Their faith is based on hearsay, second hand opinions from those who they think are believable.

The PM imagines and appears convinced that use of Sham ID, called "Aadhaar" has saved and will save huge sums of money, otherwise stolen from welfare funds. At least, he thinks that this could justify his decision to push for implementation of the scheme he virulently opposed all through.

The Andhra CM's rush to link the Sham ID Aadhaar number to all state databases has resulted in entire data in databases becoming public. Ignorance in decision-making entails costs.

During the 2014 elections, I corresponded with Subramanian Swamy, now BJP Rajya Sabha MP. I met him in December 2013 in Chennai. At the invitation of Somasekhar and myself, he came to address an election meeting in Apr 2014. I was surprised to note that he had brought with him documents that I had given to him during the meeting in Chennai 4 months previously. Even more surprising he remembered the explanations of the implications of the documents I had given to him.

He said that Nilekani should be prosecuted under the Prevention of Corruption Act. However, he too kept silent when Modi decided to implement the Sham ID, called "Aadhaar" Scheme.

During 2016 and 2017, other activists emerged on the scene. Thus there is an organization called "Re-think Aadhaar". Another is called "Aadhaar Fail".

The former, Re-think Aadhaar seems to have some foreign connection.

In 2017, I tried to contact the TMC (Trinamool Congress) MP, Derek O'Brien. Firstly, I sent him emails seeking an appointment. When I was in Delhi I went to his office.

I met his secretary, Shane. When I explained to him the reason I wished to meet the MP, he appeared confused and suggested that I meet Chetna Kumar. She came a little later and suggested that I talk to the Re-think Aadhaar group. I told her that I would do so but requested that she help fix an appointment with the MP, Derek O'Brien. She agreed. The next time when I was in Delhi, I went to the

MP's office along with Gopal Krishna, an anti-UID activist. Again, I requested Chetna Kumar for the appointment with the MP. She told me that he had gone to the airport and would take time to return. We requested her to inform us when he came back. As we were coming out of his office, we saw him entering it. We did not receive any call from her and did not get the appointment to meet the MP.

My purpose in seeking the appointment was the same as my attempts to meet the CPM leaders in Kerala. I wished that a state government ask UIDAI for the contract with BSPs, then raise the question of why the contract grants access to the BSPs and authorizes the BSPs to "collect, use, store, transfer, process and link the data to individuals." The West Bengal government had opposed the Sham ID, called "Aadhaar" Scheme. Its CM, Mamata Banerjee had publicly stated that she would not implement it in the state. So, it again astonished me that one of her most prominent MPs did not give me an appointment and his staff did not succeed in arranging one.

Through the help of Gopal Krishna, I met a number of people who I thought would be interested in making the dirty deal of the contract public. Among the people who we met were MPs [one was from the JD (U) from Bihar], a staunch supporter of the Modi government who was head of a central government cultural center and some others. I met Swamy Agnivesh and spent about an hour explaining the seriousness of handing over all data to foreign entities. At his invitation (for which, I thank him), I stayed on for lunch and we had a very interesting conversation. When I was explaining the contract and its dangers, he invited some of his staff members who were tech-savvy. One young member of his staff questioned my information. He was more concerned with my data which showed that the founder directors of L 1 Identity Solutions Operating Company Pvt. Ltd. were all formerly employed in CIA, homeland security, defense department and FBI.

Not one of the many persons to whom I gave documentary evidence of all data being handed over to foreign entities ever brought it out in public.

Once, along with Somasekhar, I had a lengthy discussion with M P Achuthan, an MP from Kerala. We explained to him at great length the Sham ID, called "Aadhaar" Scheme. He gave us a patient hearing for about two hours. We do not know what he did subsequently. We never heard from him afterwards.

UIDAI, Nilekani and many others among the Sham ID protagonists are fond of making us believe that the Sham ID, called "Aadhaar" Scheme is the same as or similar to SSN of USA. I wonder what they would say to the question whether the US Government would contractually grant access to all SSN data to private parties and allow these to collect (more data), use, store, transfer, process and link to individuals.

None of the anti-Sham ID activists, as far as I know, contacted any political party or politician for support. If they did, they have not revealed the outcome.

In discussing the games Indians play, I find something stranger than what Raghunathan describes in his book by the name.

This is the inability or rather the refusal to see the implications of handing over all data to foreign entities and authorizing them to do whatever they wish to with it. If one were to look at the blindness to the impact of the contract clauses alongside the frenzied talk about data protection, the glee in reporting data leaks or hacking, one cannot but conclude something seriously amiss with the Indian psyche. I shall discuss this while describing the role of the Indian media.

RTI

I was able to garner a lot of information through RTI. The experience was revealing how the Indian bureaucracy respects or rather disrespects the law of the land. The first response to almost all my RTI queries invariably was to either deny or pass the buck. There were a few brave souls who were prompt. However, in the majority of the queries, I had to resort to the appeal process. The *RTI Act stipulates in Section 4 (1) (c) and (d) of RTI Act, 2005 that public authorities are to "publish all relevant facts while formulating important policies announcing decisions which affect public"; and "provide reasons for its administrative or quasi-judicial decisions to affected persons."*

I have not come across a single instance wherein any public authority has acted in accordance with this law. The Government issued over a 100 notifications on making the Sham ID, called "Aadhaar" compulsory for various purposes which are neither subsidies, nor benefits nor services. For example, the amendment to the Income Tax Act making it mandatory for linking the Sham ID Aadhaar number with bank accounts. No reasons were given until people started questioning it and the answers were to the Supreme Court. Sections 4 (1) (c) and (d) of RTI Act are observed in the breach. Another example is the order issued asking the applicants for UGC scholarships to produce Sham ID Aadhaar number. UGC did not think it fit to announce the reason for the decision.

The crowning irony is that the Aadhaar Act has as its objective "transparency" while making every action of UIDAI opaque to public though Section 7 of The Aadhaar (Data Security) Regulations, 2016.

I would like to briefly share my experience and success in tackling the bureaucratic stone-walling tactics. Hopefully, this would be useful to those who wish to use RTI to ensure accountability of governments. I used cross examination techniques of successful criminal lawyers. I would send the same set of questions, suitably modified, if need be, simultaneously to different government entities. For example, I sent RTI applications on fakes/duplicates to Ministry of Petroleum and Natural Gas (MoPNG), and all three Oil Marketing Companies (OMCs). The Ministry would promptly pass the buck to the OMCs claiming that after the administrative price mechanism has been removed, the ministry has no information. The OMCs would dilly-dally before providing any information at all. By seeking answers from two or more departments for the same queries, the chance of anyone bluffing is reduced. Thus, I would ask the Bangalore office of UIDAI and the UIDAI head office the same questions in RTI applications.

I found that the Technology Division would contradict the Headquarters. A typical example is the RTI query on fakes/duplicates.

I have filed hundreds of RTI applications and it is a huge story which space and time precludes from recounting here.

MEDIA

A word about Indian media's approach to the Sham ID, called "Aadhaar" is necessary here. The media held panel discussions. Even Rajya Sabha TV did so. The media carried many articles. News reports were put out on data leaks and on militants and terrorists when arrested found to be having "Aadhaar card". Media did sting operations. 'Headlines Today' and TV 9 did so. *Yet, none of them highlighted the contracts and the handing over of all data to foreign entities.*

I was told that whenever media published any article critical of the Sham ID, they would be called by UIDAI or Nilekani personally and asked to keep off. 'Deccan Herald' published one or two of my articles and thereafter stopped doing so.

Noam Chomsky's excellent exposition of manufacturing consent, in his book by the same name, gives insights into why media behaves in this fashion. In the preface to the book, he refers to US practices in Central America and says, "These practices have not only distorted public perceptions of Central American realities, they have also seriously misrepresented U. S. policy objectives, an essential feature of propaganda, as Jacques Ellul stresses:

"The propagandist naturally cannot reveal the true intentions of the principal for whom he acts… That would be to submit the projects to public discussion, to the scrutiny of public opinion, and thus prevent their success… Propaganda must serve as veil for such projects, masking true intention."

If consent was manufactured anywhere, surely it is in India and in the Sham ID, called "Aadhaar" Scheme that manufactured consent finds it greatest success. UIDAI often claims that consent of the one who enrolls is taken. Can anything be more ridiculous considering that the poor, millions of them, enrolled under threat of denial of food? The middle class scampered to enroll when threatened with stoppage of LPG subsidies, blocking of bank accounts and mobile numbers and scholarships and even denial of entry to competitive examinations for those without the Sham ID, called "Aadhaar".

The AG repeatedly claimed during arguments in the Supreme Court that a billion people "volunteered" for the Sham ID.

UIDAI took massive advertisements and perhaps "leaked' news showing it in favorable light. Thus, news was put out on lost children being restored to their parents using the Sham ID, called "Aadhaar".

Here's an image of UIDAI's advertisement.

Fig 16: UIDAI's advertisement claiming "Reuniting lost children with their parents."

Another of UIDAI's advertisements is even worse, as it is a tissue of lies and fabrications put out as Frequently Asked Questions – FAQs.

Here is this advertisement.

Fig 17: UIDAI's advertisement on FAQs

These advertisements were put out just when the Supreme Court hearings began in 2018. UIDAI was making its arguments both inside and outside the court.

The advertisements are blunt, blatant lies. Take the one on lost children being restored to parents "using Aadhaar".

The headline of the advertisement says, "Aadhaar Reunited Missing Children with their families – A Reason to Rejoice."

It quotes 8 newspaper reports of "Aadhaar" reuniting lost children. What is left unsaid is "How?" If one reads the news reports, they too do not answer the question, "How". Firstly, the Sham ID, called "Aadhaar" does not have as one of its objectives, reuniting lost or runaway children. So, let's say that this is a bonus. Children do not have biometrics of a quality which would help identify them accurately. Hence the claim that "Aadhaar" reunited children is preposterous.

From the demographic data (which incidentally, UIDAI admits in its BSP Contracts, is so inaccurate as to be unusable) even though unreliable, some idea of who the parents could be and where to find them may be obtained. It is not then difficult to trace the parents. Does not common sense tell us that if we were to keep the demographics of all people in a database, that could be used to trace or track people? So, claiming in an advertisement that "Aadhaar" helped reunite children is merely using the brand name of the Sham ID, called "Aadhaar" to mislead readers into attributing magical powers to it. It is a half-page advertisement. Tax payers have paid for UIDAI to put out an advertisement to deceive themselves. How ironic!

The other advertisement is worse. It is titled "Frequently Asked Questions."

Let's look at some of the brazen lies in it.

One of the FAQs reads thus: "Why am I being asked to link all my bank accounts with "Aadhaar"? (The quotation marks are mine.)

The answer given in the advertisement has three statements. These are as follows.

> ➤ For your own security, it is necessary to verify identity of all bank account holders and link them to "Aadhaar" to weed out the accounts being operated by fraudsters, money-launderers, criminals, etc.
>
> ➤ When every bank account is verified and linked with "Aadhaar" and then if anyone fraudulently withdraws money from your account such fraudster can be easily located and punished.
>
> ➤ Therefore, by linking your bank accounts with "Aadhaar", your accounts become more secure and not the other way around.

From the advertisement, it is obvious that UIDAI imagines that everyone is a fool and would fall for such tomfoolery or buffoonery.

The advertisement is effectively saying to everyone, "You could be fraudster, money-launderer or criminal. Therefore, you are to link your bank account with the Sham ID Aadhaar number. Once, it is determined that you are not any of these, then linking your bank account with the Sham ID Aadhaar number would protect your account".

UIDAI is telling the nation, "Everyone is a criminal, unless proved otherwise." This is indeed ironic since UIDAI is itself involved in what could be termed criminal activity of handing over the entire data to foreign entities and lying to the people and courts that data is safe.

Fortunately, from the observations and questions by the Supreme Court, it is clear that UIDAI has not been able to pull wool over the eyes of the Court and it has seen through the UIDAI game plan.

The idiotic assumption in the statement is that banks have not verified accounts being opened. Further, UIDAI is claiming in the advertisement that once bank accounts are linked to Sham ID Aadhaar numbers, the criminals would be identified or that anyone who commits a banking fraud would be apprehended. Contrast this with the reality of the incidents described below.

In 2016, a Pak spy working in its embassy was caught while taking documents from a jawan. He was found in possession of not only a Sham ID Aadhaar number but also a bank account and an LPG connection. He was in receipt of LPG subsidies in his bogus bank account.

As recently as Jan 2018, another Pak national was caught while attempting to enter the Jaisalmer Air Force base. He was found in possession of a Sham ID Aadhaar number. He had been living in India for the past 18 years.[29]

UIDAI never comments on such cases. In fact, since the Sham ID, called "Aadhaar" is for all residents, legal or illegal, and biometrics does not differentiate between nationalities, it is impossible to prevent any foreigner or criminal from obtaining the Sham ID number.

UIDAI admits in its contracts with BSPs that its demographic data is inaccurate. Examination of the enrolment process makes it evident that there is no verification of the demographics (address, name, etc.) of Sham ID "Aadhaar" number holders.

In an RTI reply to me dated 12-11-2014, UIDAI stated that the Sham ID Aadhaar number issued to an illegal immigrant from Bangladesh is a "genuine" enrolment! A copy of the UIDAI reply is in the appendix.[30]

It baffles the mind to see UIDAI making such false claims in an advertisement. I think UIDAI deserves to be hauled up before the Advertising Standards Council of India for false advertisements. More astonishing is the fact that such frivolous and patently fallacious full-page advertisements escape the notice of the media, political parties, activists and even advocates.

Instead of singing paeans of how good is the Sham ID, called "Aadhaar", it would be useful to the public to know what on earth the use of this number is. It does not confer citizenship, it does not guarantee any rights, and it assumes

---

[29] The URLs for both these news reports are in the appendix.
[30] UIDAI's RTI reply No. K – 11013/100/2011 – RTI/ Vol. IX/502/2014-15/1699 dated 12-11-2014

that anyone and everyone could be, or already is, a potential thief, it hopes that fakes/ghosts in government databases would be eliminated and that too without any investigation into how these got into the database in the first place. UIDAI assumes, and the powers that be accept, that welfare monies are stolen using fake/ghost IDs, again without any investigation or inquiry.

Worse, the use of biometric identification is only a façade. Once the Sham ID number is generated, the biometrics is no longer used, except to pretend that the whole Sham ID, called "Aadhaar" Scheme is based on foolproof biometrics technology. For example, biometric identification was never used and is not used even now at the point of subsidized LPG cylinders delivery. UIDAI is aware that biometric identification is problematic, as explained earlier, and this fact is proved by the setting up of UBCC and incorporation of Section 5 in the Aadhaar Act.

The Sham ID, called "Aadhaar" Scheme hinges on using numbers linked to people and all their transactions. It does not matter to UIDAI that millions of people may be denied their rights and/or be defrauded. Such callous indifference to sufferings of the poor is unpardonable. And this is done in the name of good governance and efficiency and claimed to be in the interests of the poor and marginalized.

It reminds me of the children's book, "Alice in Wonderland". Alice is unable to distinguish between Tweedledee and Tweedledum, just as we are unable to make out whether UIDAI is government or government is UIDAI, or to make out the difference between the two major political combinations, the UPA and the NDA. First, to understand the confusion between UIDAI and government, let's examine the question, "Is UIDAI a creature of government?" If so, it is a state entity, with sovereign duties and powers. Then, when UIDAI says that the enrolment in Sham ID, called "Aadhaar" is voluntary, one would understand it to mean that the state/government has determined that enrolment is voluntary. When simultaneously, government issues a notification making the production of Sham ID number mandatory for receipt of a particular right, benefit or service, one arm of the government is contradicting another arm of the same government. Hence, like Tweedledee and Tweedledum one cannot differentiate between the two.

Does this seem insane? Well, it seems that the Sham ID, called "Aadhaar" Scheme and all those who promote it, those who oppose it, those who describe it, and those who publish news about it and so forth, are in a modern version of "Alice in Wonderland".

Here's why. Listen to the conversation between Alice and the Cheshire cat.

Fig 18: The Cheshire Cat

Says Alice, "Would you please tell me, please which way I ought to go from here?"

"That depends a good deal on where you want to get to," said the cat.

"I don't much care where–" said Alice.

"Then is doesn't matter which way you go," said the cat.

"—so long as I get somewhere," Alice added as an explanation.

"Oh, you're sure to do that," said the cat, "if you only walk long enough."

Alice felt that this could not be denied, so she tried another question. "What sort of people live about here?"

"In that direction," the Cat said, waving its right paw round, "lives Hatter; and in that direction," waving the other paw, "lives a March Hare. Visit either as you like: they're both quite mad."

Fig 19: The Mad Tea Party

"I am afraid I don't want to go among mad people," Alice remarked.

"Oh, you can't help that," said the Cat: "We're all mad here. I'm mad. You're mad."

"How do you know I'm mad?" said Alice.

"You must be," said the Cat, "or else you wouldn't have come here."

I could go on with Alice's story. The resemblance is uncanny.

We must all be mad to be indulging in the insanity of the Sham ID and pretending that it works, perhaps it needs some tweaking, like data protection, and believing that it is useful—for prevention of subsidy theft, it can prevent money-laundering, that lost children can be restored to parents using Sham ID, called "Aadhaar", imagining that it is ok for some purposes and people, and should be voluntary and not mandatory and so on. And finally, and most importantly, we need not worry about access provided to all data to foreign entities and its *"collection, use, storage, transfer, processing and linking to individuals"* by them is something we need not bother about. If this were not madness, then what is?

Most probably, the mind refuses to accept that UIDAI or government could hand over all data to foreign entities and lie about it.

Many of the very same people who vociferously decry data leakages and intrusion of privacy rights, ask me quite innocently, with a straight face, when I show them the BSP Contracts, "What can they (foreign entities) do with the data?"

So, continuing the "Alice in Wonderland" metaphor, let's look at how UPA and NDA themselves, and their versions of Sham ID, called "Aadhaar" are as indistinguishable as Tweedledee and Tweedledum.

Fig 20: Tweedledee and Tweedledum

"— wherever the road divided there were sure to be two finger-posts pointing the same way, one marked 'To Tweedledum's House', and the other 'To the House of Tweedledee'."

Then Tweedledee recites the poem, "The Walrus and the Carpenter".

Fig 21: The Walrus and the Carpenter

They were walking along the beach and "wept like anything to see such quantities of sand." UPA and NDA weep like anything to see such leakages of subsidies, just like the Walrus and the Carpenter.

Then the Walrus invites Oysters to join them for "A pleasant walk, a pleasant talk." Didn't both UPA and NDA invite us to join the Sham ID, called "Aadhaar" Scheme and that too, voluntarily?

Let me explain the allegory when applied to the Sham ID, called "Aadhaar" Scheme.

The metaphors in the poem are as below.

Tweedledee and Tweedledum are UPA and NDA. We, the people, are the Oysters.

The Walrus is UIDAI and the Carpenter is the government.

The sea bed is the Constitution, where we are safe. The sand is subsidy leakage.

The poem continues,

"The eldest Oyster (*old anti-Sham ID activists as per metaphor*) looked at him,
But never a word he said:
The eldest Oyster winked his eye,
And shook his heavy head –
Meaning to say he did not choose
To leave the oyster-bed.
But four young Oysters hurried up, (*yuppies in metaphor*)
All eager for the treat:
Their coats were brushed, their faces washed,
Their shoes were clean and neat –
And this was odd, because, you know,

They hadn't any feet.
Four other Oysters followed them,
And yet another four;
And thick and fast they came at last, (*Mad rush for LPG!*)
And more, and more, and more –
All hopping through the frothy waves,
And scrambling to the shore.
The Walrus and Carpenter
Walked a mile or so, and then they rested on a rock
Conveniently low:
And all the little Oysters stood
And waited in a row.
"The time has come," the Walrus said,
"To talk of many things:
Of shoes – and ships – and sealing wax–
Of cabbages – and kings –
And why the sea is boiling hot – and whether pigs have wings."
(This is the intermission when 103 notifications were issued. The constant
refrain of "development" by both parties is all too familiar – they talk of many things
– of cabbages and kings!)
"But wait a bit," the Oysters cried,
"Before we have our chat;
For some of us are out of breath,
And all of us are fat!"
"No hurry!" said the Carpenter.
They thanked him much for that.
"A loaf of bread," the Walrus said,
"Is what we chiefly need:
Pepper and vinegar besides
Are very good indeed –
Now if you are ready, Oysters dear,
We begin to feed."
"But not on us!" the Oysters cried,
Turning a little blue,
"After such kindness, that would be
A dismal thing to do!"

"The night is fine," the Walrus said
"Do you admire the view?
It was so kind of you to come!
And you are very nice!"
The Carpenter said nothing but,
"Cut us another slice:
I wish you were not quite so deaf –
I've had to ask you twice!"
"It seems a shame," the Walrus said,
"To play them such a trick,
After we brought them out so far,
And made them trot so quick!"
The Carpenter said nothing but,
"The butter's spread too thick!"
"I weep for you," the Walrus said.
"I deeply sympathise."
With sobs and tears he sorted out
Those of the largest size.
Holding his pocket-handkerchief
Before his streaming eyes.
"O Oysters," said the Carpenter.
"You've had a pleasant run!
Shall we be trotting home again?"
But answer came there none –
And that was scarcely odd, because
They'd eaten every one.'

Fig 22: The Walrus and the Carpenter – after they had eaten the Oysters

I hope that the metaphor makes sense. If we don't watch out, like the Oysters, we will all be eaten up by Tweedledee and Tweedledum – UPA and NDA, with active participation from UIDAI (Walrus) and the Carpenter (government).

The media, as expected, played its presstitute role to perfection. Two experiences during my campaign are worth narrating.

In 2012, the Canadian Broadcasting Corporation (CBC) contacted me through Anil Lula, a journalist. They interviewed me for about an hour or more. The interview was video recorded, walking round a park in Domlur. Later I found that they did not broadcast my interview at all, but only carried Nilekani's promotional pitch on the Sham ID, called "Aadhaar" Scheme. I also came to know that CBC was supporting a similar proposal, to biometrically identify Canadians. The Canadian Parliament shot it down.

Another journalist, Aria Thaker, of 'Caravan' magazine, interviewed me in January 2018. I am thankful to her for it. I spent about three hours and provided her with documentary evidence of the BSP Contracts. I also gave her a number of RTI documents which proved the deceit of UIDAI in hiding the contracts as well as documents pertaining to other aspects of the Sham ID hoax.

Her article, which I must say is painstakingly well researched, is published in 'Caravan' of May 2018. It is kind of her to send me a copy on request. I thank her for this too.

The Cover Story titles it as, "The Private Powers Behind Aadhaar."

Her article is titled, "Aadhaar mixing of public risk and private profit." Its theme is that private parties are profiting from the use of the Sham ID "Aadhaar" data and secondly, it leads to surveillance. These are no doubt true.

Aria has done enormous work. It is quite useful. At least we know those who worked for UIDAI have, or imagine, they have, a business opportunity in using the UIDAI database.

The very idea that former employees, many of them "volunteers", should seek to set up businesses to use the data collected, all of it illegally, as many of us know, is disgusting.

That they approached the Supreme Court in an attempt to intervene in the Sham ID, called "Aadhaar" case, shows how brazen one can get when the conscience is seared and no longer values ethics.

Aria has interviewed a large number of people. The interviewees include Piyush Peshwani, one of the founders of "OnGrid", Saranya Gopinath, counsel for Khosla Labs, Rachita Taneja of Mozilla Foundation, Srinivas Katuri of

Transaction Analysts, Reetika Khera, Professor, IIT Delhi, Nitin Pai of Takshashila Institution, Tanuj Bhojwani with iSPIRT (Indian Software Products Industry Round Table) and India Stack. One, Sanjay Swamy tells her that Aadhaar number is not sensitive data.

She has not mentioned that UIDAI invited applications/proposals for "Application Development using the Aadhaar Platform." This invitation too seems to have been taken off from the UIDAI website.

Most people do not realize that the Sham ID, called "Aadhaar" database is NOT a platform on which one may build applications. Unlike computer languages like UNIX, or software like Oracle which may be customized for use by specific customers, the Sham ID, called "Aadhaar" is a database. The only way in which to use the database is to use the data therein. One cannot say that the data is confidential and at the same time allow it to be used.

What she misses out is that the UIDAI-government pitch promoting the Sham ID is plainly deceitful. She has also not understood the so-called businesses being set up by the numerous people and organizations she talked to. What the so-called businesses are doing is to write a simple code to use the Sham ID number for a certain purpose, for say, an online payment. The code would check up whether the number exists in the Sham ID "Aadhaar" Database. To do so, UIDAI allows these entities to query the database. These agencies are called AUAs (Authorized User Agencies). Only permitting selected organizations to do this work creates a monopoly.

Secondly, the business model of the AUAs is two-fold. One, they charge a fee for authentication of ID. Next, they can, and would, (protestation to the contrary are to be taken with barrels of salt) collect the type of data (perhaps, metadata) of each authentication transaction. It could be a bank that is asking for authentication of a customer. It might be an insurance company or a Food Department. The nature of the entity asking for authentication provides a clue to the purpose of authentication. This is valuable commercial information.

It is more serious that she ignored or rather did not emphasize the danger of authorizing foreign entities, like L 1 Identity Solutions Operating Company Pvt. Ltd. to "collect, use, transfer, store, process, —- information that pertains to specific individuals and can be linked to them." This quote in her article is from the copy of the BSP contract that I gave her. It is in Clause 3.1 of Annexure 'B' of UIDAI's contract with M/s. L 1 Identity Solutions Operating Company Pvt. Ltd. The quote is in a paragraph on page 42 of the magazine carrying the article.

The paragraph is placed within brackets. I don't know why. While she adds, "Critics have pointed out that such sharing of data violates provisions in the Aadhaar Act," there is no comment or explanation of the implications of the grant of access to all data to foreign entities, the dangers to the people and the nation in doing so, and that this, (access of all data to foreigners) is tantamount to treason.

It is this hesitation to call a spade a spade that is puzzling. Not only Aria, but almost all people who I met and showed the contract to, are uncomfortable facing the terrible fact of our government lying to people about data not being shared while providing access to all data to foreigners. One minister in Karnataka, when I showed him the relevant clause of the contract remarked, "This is for the high command to take action. I cannot do anything." He too, as a minister of government, did not understand treason when he saw evidence of it!

I had an interesting exchange of WhatsApp messages with Aria on this. She told me that the story on access to data to foreign entities has already been covered. She referred to Govind's article in 'Fountain Ink' and the 'Times of India' news story by Chetan Dash (Kumar). She did not know that both of them had been given the documents by me. She told me that there were constraints on the length of her piece of writing. That's understandable.

The 'Fountain Ink' article did mention L 1 Identity Solutions Operating Company Pvt. Ltd.

The question of misplaced priorities and inability to appreciate the seriousness, indeed, to have even a basic understanding of what the real issue is, is the fundamental problem. The issue is far greater than using the Sham ID "Aadhaar" Database for authentication and collecting data for later commercial exploitation or providing access to all data to foreign entities.

The issue is not about *sharing* data. The issue has two facets.

One facet is that apart from access to all data, there is the **contractual authorization** to *collect (more data), use, store, transfer, process and link (the data) to individuals.*

The *second aspect is the lying being done by both UIDAI and the government about it.* Both keep repeating that the data is safe, that it is not shared. As mentioned earlier, the AG is on record in the Supreme Court stating how safe the data is, informing with his own limited understanding of informational data security, that the UIDAI servers are safe behind 13-feet-high walls. The CEO,

UIDAI informed the Supreme Court that the foreign BSP Contractor's officials are escorted into and out of the UIDAI data center and by inference argued that the possibility of these official taking out data is extremely low.

Aria in 'Caravan' and Govind in 'Fountain Ink' are completely off the mark on the real issue. Aria's theme is on commercial exploitation of the data. She has not understood how such commercial use of UIDAI data is not just about private profits at public expense, or about revolving doors, or security of data, but about garnering metadata from transactions that pass through the APIs.

Govind has expounded on how US military-industrial complex and its intelligence agencies collaborate to collect data from numerous sources. This has been so well documented by Glen Greenwald in his book "No Place to Hide" on Snowden, that there is no need at all to push the theme of US intelligence collection.

Both Aria and Govind have done painstaking work – interviewing people, researching the Net and so on. Their laudable effort unfortunately actually diverts attention from the real issue.

THE REAL ISSUE THAT IS MISSED OUT

For me the anti-sham ID campaign has been a great learning experience. It taught me how people make decisions. Observing this was enjoyable as a first-hand experience in behavioral science.

Dan Ariely, as mentioned earlier, has authored a book titled, "Predictably Irrational." It gives lovely insights into human irrationality. While so, I believe that his thesis and hence the title is wrong. People are "Differently Rational." One person's rationale is different from another's. So, we erroneously think that those not in tune with our rationality are irrational.

Is there an absolute rationality? Probably yes, but we find even God unpredictable, un-understandable and hence, to our mind irrational.

This different rationality, perhaps explains why most people missed out the essence of the issue in the Sham ID, called "Aadhaar", as I see it.

I think that Aria, Govind, all activists against the Sham ID, called "Aadhaar" Scheme, the advocates who represented them in the Supreme Court and the judges who heard the case (as seen from lack of observations and questions from the court), politicians, national security officials and cyber-security experts and media have not realized the implications of these clauses in the BSP Contracts. I found all of them superbly irrational by my line of analysis and thinking of the central issue of the Sham ID, called "Aadhaar". All of them are rational in their own way, only their rationality is different from mine. For understanding my rationale in approaching the crux of the issue in the Sham ID, called "Aadhaar", let me put some questions.

Here are the questions that I think arise, and that need extremely serious, careful consideration.

Why does the contract not only provide access to all data to foreign entities but also authorize them to collect additional data, use the data, store it, transfer it and process it for linking to individuals?

Who sanctioned such clauses in the contracts?

Did these clauses in the contract have government sanction? After all, the decision to provide access to all data of the people of this country and to authorize its unrestricted use by foreign firms, is not a decision taken lightly or one that could be taken by a bureaucrat.

Can any government sanction a contract authorizing foreign entities to not only access all data of its people but also to use the data in any manner these entities wish to?

The contract was signed during the previous UPA government. It is quite unlikely, though not impossible, that Manmohan Singh, then prime minister saw the contract or gave his consent. However, there can be no doubt that Nilekani and the top bureaucrats who were at the helm of affairs of UIDAI were aware of the contract.

Now, let's analyze the NDA's attitude to the Sham ID, called "Aadhaar". I don't think the NDA politicians realize the consequences of the contract. Most politicians are not technical people and hence are ignorant of technological dangers. Many are complacent about such ideas of national security, which to them is a vague concept, unless they come to know that the enemy is marching across borders or is blowing up trains and buildings or hijacking planes.

That said, NDA has less of an excuse than UPA. I addressed their Parliamentary party. I met most of the top leadership, except the present PM and the party chief. I have given documentary evidence to these leaders. I do concede that they would neither have the time nor inclination to read the evidence, let alone grapple with the technical jargon of the contracts; but then, BJP has an IT Cell. They are masters at Tweeting and perhaps, trolling. Do they not have the expertise to unravel the contracts? Among the MPs, over a hundred, to whom I had sent my first monograph on the Sham ID, only one – Advani – acknowledged it. After my brief presentation to the Parliamentary party, he held up the monograph and pointing to it, told the party, "Read this. Never use the word, 'Aadhaar'. It is the name of a private Trust of Nilekani."

After the NDA assumed office, I wrote to both the PM and the NSA. It is quite possible, perhaps most likely, that the babus in the PMO filtered my mail and the PM never got to see it. Yet, it is not possible to absolve him of all responsibility. He too is naïve as far as technology is concerned and enamored of it. He has fallen prey to the machinations of foreign IT giants. He hugged Zuckerberg when they met, perhaps the only PM to do so. He fell for Tim Cook's iPhone and App. Here's his photo showing Tim Cook how he is using the App Cook gave him.

Fig 23: Modi and Tim Cook (Author – Anonymous)

Such naivety stems from the fascination for technology and admiration for the West.

Modi did not rest content with this. He went ahead and insisted that his cabinet ministers use the App and their performance is assessed on their usage of the App. The PM has evidently not read Glen Greenwald's book on Snowden or anything on US snooping.

Here is a picture of the App.

PM's Personal Platform
Who is Most Active?

	Activity Points	Followers
BJP	6978	4705
Narendra Modi	5253	6511
Piyush Goel	4887	3568
Jitendra Singh	3028	1963
Radha Mohan Singh	2180	1378
Nitin Gadhkari	1016	1816
Kalraj Mishra	1012	790

'Cool' Badges

On Signing up: Go-Getter Batch	200 Points: Pro Active	500 Points: The Doer
1000 Points: The Explorer	2000 Points: The Know It All	5000 Points: Super Fan

Unspecified Threshold: Orange Tick on Profile

Fig 24: Modi's Personal Platform given to him by Tim Cook[31] (Author – Anonymous)

In sharp contrast is the mobile phone US presidents are allowed to use. They are given a phone which may be used for talking only. Their phones cannot even be used for texting. Obama called the phone given to him by the US security establishment, a toy!

Let's get back to the clauses in the BSP Contracts. The fact that there are four clauses in three annexures of the contract makes it evident that the decision to provide access of all data to the BSP Contractors, and incorporation of the clauses which leave no room for doubt at all, was deliberate and premeditated.

The Apple app enables Apple Inc. and by its contracts with US NSA the latter too, to have real time access to all communications between Modi and his cabinet colleagues! While Apple may access what the PM and his cabinet are doing or saying to one another, the BSP Contracts enable access and use of the data pertaining to all the people of the country.

Coming back to the BSP contract clauses, so far in public, I have only dealt with three of them. These are in Annexures, 'A', 'B' and 'E'. They deal with grant of access to all data, the storage of the data by the BSPs and the handing over of demographic data with the cautionary statement that the data is inaccurate and not to be used for de-duplication. First, I shall once again explain these three

---

[31] The URLs of these news reports are in the appendix.

clauses and point out the meticulousness with which they have been worded. After that I shall deal with more clauses in the contracts which reveal the extent to which the *BSPs have not only access and contractual right of use but also, absolute control over the inputs and outputs into and from the database.*

The wordings of the clauses are so specific and emphatic that they clearly prove great care. There can be no doubt at all that the contractors too were involved in the drafting of the clauses. The BSP Contractors have safeguarded themselves from any penal consequences, as the acts they are authorized to do could lead to criminal prosecution. Thus, the first clause, Clause 15.1 of Annexure 'A' of the Contract between UIDAI and L 1 Identity Solutions Operating Company Private Limited provides access to all data. Clause 15.3 of Annexure 'A' of the Contract directs L 1 Identity Solutions Operating Company Pvt. Ltd. to store the data for a period not more than seven years. Are we to understand this as meaning that the Company is to store the data in UIDAI servers? That would be ridiculous. Again, is it possible to imagine that the Company is to store the data but not look at it?

The next clause, Clause 3.1 of Annexure 'B' of UIDAI's contract with M/s. L 1 Identity Solutions Operating Company Pvt. Ltd. is in an ironically titled paragraph. The paragraph title is "Privacy of data". As mentioned earlier, the clause authorizes the BSP Contractors to *collect, use, store, transfer, process and link (data) to specific individuals.*

Clause 4.1.1 of Annexure 'E' of UIDAI's Contract with L 1 Identity Solutions Operating Company Private Limited is the one on demographic data. In this clause, UIDAI admits that the demographic data is so inaccurate that the BSPs are cautioned against the use of demographic data for de-duplication.

Now, let's see what else is in the infamous contracts. Annexure 'C' is the Service Level Agreement (SLA). Clause 6.1.2 of Annexure 'C' of the Contract between UIDAI and M/s. L1 Identity Solutions Operating Company Pvt. Ltd. stipulates the "Responsibilities of Biometric Suppliers". It merely states that the Suppliers are responsible for delivering services described in Annexure 'E'.

UIDAI's BSP Contracts have 9 annexures – 'A' to 'I'.

Annexure 'E' gives the "Scope of Work". Clause 1.1 of Annexure 'E' of the Contract between UIDAI and M/s. L1 Identity Solutions Operating Company Pvt. Ltd. is about the "Objective" of the scope in the said annexure. The objective as stated is to select three BSPs who are to *"design, supply, install, configure, commission, maintain and support (a) multi-modal Automated Biometric Identification System (ABIS) and (b) multi-modal Software Development Kit (SDK).*

There is nothing that UIDAI has to do, except use it. It is a turn-key job not just for setting it up but for maintaining it in perpetuity.

Clause 1.2 of Annexure 'E' of the Contract between UIDAI and M/s. L1 Identity Solutions Operating Company Pvt. Ltd. is titled, "Background". It says, "UIDAI has been set up by Government of India with a mandate to issue Unique Identification *numbers (UID numbers)* to all residents in the country." It adds, "These *numbers may* then *be used for authentication*. This can be used by several Government and *private organisations* for better delivery of services to residents."

The concept of the Sham ID, called, 'Aadhaar' Scheme is therefore to *use biometrics ONLY to generate* ostensibly unique *numbers* which, are then *to be used by* both government *and private organizations*.

Clause 1.3 of Annexure 'E' of the Contract between UIDAI and M/s. L1 Identity Solutions Operating Company Pvt. Ltd. says, "The purpose of UIDAI is issue UID numbers that are (a) robust enough to *minimize*/eliminate *duplicate and fake identities* and (b) can be verified and authenticated in an easy and cost-effective way." UIDAI is not sure whether the system can eliminate duplicate/fake identities. Hence, the precaution is taken to have the alternative goal of minimizing spurious IDs. Here is yet another unfounded assumption that there are duplicate/fake identities. If there are indeed duplicate/fake identities, several questions arise, "Who created these in the first place?" "Have the criminals who made these counterfeits been apprehended?" "If not, why?" I am not for a moment saying that there are no duplicate or fake IDs. Of course, there would be some; but to assume that there are very large numbers of duplicates and fakes is silly. And to base an entire public (governmental) program costing several thousands of crores of rupees, on such unsubstantiated whimsical thinking, is unimaginable.

Mere preparation of a duplicate or fake ID is not sufficient. The details of these IDs – name, address, age, date of birth, gender and other details, depending on the agency that requires the ID – are to be then entered into or input to a government database. For example, for pensioners, there would be employment details, if they are retirees. These details are provided to the pension disbursing organization by the employing department from where they superannuated. If the duplicate/fake identities are of those drawing social welfare pensions, then too there are government employees who are to physically verify the identity and demographic particulars and also the eligibility criteria. Biometrics cannot minimize, let alone eliminate these, especially in large populations. UIDAI accepts in its BSP Contracts that "*BSPs are yet to build systems to such a scale. Consequently, it is not possible to predict scalability of the present offerings against the demographics of India.* As the *quality and scalability of biometric measures across the population is currently not known,* alternate[32] methods for de-duplication and fall-back strategy must be incorporated in the design should the primary strategy fall short of the UIDAI goals." This is the wording of paragraph 5, titled "Risk Management" of Clause 3.2 of Annexure 'E' of the Contract between UIDAI and M/s. L1 Identity Solutions Operating Company Private Ltd. Astonishingly, knowing that the BSPs had no experience of applying their biometric technologies to large populations, UIDAI went ahead with the contracts and bluffed the political leadership and bureaucrats to draw them into this make-believe world of allegedly Unique identities. They fell for it hook, line and sinker. Even the judges of the Supreme Court were not immune to the bluff and bluster of UIDAI's brand promotion campaign with thousands of crores of rupees public money spent on it. Thus, as mentioned earlier, when PUCL in a PIL, drew the attention of the Supreme Court to food grains damaged in storages, and the government explained the difficulties in ensuring the food reaches the real beneficiaries, the court remarked, "Why don't you use Aadhaar?" UIDAI, very early in the Sham ID Project, made it convenient for judges in the higher courts to enroll. It is believed that enrolments of judges were done in the court premises. They were probably beguiled by the technology.

THE BSP BLACK BOX

Clause 3.2 of Annexure 'E' of the Contract between UIDAI and M/s. L1 Identity Solutions Operating Company Private Ltd. titled, "Vendor lock-in" deals with *proprietary algorithms.*

(Here is a brief explanation of what algorithms are. Algorithms are procedure or rules to be followed in calculations or problem-solving, especially in computer technology. In the case of biometric technology, the algorithm converts the biometric images of fingerprints or iris scans into a machine-readable template. For example, in fingerprint reading, the curves on our fingers have features like ridges, high-points, bifurcations, valleys, ridge-terminations and so on. The algorithm creators choose a certain number of points on the finger. This could be 8 or 12 for most applications. The features at these points are then converted by the algorithm into a binary string of 0s and 1s. The converted binary string is called a template. Computers compare these templates to decide whether

---

[32] The word used in the Contract is "alternate". Those who drafted the Contract do not seem to know the difference between, "alternate" and "alternative".

the fingerprints of a person match fingerprints taken from a crime scene or at an ATM. In the matching process another parameter is used. This is called, "Hamming distance". **Hamming distance** between two strings of equal length is the number of positions at which the corresponding symbols are different. For example, if we have two binary strings, 01101010 and 11011011 of equal length, 8 digits, and we find that there are 4 positions where the two strings have different symbols, then we say that the hamming distance is 4. The manufacturer of the biometric device and the algorithm owner specify the hamming distance. This is used to decide whether a match occurs between two sets of biometric templates or not. The specification of hamming distance and the string length determine the accuracy of the system. If the specification is too tight, it will result in many false rejects. On the other hand, if the specification is loose, it will result in many false matches, i.e., one person being mistaken for another because their fingerprints or other biometric characteristics match, as per the computer output).

Now, back to the black box of the BSPs. Paragraph 3 of Clause 3.2 of Annexure 'E' of the Contract between UIDAI and M/s. L1 Identity Solutions Operating Company Private Ltd. states, "The system is designed such that these algorithms and data representation form a part of the *black box, and the entire box or subsystem can be replaced without any impact on the other biometrics black boxes.*"

What is a black box?

The Business Dictionary defines it thus:

Device, process, or system, whose inputs and outputs (and the relationships between them) are known, but whose internal structure or working is (1) not well, or at all, understood, (2) not necessary to be understood for the job or purpose at hand, or (3) not supposed to be known because of its confidential nature.

Read more: http://www.businessdictionary.com/definition/black-box.html

Here is a picture of a black box.

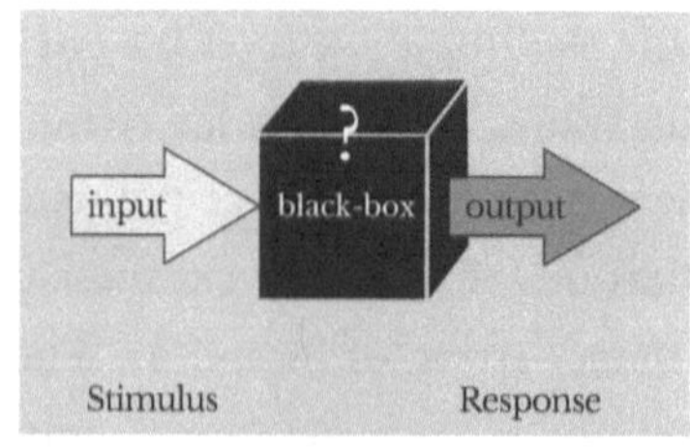

Fig 25: Sample of a Black Box

As we see here, it has an input and output, a stimulus and a response. Something goes into the black box and something comes out of the black box. What happens inside the black box is not known.

In the case of the Sham ID, called "Aadhaar", UIDAI sends the biometric and demographic input into the black box. The processes installed by the BSPs do something with the inputs and out comes the result or output, which says the input is a duplicate or fake. UIDAI does not know what the BSP's algorithm and software did with UIDAI's input data.

In RTI replies to me UIDAI confirmed that it has no idea of whether an enrolment is a false one or whether it is a duplicate. UIDAI also confirmed that the de-duplication is done by a consortium of companies, admitting that it has no role at all in this exercise.[33]

What is the implication of this? It means that UIDAI has no clue as to what happens inside the **black box** which contains the algorithm, which in turn, decides whether a match between two sets of biometrics has taken place or not. It means that the decision to accept an enrolment or reject it or to accept or not accept an authentication (if biometrics is used in authentication), rests in the **black box**. The BSPs know what is in the **black box** and have access to it. Thus, the control of who enrolls and who is authenticated is solely under the control of these foreign companies who are UIDAI's BSP Contractors. In other words, the so-called targeted delivery of our government's services is under foreign control and domination.

Hence, it is clear that the Sham ID, called "Aadhaar" Scheme is not a simple case of data breach or data sharing or intrusion into privacy but one of absolute surrender of our cyber space and all government services into foreign hands.

Why then has this surrender of sovereignty not caught the attention of anyone? Even those who refer to it seem to be almost apologetic about mentioning such perfidy. One may concede that most people would not have access to the contracts, or would not have read them in depth even if they had access to them. However, when these facts are brought to the attention of those responsible, it is unpardonable if they fail to act. It appears that they are unable to differentiate between data security/ leaks and data sharing or controlled access for purposes of maintaining licensed software on the one hand, and complete surrender of control to foreign agencies.

---

[33] The RTI replies dated 08-02-2013 and 25-05-2016 are available in the appendix.

There could be a probable, plausible or possible explanation.

<table>
<tr><td>There Are None So Blind As Those Who Will Not See:</td></tr>
<tr><td>According to the 'Random House Dictionary of Popular Proverbs and Sayings' this proverb has been traced back to 1546 (John Heywood) and resembles the Biblical verse Jeremiah 5:21 ('Hear now this, 0 foolish people, and without understanding; which have eyes, and see not; which have ears, and hear not').</td></tr>
</table>

<**http:**//www.actualfreedom.com.au/richard/abditorium/nonesoblind.htm>

People refuse to see that which, to them, is unpalatable. It would be very uncomfortable and highly disconcerting to think that a government or a high corporate official or bureaucrat would be involved in handing over data of the nation to foreigners and then lie about it. It is, as many would say, unimaginable. The best way out of facing the disturbing truth is to, ostrich-like, ignore it or pass it by. This could be one explanation of why so many people who have been given incontrovertible documentary evidence have remained silent on it or say it in a manner that indicates that this is just one more reason to junk the project.

Another way out is what Dan Ariely calls, the "Decoy Effect". The surveillance and privacy angles make for the perfect "decoy". It diverts attention from the discomfiting need to accuse people at "high levels in society" of so horrible a crime, almost like treason.

Hence, the apparent inability to differentiate between the two—data sharing and data leaks on the one hand and data handed over to foreign entities with no control over what is done to or with the data, and blind acceptance of the processed results for entry into UIDAI database on the other hand. This behavior, although puzzling, is after all part of common human behavior. In any other developed nation in the world, there would be a furor, and the governments who indulge in such acts would be unceremoniously thrown out.

Is this the reason why this aspect of the case in the Supreme Court and in media was just a footnote? It is too difficult to accept or even imagine such wrong doing. Everything else but this hit the headlines. Thus, all were happy when the privacy-as-fundamental-right issue was referred to a larger bench. The Supreme Court—successive "Masters of the Rolls" did nothing to constitute the 9-judge bench for more than two years. Finally, when the "privacy bench" was set up and gave its judgment, activists were thrilled when the Supreme Court held that privacy is indeed a fundamental right, albeit not an absolute one.

13-FEET-HIGH WALL IN THE CLOUD

There is more. Remember the AG's pitch to the Supreme Court, mentioned earlier: "Data is safe behind 13-feet-high walls". The CEO, UIDAI categorically affirmed that data cannot be taken out by the BSP Contractors. When asked by the correspondent of the 'Times of India', after persistent pursuit for an answer, he said, "Not all clauses of contracts are always exercised"! Really?

Clause 6.1.10 of Annexure 'E' of the Contract between UIDAI and M/s. L 1 Identity Solutions Private Ltd. titled, "Cloud Enabled", states: "The solution should support the ability to deploy and run the application– (meaning the ABIS [Automatic Biometric Identification System] and SDK [Software Development Kit], that is the biometric solution for de-duplication, authentication and verification–within a **<u>private</u> cloud platform** to take advantage of next generation cloud features."

The contracts and these clauses must be considered in the context of repeated attempts to hide information regarding the BSP Contractors and the contracts. UIDAI repeatedly assures people that data is safe since it is encrypted and not transferred over the Internet from the enrolment centers to UIDAI. Notice how the Contract talks of storing the data in a *private cloud!* Is this not deceitful?

It (the deceit) started with the denial of knowledge of the country of origin of the contractors. Next, UIDAI made valiant but futile efforts to prevent the contracts from becoming public. The circumstances of the case were described earlier in this book. However, here's something that I have not mentioned so far. It is in the context of the attempt to hide the BSP Contracts from the public eye. It may be recalled that having issued a letter to the CIC (Ms. Sushma Singh) agreeing to furnish the contract copies, UIDAI surreptitiously removed certain pages (annexures) while handing them over to me. The UIDAI officials cheated both the CIC and me. They pretended that they were handing over the contract copies but did so, after removing some annexures.

And what did these annexures contain? They contained the "Technical Bid" of the BSP Contractors. Why did the UIDAI officials do such a willfully deceitful and perhaps criminal act? The motivation for the crime could be known from the clauses in the contract so strenuously attempted to be hidden from the public eye, even if the Technical Bid is not immediately available, I am certain that the Delhi High Court will order the disclosure of the Technical Bid.

Now, let's look at the relevant clause.

After Clause 4.2.2.3 of Annexure 'E' of the Contract between UIDAI and M/s. L1 Identity Solutions Operating Company Private Ltd. is a paragraph which states as follows: "BSP shall supply the UIDAI with a perpetual, fully paid-up, enterprise/world Server and Desktop license to use the *BSP's proprietary* Multi-modal SDK for use within the applications developed by UIDAI *or by its authorized contractors/subcontractors* for the purpose of the UID program. As provided in L 1 Identity Solutions Operating Company's licensing policy in its *Technical Bid*, the Purchaser (including its authorized contractors/ subcontractors) are permitted to: (a) *make and install copies of the Multi-modal SDK software on Purchaser owned or controlled server* and desktop computer system hardware (the system or systems) *located at UIDAI owned or controlled facilities*; (b) *use the Multi-modal SDK software and related documentation for Purchaser's own internal use in developing 1:1 and 1:few custom solution applications* (the "*UIDAI Custom Applications*") containing Multi-modal SDK software components in furtherance of the UID programs; (c) use the UIDAI Custom Applications solely in furtherance of the UID program; (d) *publicly demonstrate the UIDAI Custom Applications on Systems*; and (e) *make and deploy copies of the UIDAI Custom Applications* to government and *non-governmental entities and grant such parties a limited sublicense to use UIDAI Custom Applications* solely in furtherance of the UID program."

A plain reading of the clause in the contract shows the diabolical attempt at setting up a database of the personal details of the people of this country (and of those who happen to stay here for a time), at public expense, link it to every other database (bank accounts, school, college and university and hospital records, pensions, voter ID lists, phone numbers, passports – you name it, it is there) through the Sham ID Aadhaar number, and with no thought at all for safety of the people, and to allow others to use the data. Cambridge Analytica's intrusion into privacy pales into insignificance in comparison with the brashness and sheer foolhardiness of the attempt.

I made a comparative table between Cambridge Analytica and UIDAI and here it is:

A Comparison – Cambridge Analytica and UIDAI

Sl. No.	Parameter	Cambridge Analytica	UIDAI
1.	Data collection	From Facebook which is voluntary.	Directly from people through compulsion, threats of denial of food, blocking of bank accounts, etc.
2.	Resources	Uses private funds.	Uses public money
3.	Type of data	Social interactions – holidays, hobbies, purchases, etc.	All sensitive personal data– biometrics, demographics, bank accounts, mobile phones, financial status, etc.
4.	Use of data	For commercial and political purposes	Ostensibly for targeting subsidies, preventing money-laundering and tax evasion, fighting terrorism
5.	Linkages	Not linked to individuals. Social profiles of group spending to decide marketing strategies and political concerns to decide poll strategies. Not linked to government databases	Linked (specific) individuals and to all government databases
6.	Power over people whose data is collected	No power over people whose data is collected	Power to block bank accounts, mobile phones, scholarships, etc.
7.	Parties involved in data collection	Private parties and people who voluntarily upload data	Government through use of private and government entities
8.	Technology	Big data analytics – own technology	Fallible biometrics licensed technology. Conceptually flawed IT systems
9.	Type of crime	Perhaps a misdemeanour—violation of European Privacy Regulations	A felony—entire data handed over to foreign private companies and they authorised to do whatever they wish to do with it. Lying to the people that data is not shared, hiding the contract, deceiving CIC
10.	Usefulness	Commercial and political uses	Largely useless for legal purposes, but can be used for crimes against people.

There is not a shadow of doubt about the intentions of UIDAI. Lest anyone think otherwise, UIDAI itself removes any shred of uncertainty though the Clause 1.4 of Annexure 'E' of the Contract between UIDAI and M/s. L1 Identity Solutions Operating Company Pvt. Ltd. The Clause reads, "The UID will serve as a universal proof of identity, (My comment: UIDAI expects every nation to recognize the

Sham ID) allowing residents to establish their credentials (My comment: Is the identity of a thief proof of her/his credentials?). It will *give the Government a clear view of India's population* and enable it (it refers to the *Government*) *to track* and **deliver services** and resource flows effectively." (The emphasis is mine.)

The purpose is made absolutely unambiguous. It is *to enable the Government to track us and everything we do.*

Here is a question worth pondering about. Payments of salaries, pensions, provident funds, issue of voter IDs, a private company providing a phone connection–are all these services that the Government needs to track?

All this has been kept under wraps, shielded from the public eye. I am certain the government, the PM, the cabinet, and most of the bureaucrats would not know of this. In contrast, many of the architects of the Sham ID Project would be certainly aware of what they are doing and the reasons therefor.

What the people behind this satanic evil are doing is cashing in on the ignorance of people in general about technology and its uses.

One of the arguments made by its protagonists for the Sham ID, called "Aadhaar", born of ignorance, goes something like this. "We give our data to so many people and organizations. We give our biometrics for travel to USA. Facebook and Google have more data than what UIDAI is collecting." Of course, this is true to an extent. It is also a fact that these US IT companies have signed agreements with US intelligence organizations to provide access to their servers. The former argument has been made even in the Supreme Court. I have seen many tweets making this pitch. I have replied to most of these. I never received a response to my reply tweets. They are either unable to understand the fallacy of the argument or refuse to understand it.

I would like to make a submission on the intrinsic difference between the two. Firstly, people choose Facebook and/or Google. Then they choose what they put into these Internet pages. There is no compulsion under threats of denial of food or scholarships or anything else. Facebook and Google cannot block our bank accounts. Facebook and Google do not spend public money to collect data. Chalk and cheese, apples and oranges? Your choice. The analogy woefully misses the mark.

Another silly argument made is the allusion or comparison of the Sham ID, called, "Aadhaar" to the US SSN. Nilekani has done so on numerous occasions. However, he and UIDAI also say that the U.K. National ID Card and its Act are different from the Sham ID, called "Aadhaar". Why do they often make this false statement? Their argument is two-fold; one, that the U.K. National ID Card contained data, whereas the Sham ID is not a card at all. But tongue in cheek, they call it Aadhaar card. Second, the U.K. National ID Card Act was meant to prevent illegal immigration. On the first point in the argument, while the U.K. card did contain some data, it was not linked to every database of the country. Ironically, while UIDAI and Nilekani try to make the distinction that the Sham ID, called "Aadhaar" is not a card, they promote the lie calling it "Aadhaar card". This is to keep the pretense of the Sham ID, called "Aadhaar" being an ID card, which is what people were looking for. This is another ruse of UIDAI that has even taken the Supreme Court for a ride. Judges of the Supreme Court often use the phrase "Aadhaar card" without knowing that there is no such card. Go any place where you are required to produce your ID, a bank, a phone company, anywhere, and you will find the same phrase, "Aadhaar card". The person asking for your ID will invariably ask for "Aadhaar card". Almost all people and organizations have been fooled into believing that the Sham ID, called "Aadhaar" is an ID card. Lies spread faster than truth.

For those interested in probing further the UIDAI lie, Anumeha Yadav's excellent article in www.scroll.in (Dec 20, 2016) is a good starting point. The URL of the article is in the appendix of list of URLs.[34]

Why do people behave in this manner? Apart from the "Predictably Irrational" thesis of Ariely, there is an interesting analogy in the Bible. In this people are often referred to as sheep and God as the Shepherd. I often wondered, why? Then it dawned on me. I have never seen a sheep in a circus. Have you? As I studied the reasons for this singular lack of the presence of sheep in circuses, I found that the sheep is one of the dumbest of animals. It cannot be trained. It does not even know how much to eat and for how long. Left to itself, it will either choke to death eating or overeat itself to ill health. (Is it any wonder that humans too overeat themselves into obesity and death? And so, the analogy is not without reason.) I also noticed that sheep just herd together and follow other sheep. If one sheep runs across the road, all others will rush behind it. Sheep like behavior in humans, perhaps explains why so many of our country folks could be so deluded into belief in the Sham ID, called "Aadhaar".

Perhaps, a look at legal issues surrounding the subject of this book is warranted now.

---

[34] **Despite the comparisons, India's Aadhaar project is nothing like America's Social Security Number**
<https://scroll.in/article/823570/despite-the-comparisons-indias-aadhaar-project-is-nothing-like-americas-social-security-number>

Legally Speaking

Fig 26: Depicting the titled Balance of Justice

"In a free society, State does not conduct the affairs of men. It administers justice among men who conduct their own affairs." – Walter Lippman

The torturous progress, if it may be called "progress," or more appropriately, meandering, through our judicial system and finally into the hallowed halls of the Supreme Court were described earlier in Chapter IV. It would be useful to say something about the legal issues as seen by a layman, who as petitioner, studied various legal aspects of the case and interacted with the advocates who argued it.

I have no qualifications in the discipline of law. I have always had an abiding interest in law and justice. It stems from my hatred of injustice. I have had some training in the Army on military law. I have successfully defended Army persons in Courts Martial. My experience as member of Military Courts of Inquiry into fraud and theft has come in handy in understanding the nuances of law. Primarily, I approach law and legality from a common sense, pragmatic, "as the common man's" (for whom the law is meant) point of view. After my military career, I had the opportunity of handling cases in Administrative law and Company law in high courts, the Supreme Court and in arbitration. I never lost a case. In every one of them, I drafted the complaints, petitions, briefed my advocates, prepared arguments for them and assisted them in many ways. Thus, I have some familiarity with both law and court procedures.

As I mentioned earlier, as far as I know, two books have been written about the Sham ID, called "Aadhaar" Scheme. The first one, by Shankkar (with the double 'K') Aiyar, titled "Aadhaar", and subtitle "India's 12-digit Revolution" eulogizes the evil scheme and extols those who ideated and pushed it through, as a one-stop-solution, a digital utopia, until it almost became an all-pervasive blanket of digital dystopia, through ignorance, complacency and foolhardiness of people in power and outside it.

The second one is a more dispassionate work of an eminent advocate and writer of books on law, Mr. Pavan Duggal. It is a scholarly work.

Duggal had an opportunity in his book to speak about the legality or otherwise of the Sham ID, called "Aadhaar" Scheme. He has not done so.

He has made no arguments for or against it. Before looking at what he says, it is useful to briefly recapitulate the arguments in the Supreme Court so that when I give my legal reasons against the scheme and the Act, it would be properly understood.

The arguments in the Supreme Court centered on right to privacy, surveillance, exclusion due to failure to authenticate, passing the Act as Money Bill being *ultra vires*, questioning the savings claims, lack of security, data protection, various defects in the system/implementation, excessive delegation and so on. Article 73 of the Constitution was the crux of the argument in the first petition, and this is attributed to Kuppuswamy.

Shyam Divan, once early in the hearings, perhaps in 2014 or so, in response to a query from the Bench, did say that even if the Constitution were to be amended, that too would be void as it would violate the basic structure of the Constitution. Neither did the Bench ask him to elaborate, nor did he do so, as far as I know. Apart from him no one else mentioned this point. All arguments were largely on violations of Articles 14, 16 and 21. I did not notice anyone mentioning Article 13.

Duggal does not mention any of these in his book. He only explains various sections of the Aadhaar Act. He has not commented on the legality of the Act or the provisions of the Act, probably because the issue is under consideration by the Supreme Court.

He has also not stated his views on the passing of the Act as a Money Bill. He has merely explained what a Money Bill is, and the roles of the Lok Sabha and Rajya Sabha in respect of such a Bill.

Not being a scientist or engineer, Duggal assumes that biometric identification is unique, and hence he does not discuss an important aspect of the legality of the Act, namely, whether it is rational; and the legal implications, if it is shown to be irrational.

In dealing with Section 5 of the Aadhaar Targeted Delivery Act, Duggal missed the crux of the section. He lists the categories for which UIDAI is mandated to take special measures. He states in his book, "Thus the law recognized the fact that a number of categories of persons coming within the ambit of residents in India who are residing for more than one hundred and eight(y) two days in one calendar year, prior to making the application *may not have permanent dwelling house. Therefore*, the Unique Identification Authority of India (UIDAI) has been mandated to take special measures to get the said categories of people within the fold of the Aadhaar ecosystem (?)[35] (The emphasis is mine.)

Duggal mistook Section 5 as meant only for people who may not have a permanent dwelling place. Those who do not have permanent dwelling places are a separate category among the categories listed in the Act as those for whom special measures are to be instituted.

As mentioned elsewhere in this book, the categories listed as those requiring special measures are those for whom biometric identification does not work because of poor quality of fingerprints and iris. The list would comprise over 85% or 95% of the population. That's why I said that the section is an admission by UIDAI of the impossibility of providing unique IDs to the vast majority of the people of India. The basis of the Sham ID, called "Aadhaar" Scheme is scientifically impossible. Hence also the fraud of pretense of unique IDs. The silence of the Act and of UIDAI in spelling out these "special measures" is the devious ploy to trick the public and the courts into imagining that great care is taken to avoid distress to people due to non-recognition of their biometrics.

Unfortunately, Duggal assumes that the Sham ID, called "Aadhaar" somehow or other provides unique IDs. He is one of many with this misconception that this book hopes to dispel. Hence, in the Preface to his book, Duggal states, "As an author, I believe that with the implementation of the Aadhaar (Targeted Delivery of Financial and Other Subsidies, Benefit, and Services) Act, 2016, the process of growth of evolving jurisprudence on Aadhaar is likely to continue at a rapid

---

[35] There are two typo errors in the first edition of the book, on page 41. The first is the word "eight" should be "eighty". The second is the question mark (?) at the end of the sentence on Aadhaar ecosystem.

space. It will be interesting to see how this jurisprudence evolves over a period of time." He is convinced that the Sham ID, called "Aadhaar" Scheme is here to stay, and hence he hopes that there will be "growth of evolving jurisprudence on Aadhaar." This view, which is based on the belief that the Sham ID, called "Aadhaar" Scheme will exist because of lack of knowledge of the capabilities of biometrics and Information Technology, is indeed a pity.

As a layman, I know that no law can legitimize a scientific and mathematical absurdity. King Canute was perhaps the first in recorded history to tell his sycophants that he can't stop the tide. Our government and people seem to believe that government is more like Louis XIV and prefer to paraphrase him as, "I am the Law." UIDAI could well rescript Marie Antoinette to say to the poor, "If you don't get rice (because biometric identification doesn't work), eat cake."

To my mind, rationality is fundamental to both executive and legislative power.

My view is that the Rule of Law is the aadhaar (foundation) on which democracy rests. And Rule of Law in turn is based on rationality in law, and executive action guided and constrained by it. One normally attributes need for rationality and avoidance of arbitrariness to executive action and constrains it to the executive sphere. Since executive action is to adhere to law, the law itself has to be based on rationality.

I had an interesting exchange of emails with Usha Ramanathan (of the 'Say No 2 UID' group,) on the Rule of Law. When I advocated that the case should focus on the Rule of Law, she suggested Dworkin. The Group must have been foxed by the name. I decided to play the game and responded with the name, Dicey.

Let me explain these names and what they stand for. The explanation is best done by quoting Wikipedia. Here's what it says about Dworkin.

"Law as rule and principle

Dworkin as a critic of HLA Hart's legal positivism has been summarized by the *Stanford Encyclopedia* which has stated that:

Dworkin, as positivism's most significant critic, rejects the positivist theory on every conceivable level. Dworkin denies that there can be any general theory of the existence and content of law; he denies that local theories of particular legal systems can identify law without recourse to its moral merits, and he rejects the whole institutional focus of positivism. A theory of law is for Dworkin a theory of how cases ought to be decided and it begins, not with an account of the political organization of a legal system, but with an abstract ideal regulating the conditions under which governments may use coercive force over their subjects."

Wikipedia also explains what legal positivism is.

It says, "**Legal positivism** is a school of thought of analytical jurisprudence, largely developed by eighteenth- and nineteenth-century legal thinkers such as Jeremy Bentham and John Austin. While Bentham and Austin developed legal positivist theory, empiricism and logical positivism set the theoretical foundations for such developments to occur. The most prominent legal positivist writing in English has been H. L. A. Hart, who in 1958 found common usages of "positivism" as applied to law to include the contentions that:

1. laws are commands of human beings
2. there is no necessary connection between law and morals—that is, between law as it is and as it ought to be
3. analysis (or study of the meaning) of legal concepts is worthwhile and is to be distinguished from history or sociology of law, as well as from criticism or appraisal of law, for example with regard to its moral value or to its social aims or functions
4. a legal system is a closed, logical system in which correct decisions can be deduced from pre-determined legal rules without reference to social considerations
5. moral judgments, unlike statements of fact, cannot be established or defended by rational argument, evidence, or proof "noncognitivism" in ethics"

Dworkin did a lot of harm by advocating an "abstract ideal regulating the conditions under which governments may use coercive force over their subjects."

If one were to agree with Usha Ramanathan and base our arguments in the Supreme Court from Dworkin, one would be accepting the Sham ID, called "Aadhaar" Scheme as legitimate if "conditions under which, government could use coercive force over their subjects" exist. This line of thinking would let the Sham ID Scheme continue. Hence I disagreed with her and suggested Dicey and his theories as the ones to which, we should go. Dicey was the first to advocate Rule of Law, albeit in a narrow way. Here's what a website – IAS SCORE - says about Dicey.

"A V Dicey in his book **The Law of the Constitution (1885)** has given the following three implications of the doctrine of rule of law.

1. **Absence of arbitrary power,** that is, no man is punished except for a breach of law
2. **Equality before the law,** that is, equal subjection of all citizens (rich or poor, high or low, official or non-official) to the ordinary law of the land administered by the ordinary law courts
3. **The primacy of the rights of individual,** that is, the constitution is the result of the rights of the individual as defined and enforced by courts of law, rather than constitution being the source of the individual rights"

I think Dicey confined, or rather emphasized, Rule of Law to executive actions, although he did accord primacy to individual rights. Rationality either in law or in executive action was not the focus.

The title of this book is, 'Sham ID, called "Aadhaar".' The subtitle is, "Extraordinary Indian Delusion". Why did I title it so? Simply because it is the truth. Millions of people have been deluded into believing that the Sham ID is a unique ID. A Google search gives you meanings for the word "sham". All of these fit the Sham ID, called "Aadhaar" Scheme.

Here are they:

"Fake, pretended, feigned, simulated, false, artificial, bogus, synthetic, spurious, ersatz, insincere, not genuine, manufactured, contrived, affected, plastic, make-believe, fictitious."

The Cambridge dictionary gives the meaning of the word, "sham" as:

"Something that is not what it seems to be and is intended to deceive people, or someone who pretends to be something they are not".

A law, an Act of Parliament, that seeks to legitimize such deception or deceptive scheme is against the Rule of Law. After all, the Rule of Law is not only about rationality in law and in executive action but also presupposes honesty.

Why is the Sham ID, called "Aadhaar" Scheme a pretense and a fraud on the people of India? It is supposed to be providing a unique ID to all *residents* of India. The provision of IDs to all residents, as opposed to all citizens, is not a simple idea of helping everyone. It is a device to camouflage the fact that neither biometrics nor UIDAI can determine who is a citizen and who is not. This is the duplicity, the craftiness, the trickery of UIDAI. The Government has fallen for the ruse. This is the same party which amended The Citizenship Act, 1953 to set up the National Register of Citizens. Advani, who spearheaded this initiative, is an honest man who wanted to weed out people who illegally enter India and merge into its citizenry.

The reader will remember the controversy surrounding this issue which media termed a "turf war" between the Home Ministry and the Planning Commission – UIDAI. It is anything but a turf of war. Consider the objectives of Aadhaar Act. It is meant "to provide good governance, efficient, transparent and targeted delivery of subsidies, benefits and services." The enrolment cake was divided equally between the proverbial monkeys. UIDAI was to enroll one half and the Registrar General of India (RGI) was to enroll the other half. A Group of Ministers (GoM) decided this. The RGI is tasked with preparation of the National Register of Indian Citizens (NRIC). This also goes by different names– Population Register, Citizenship Register, etc. Plainly the GoM decision was a blunder. They either did not know and were not told that the UIDAI is enrolling residents, including non-citizens, or they took the plunge to get away from the issue thinking, "We will cross the bridge when we come to it."

I raised some RTI queries on the matter, all of which were as usual taken on the RTI merry-go-round. My main query was how the two databases, one of citizens and the other of non-citizens would be merged. RGI appointed Bharat Electronic Ltd. (BEL) as the enrolling agency for its share of enrolments. I found officers in BEL most forthcoming. Did UIDAI trick BEL into automatically sending all its enrolment data to UIDAI? It would appear so, if the RTI reply of BEL is true. I believe it is. As reported to me and confirmed in an RTI reply, UIDAI gave BEL a software to install on their scanners capturing biometrics and systems collecting demographic data. BEL installed it as advised. The software automatically transmitted the data to UIDAI. What UIDAI did with the data is not known. The problem of merging the two databases and finding out who are Indian citizens in UIDAI's database is not solved.

The amendment to The Citizenship Act for setting up NRIC did not have provision to collect biometric data. Why BEL chose to do so and under what authority is unclear. Why no one questioned this is equally mystifying. One of the petitions, apart from mine, pointed out that the UIDAI database does not distinguish between citizens and non-citizens and hence using it to target welfare and benefits is problematic. This was the petition of Rajeev Chandrasekhar, MP. My petition, at the suggestion and advice of Gopal Subramanium, impugned The Citizenship Act itself as well as NRIC. These averments are in the petitions. I do not know whether the advocates drew the attention of the court to them and if so, how the bench reacted to it. None of the activists have shown any interest in this line of argument. The NRIC has been given a quiet burial. This is the power of the invisible lobby pushing the evil into India.

A point that I had mentioned in my petitions is the illegality of the BSP Contracts. The question I raised was, "Can a government collect personal data of all people—and that at public expense—and hand it over to foreign private companies for their use in any manner they desire and enter into a contract for such purpose?" Under what provision of law or Constitution could a government do so? Since doing so is tantamount to a crime, if done by anyone else, he/she would be arrested and charged with treason/offense under Official Secrets Act!

Worse, the more important question is, "Can a government lie to the people who they represent?"

Both these, the handing over all data to foreign entities and the lying about it, are gross violations of the Rule of Law. When a government utters falsehood, the entire edifice of people's trust on which the legitimacy of government rests is destroyed. When the government filed affidavits in the Supreme Court making averments and arguments on its behalf, including a Power Point Presentation, that the data is not shared, it is safe and so on, and asserting robust data protection, it was nothing but perjury. Incredibly, these astonishing facts and inferences therefrom and their legal implications have eluded the petitioners' advocates, and hence the attention of the Supreme Court. However, should their Lordships read the affidavits and the petitions, they would find the issues highlighted (in this book) and mentioned in them are irrefutable, absolutely true and cry out for urgent attention and action.

If the Sham ID, called Aadhaar is not the solution for subsidy theft and other such ills, what is the way forward. To this, we may now turn our attention.

Fixing Governance – The Alternative Solution

The first requirement for fixing governance is honesty at all levels, especially at the top. Technology cannot help the dishonest technologist to become honest.

Fig 27: Using Technology Appropriately

Fig 28: Inappropriate use of Technology

I am all for use of technology. Information Technology is a powerful tool in the hands of the honest and knowledgeable. I have used technology both for the design and manufacture of missiles and for areas of business management such as finance. I am no Luddite.

However, when technology is a pretense for deceit, it harms rather than helps. This is the case with the Sham ID, called "Aadhaar" Scheme. Let's look at the Act itself. That's where we see the beginnings of the dishonest intention.

The Aadhaar Act begins with lofty words of its objectives – "An Act to provide *for, as a good governance,* efficient, *transparent,* and targeted delivery of subsidies, benefits and services, the expenditure for which is met from the Consolidated Fund of India, to individuals residing in India through *assigning* of unique identity *numbers* to such individuals and matters connected there with or incidental there to."

Firstly, I wish the drafters had got their grammar right. What is '*as a good governance*? Why the singular article, "a"? What is *a good governance*?

Next, the Act proclaims "transparency" as its objective. I am in absolute agreement. Transparency is the antidote to crimes of dishonesty, theft, misappropriation and so forth. Yet, what do those who pass the Act do? They proceed to make Rules and Regulations under the powers conferred by the Act to make everything opaque. Section 7 of The Aadhaar (Data Security) Regulations, 2016 does exactly this. We may excuse those who enacted the legislation since it is our misunderstanding that they want what they do to be transparent to us. Sorry. That's not the case. As the BSP Contracts show, they want to *"give a clear view (of us) to the government."*

The next bit of dishonesty is in the method prescribed for providing the allegedly good governance. It is, as the objectives of the Act say, *"through assigning of unique identity numbers."* While all along, UIDAI and government have been shouting themselves hoarse that the purpose is to *provide unique IDs* to those who do not have IDs and hence are denied access to government welfare, in their writings, here in the Act and on the UIDAI website, the objective is to assign *unique identity numbers to all residents.* Hence, instead of providing IDs, they assign numbers to individuals much as is done for prisoners.

The dishonesty is also in the pretense of using biometric technology for unique identification. Biometrics is used largely for assigning what UIDAI claims to be unique identity numbers. Once the numbers are assigned, only these are used by linking them with various databases. The pretense of use of biometrics continues only in areas wherein the hapless persons subjected to the vagaries of biometric technology have no voice–like in NREGS, PDS-ration-shops, etc.

The enactors of the law have dishonestly sheltered themselves from the onslaught of aggrieved persons who would certainly be at the receiving end of the faulty technology and worse implementation. Thus, we find Section 47 of the Aadhaar Targeted Delivery Act. By this section, the victim cannot file a complaint in a court of law or in a police station. He/she can only complain to UIDAI, who then has the sole discretion of what to do.

The shelter extends to expanding the scope and spread of the Sham ID, called "Aadhaar" Scheme by not restricting it to a narrow reading of the objectives. Thus, even if the expenditure is not incurred from the Consolidated Fund of India, for example, if the government wants to link the Sham ID number to say, phone numbers, then Section 57 of the Aadhaar Targeted Delivery Act comes in handy. It shamelessly proclaims that the "Act (is) not to prevent use of the Aadhaar number for other purposes." As a measure of abundant caution, the words, "under law" are added at the end of the title of the section.

Apart from the legal gimmicks of the Act, the worst act of dishonesty is in the unstated assumption on which the whole edifice of the Act and scheme rests. This is the unfounded assumption that subsidies are "leaked" because the identities of the beneficiaries are not established well enough. The very use of the word, "leakage(s)" for what is evidently theft, is dishonest. By using innocuous words for what is obviously a crime, the dishonest hope to preclude the need for investigation. It is a pretense that there is no crime but some defect that could be fixed by technology alone.

THE SOLUTION

I am one who not merely criticizes but would also propose solutions. I would also help implement the suggested solutions.

Every problem has a solution. Some take time to resolve, while other could be quickly sorted out.

Let's look at the problem of ensuring good governance. Firstly, we may ask the question, "Good governance - What is it"?

How may 'Good governance' be defined?

One definition could be–"Good governance is when the recipients of effects/results of governance, not only perceive it as good but also, in quantifiable terms, governance is indeed good; it meets international standards of good governance and exceeds them."

Quantifiable indices of good governance are Human Development Indices (HDI) and such parameters as health (percentage of population who die of preventable diseases), longevity, infant mortality, pre and post-natal and maternity death rates, absence of corruption, education and literacy, access to justice, employment rates, etc.

Apart from good management of health services, education, etc. it is essential that corruption be reduced to an extent that it does not radically affect management and achievement of objectives. This is quite easy if politicians and bureaucrats are reasonably honest. It may yet be done even if there is a low degree of the dishonest among this lot. How reduced corruption could be achieved will be described below, but before doing so, it is important to understand how crimes involving syphoning of welfare monies, in kind or cash, are carried out. It is also necessary to know what corruption is.

CORRUPTION

Corruption has three levels or types. The first is at the policy level or type. This happens at the highest levels of government. The 2G scam, allowing mining in a forest area, a nuclear power plant agreement, dubious defense purchases are examples of policy level corruption.

The next type is the medium scale corruption. Examples of these are the Asian Games scam, fodder scam, Nirav Modi or Mallya fleeing the country, Bellary mining scam, and Land acquisition scams.

The last type is at the lowest level. A traffic policeman accepting a bribe, a ration shop owner bribing a government official, fixing tenders or taking bribes in government purchases are of this type.

There is vast difference in value and frequency between the various types/levels of corruption described above. The higher the level of the type of corruption, higher is the monetary value and lower is its frequency of happening. This is the most difficult type of corruption since it involves the highest levels of political leadership. The old question, "Who will guard the guardians?" comes back to haunt us when we try to tackle this type of corruption.

The lower levels/types of corruption are the easiest to eliminate.

What the Sham ID, called "Aadhaar" Scheme appears to tackle, is the last type, since the concentration seems to be in preventing theft of PDS rations or frauds in NREGS wage payments. Of course, some may claim that the Sham ID, called "Aadhaar" could also address the two other higher levels of corruption through linking it with bank accounts and PANs. The futility of such thinking was dealt with in an earlier chapter.

Hence, the solution described here is focused on the last type of corruption leading to good governance in the sphere where the Sham ID, called "Aadhaar" is supposed to operate to achieve the objectives of the Aadhaar Act.

INVESTIGATION OF SUBSIDY THEFT AND USE OF TECHNOLOGY TO PREVENT IT

The first thing to be done for this is *investigation* to find out the *modus operandi*. One can't have a solution without knowing what the problem is. You will not be able to solve a differential equation using the best of computers and IT experts, unless you know mathematics. However, while investigation of the crimes in welfare theft is important and inescapable, one could make a start with the use of technology to reduce the loopholes that may be used for the crimes.

Investigation is simple if one knows how to go about it and where to look for the evidence. The investigation is not only to apprehend the criminals but also to find out the loopholes used by criminals and plug these. In the case of PDS, there is huge documentary evidence and the trail left behind by the thieves. The RTI reply to me, mentioned earlier stated that there were no fake ration cards. The Food and Civil Supplies Department in Karnataka found only ineligible ration cards. So, check whether these ration cards were used for drawing rations. Who issued these ration cards? Who entered the data pertaining to these ration cards in the PDS database? How are ration cards allocated to ration shops? Who authorizes the data entry operators to accept the data pertaining to issue of new ration cards? Does the reduction in stock figures at ration cards tally with issues shown against these ineligible ration cards? What is the quantity of food grains written off as damaged? Who determined the quantity and who certified it? What steps have been taken to prevent damage in future? How is the transportation organized? Check figures of quantities transported and stocks in ration shops. How is weighment of grains done while loading into trucks for distribution to ration shops? Who orders dispatch to ration shops and who supervises weighments and loading? What documents are issued to transporters? What receipts do they produce to accounts? The answers to these questions and those that develop as the investigation proceeds would lead to the criminals and their *modus operandi.*

Common sense dictates that thieves are as efficient as anyone else and would seek to maximize their effort-result ratio. Hence, we may ask ourselves,

"Where would the theft take place?" If efficiency is what the thieves are hoping to achieve, they would naturally target the location where the bulk of the goods are stored. It makes more sense for a robber to steal from a bank than from a house.

Fig 29: Maximizing Efficiency of Theft

This is a picture of a bank robbery. Robbers target the place where they could maximize the gains from their criminal acts.

So also, it is reasonable to presume that welfare food thieves would target places where such food items are stored or are available in bulk. Hence, the place to look for in investigating the crime of food subsidy theft would be the grain storages and the transportation trucks.

Here are two pictures of grain storage in India. Both are open storages. In the second picture one may see the black color tarpaulin cover partially covering the grains.

Fig 30: Transporting Subsidized Food (Author – Anonymous)

Fig 31: Miserable Conditions of Food Storage (Author – Anonymous)

In the first picture, a truck is loading the grains. The open storage is an invitation to steal. So also, in bulk transportation the ease of stealing is high, and hence too the probability of the theft taking place during transportation.

How do we prevent this–stealing from storages and during transportation?

Transparency, accurate accounting, and use of technology for these, are the keys to unlock the mystery of the missing subsidized food. Policy changes too could help. For example, universal PDS would reduce a lot of corruption in deciding eligibility.

I have not attempted to describe in detail the entire suggested solution to eliminate theft of PDS food grains, in the interests of brevity; neither is it necessary to do so. Hence, a brief outline is provided below as bullet points.

- Make the process of application, issue of ration cards and allocation to ration shops transparent. Every application should be given a serial number. It could have barcodes for locating it and for ensuring input to database. The date of the application, the seniority in the queue of applicants, the number and date of the application, whether through hard copy or online, must be publicly available.

- Trucks transporting PDS food grains must be ordered to follow predetermined routes, tracked using GPS and deviations penalized.

- Weighment of empty and loaded trucks should be automated and done within the FCI storage area.

- Ration items could be packed in easily identifiable, disposable packages, in specified quantities and barcoded so that there is no need for weighing at the ration shops and "quantity fraud" is eliminated. The cost of packing would be more than compensated by the reduction in cost of stolen grains.

- Storage at ration shops should be standardized to facilitate stock checking and ease of accounting.
- Data on issue of stocks to ration shops should be made public immediately upon issue.
- Stocks at each ration shop should not only be mandatorily displayed in front of the shops but also be available in the state PDS website.
- Data of sale at ration shops should be automatically captured and the data transmitted to the state and central PDS database.
- Have periodic statutory and social audits.
- Ensure profitability of ration shop owners. They may be allowed to sell non-subsidized items, but store subsidized goods in clearly demarcated areas within the shops.
- Selection of ration shop vendors should be through public tenders.
- Names of shop owners and contact numbers should be displayed prominently in front of the shops.
- An effective public grievance mechanism, and in addition, "adalaths" ("town hall" type) meetings with people is to be held periodically. The action on complaints must be immediate, within minutes. The action should be to immediately carry out an on-the-spot investigation. Since the poor are the ones most affected by flaws in implementation of PDS, an officer specially trained and empowered to take remedial action must be designated and her/ his contact details and place where the complaint is to be registered must be publicly available to the poorest of the poor who have no access to Internet or mobile phones. These details should be displayed at every ration shop. In fact, if the system is monitored adequately, there should be no need for complaints and grievances.
- CCTVs must be used for real time monitoring of opening and closing of ration shops and activities within them. A team at the Food and Civil Supplies Department should monitor the CCTVs and report irregularities.
- Daily data of off take from ration shops, issue and replenishment of shop stocks, stocks purchased, available in storage, etc. should be available in real time on the state website.
- Open storage should be totally replaced with proper storage protected from the elements and pest infestation.
- This, increasing storage, must be done on a war footing with time bound date of completion and budget for the same. The money saved by

scrapping the Sham ID Program could be used for this purpose. Allowing precious food items to rot or be infested is a crime against humanity, especially so in a country with millions of people under starvation.

> Similar transparent (to public, without compromising on privacy rights) systems is the ONLY antidote to prevention of pilferage and frauds in welfare schemes, be it in health care, education or anywhere else.

> Big data analysis and pattern recognition should be used to discover fraud for further investigation.

These suggestions are not utopian or theoretical. I am willing to work free of any fees or charges to set up such systems with any state government wishing to implement the suggestions.

A Call for Action

"Aadhaar" Sham Unravelled and exposed
What should Patriotic Indians Do?

Now that the Sham ID, called 'Aadhaar' has been exposed, what should all patriotic Indians do? Surely, we are not to remain passive treating it like any other scam.

To decide on the course of action, let's summarise what the peeling of the Sham ID, called 'Aadhaar' "onion" has revealed.

> "Aadhaar" is unlike any other national or even other identity document. It is not an identity at all.

> It is an allegedly unique number assigned to all residents of India, which purports to identify individuals.

> *Unlike any other identity document, there is no ID card.* Instead, you are told to laminate and use the enrolment acknowledgement letter as an ID card.

> *The use of the phrase, "Aadhaar card" keeps alive the charade that this self-laminated letter is an ID card.*

> The self-laminated letter has *no signature* of any government official or authority, unlike any other ID card. Again, unlike any other ID card, it has *no security feature*, such as, a hologram or a magnetic strip.

> So, it can be easily cloned. All one needs to do is to replace the photo in the self-laminated letter.

> It is *meant for all residents* and makes *no distinction between a citizen and non-citizen.*

> Hence, although various authorities and institutions like banks are told to accept it, something else is required to prove that the holder of the Aadhaar number is a citizen.

> Due to the aura created by the brand name promotion through massive advertisements and pronouncements by government spokespersons, chances are that no one will ask the Aadhaar number holder to prove

her/his citizenship. The result will be that any foreigner or illegal immigrant will be treated as a citizen.

➤ The *entire data collected by UIDAI with public money is being contractually and systematically handed over to foreign entities.*

➤ *Not satisfied with mere handing over of the data, UIDAI has authorised these entities to collect (more data), use, transfer, store, process and link to individuals.*

➤ UIDAI admits in its contracts with these foreign entities that the demographic information provided to them is so inaccurate that demographics are not to be used for de-duplicating.

➤ UIDAI pretends to be using sophisticated technology, when in fact, the biometric technology being borrowed and used under license is so fallible that it generated huge numbers of false matches. As per UIDAI's affidavit in the Supreme Court, 80 million enrolments were deleted as duplicates/fakes. In two separate replies to RTI queries; UIDAI stated in one reply that the later dated enrolment was the one which was deleted. In its second reply, UIDAI stated that demographics were used for detecting the alleged duplicate/fake.

➤ This is false, since, in its contracts with BSPs, UIDAI has admitted that the demographic data is inaccurate and is not to be used for de-duplication.

➤ In the RTI reply, UIDAI confessed its inability to distinguish duplicates from fake enrolments. The majority of these alleged duplicates and fakes are actually false matches.

➤ It has been mathematically proven using UIDAI's specifications that the numbers of false matches would be 1 in 10 as the last 100 million of the 1 billion population are enrolled.

➤ *The data collected – biometrics and demographics – is sent by UIDAI to the BSPs for de-duplication. The de-duplication is done through and inside a "Black box". UIDAI has no clue what is inside the black box. Thus, the control of who is in the UIDAI database rests with these foreign entities.*

➤ This database is linked through the Sham ID Aadhaar number with almost all government databases. Hence, *the cyber space of the country is made accessible to the foreign private companies – the BSPs.*

➤ Through this, *the deployment and movement of the Armed Forces will be known to foreign nations.*

➤ Hence, the *UIDAI database and Sham ID system can, and will be, used by spies, illegal immigrants, terrorists,* etc. to infiltrate.

> Due to its inherent fallibility the *Sham ID number cannot be used for any purpose such as targeting of subsidies,* apart from other criteria like eligibility, citizenship, etc.

Let me quote Sir Walter Scott here to stir to action all right-thinking Indians who read this book.

> "Breathes there the man, with soul so dead,
> Who never to himself hath said,
> This is my own, my native land!
> Whose heart hath ne'er within him burn'd,
> As home his footsteps he hath turn'd
> From wandering on a foreign strand!
> If such there breathe, go, mark him well;
> For him no Minstrel raptures swell;
> High though his titles, proud his name,
> Boundless his wealth as wish can claim;—
> Despite those titles, power, and pelf,
> The wretch, concentred all in self,
> Living, shall forfeit fair renown,
> And, doubly dying, shall go down
> To the vile dust, from whence he sprung,
> Unwept, unhonour'd, and unsung."

Sir Walter Scott Lay of the Last Minstrel, Canto VI, [My Native Land]

Those who do not wish to go to the vile dust, unwept, unhonoured and unsung, must act and act now.

What could you do?

Here are some suggestions.

> Expose the fraud played on the people of India
> Write to the Prime Minister, his cabinet, your MP, your MLA explaining the facts and asking them to stop this evil
> Write to your banker, your mobile phone company
> Post the facts in your social media – Facebook, Twitter, Instagram, WhatsApp, your professional groups – advocates, doctors, engineers, chartered accountants
> Write to leaders of political parties to make this an election issue.

Apart from taking action to prevent the mischief of the Sham ID to harm us and our country in general, we may also take steps to protect ourselves against possible crimes and abuse. This is described next.

HOW TO PROTECT YOURSELF

Even if you do not wish to be an activist, the least you could do is to take some steps to protect yourself, especially if you have linked your bank account and mobile phone with the Sham ID number. You receive OTP (One-Time-Password) for online banking transactions on your mobile number registered with your bank.

Your Sham ID number and your biometrics are passwords used to access your bank account or make online payments through the National Payments Corporation.

Unfortunately, you are asked to give all these – Sham ID number, mobile phone number and biometrics to all and sundry – schools, hospitals, ration shops, banks, etc. The persons to whom you give the data could be private employees unknown to you, although you may think that they are government officials. Usually they are contract employees.

Snowden was a contract employee of a US NSA contractor. He was able to extract highly classified information form the NSA database by faking security clearance of the highest NSA officials.

Using these data, criminals could swipe your bank account.

Under Section 47 of the Aadhaar Targeted Delivery Act if someone takes out money from your bank account using the Sham ID Aadhaar number, you cannot even file a police complaint. Only UIDAI may do so as per this law!

You should therefore de-link your bank accounts from your Sham ID number. You should also inform your banker in writing that you would not use your biometrics for banking or payment purposes.

Now, let's move on to the Epilogue.

Epilogue

By the time you have come here, you would have got a fair idea of how so many people of our country have been deluded into a false belief and false hope of good governance and efficient delivery of government services. It is sad that such a shameful thing has happened. It is even sadder to note that those who opposed the Sham ID Scheme suddenly turned round and vigorously pushed its implementation. Colossal sums of money have been squandered in the mad rush to pull in all and sundry with false justifications. Varied motives were at work. Some thought that it would be genuinely useful. These people did not care to examine or study the scheme. They simply accepted whatever was dished out. The media-image of its first proponent aided the hoax in no small measure.

Those who practiced deceit and indulged in criminal acts and did so either under orders or of their own will, must not be left unpunished.

It would be interesting to see how the court case would end up.

If the court tries to "balance" its judgment between the petitioners and the government, or divide the cake judicially, it would leave many critical issues un-addressed to the detriment of the safety of the people and the nation.

Ultimately, irrespective of the Court's decision, the scheme will collapse, since it is scientifically and mathematically impossible. Unfortunately, by then, many would have suffered incalculably. The data cannot be used. By its own admission in the BSP Contracts, demographic data is so inaccurate that the contractors are asked not to use the data. Biometrics is scientifically proven to be unworkable as an identification method across large populations. Millions of people who enrolled, 180 million at last count, 80 million as per UIDAI's affidavit in the Supreme Court, were deleted as alleged duplicates/fakes. These are largely False Positive Matches, an inherent characteristic of biometric identification systems. The UIDAI database does not and cannot distinguish between citizens and non-citizens. Hence it cannot be used for targeting subsidies, benefits and services to which only citizens are entitled. However, the data can, and will be used, for crimes, like bank frauds, illegal immigration and intelligence activities. There is hence no alternative but to destroy all data, wherever it may be. That is the difficult part. One can never know where all the data is or has gone. Therefore, additional safety measures are required. The wasted money cannot be recovered. At least a part of it should be from those responsible.

Another inescapable imperative is not only to scrap this boondoggle and destroy all data everywhere, including that with the BSP Contractors, but also to take steps to protect over a billion people whose data is all over the place.

It is necessary to delink all bank accounts and mobile phone numbers that have been linked with the Sham ID Aadhaar numbers. This by itself may not be sufficient, since bank account numbers and mobile phone numbers to which, banks send OTP (One-Time-Password) are the linked mobile numbers. It is essential to issue new and different bank account numbers as well as mobile phone numbers to people who linked them.

Secondly, the law on the use of biometrics in courts (criminal or civil) is to be amended to make it necessary for those who wish to use biometrics as evidence, to prove that they did not obtain it from some database.

THE MARK OF THE BEAST

Let me now narrate one of the interesting incidents during the long campaign. A gentleman, John Abraham, from Mumbai, contacted me in 2017. He had heard about me and the campaign. His son, Isaac, had been threatened with denial of admission to the X class for not possessing the so-called "Aadhaar". He did not know my contact details. Having heard that I live in Bangalore, he travelled to the city. He also knew that I was with Citizens Action Forum. So, he went to the Forum's office in Padmanabha nagar. There it was suggested to him that he contact Rajasekhar, the Forum's current president. He met Rajasekhar in Banaswadi who gave him my mobile number, and thus he was able to contact me after trying for 2 years, as he told me.

After telling me his woes with the Sham ID, called "Aadhaar" regarding his son's admission, he told me that his objection to the scheme is religious, since he believes that it has something to do with the "number of the beast" described in the Bible. Well, "Aadhaar" is not the number of the beast. However, it is a prelude to it.

I helped John Abraham to intervene in the Sham ID, called "Aadhaar" case in the Supreme Court. In his petition he says that he would not enroll for "Aadhaar", since it is against his religious beliefs, and he, as conscientious objector should not be compelled to enroll. I wonder whether the Supreme Court would rule on his plea and if so, what would it be.

For those who may not be familiar with the "number of the beast," let me briefly explain it. The Bible is a book of the prophetic history of the Jews/Israel. It has many prophecies and all these, as per historical and archaeological evidence, have all been fulfilled. The scattering of the Jews, their persecution and regathering as nation is prophesied in the Bible. Hence, the Christian expectation is the remaining prophecies would also be fulfilled. Some prophecies are yet to be fulfilled. These pertain to the end of the world.

The last Book of the Bible is the Apocalypse. It is about the end of the world as prophesied by Lord Jesus, written by the Apostle John who says that this is what the Lord Jesus told him.

It describes the end days of the world, the destruction of the earth.

Fig 32: The Apocalypse

Some aspects of the end of the world are also prophesied in other Books of the Bible. The Book of Daniel, for example, speaks of one who will be instrumental in Israel signing a peace treaty. Terrorism, the most terrible problem confronting the world today, is caused by the "Palestinian issue", the dispute between Israel and the Arab states. The peace treaty would rid the world of the problem of terrorism. The (political) leader who is recognized as the architect of the peace treaty would be hailed as the savior of the world. It is prophesied that this leader would reopen the worship in the Jerusalem temple. After three and half years, he would declare himself as god and order people to worship him. He is called the (first) beast in the Book of Revelation. There is a second beast in the Book of Revelation. He wants everyone to worship the image of the first beast. This second beast causes everyone to have a mark on their right hand or forehead. *No one can buy or sell unless he has the mark or the name of the beast or the number of his name.* This is the *number of the beast* which, conscientious (religious) objectors would not receive.

It appears that the prophecy is saying that there will be a cashless world. All transactions—"buy or sell"—will be only using the mark or number or name of the beast.

For those who understand the prophecies of the Bible, the Sham ID, called "Aadhaar" number cannot be the number of the beast. If the Biblical prophecy is to be fulfilled, then, the Sham ID *Aadhaar number* will have to be replaced with the *number of the beast*. Hence, whether the Supreme Court allows the "Aadhaar" to continue or not, it will ultimately be set aside by the number of the beast.

Let's wait for both—to see what the Supreme Court orders say and to see whether the Aadhaar number will be replaced by the number of the beast.

– The END is NOT Yet! –

Appendices

List of Documents

1. RTI reply of Food and Civil Supplies Department Karnataka Government No: CFS/AMC/RTI/50/2011-2012 dated 22-01-2013 (page 7)
2. RTI reply of UIDAI to Mr. Veeresh Malik Letter No: 12013/13/2011/RTI-UIDAI dated 21-07-2011 (page 17)
3. Scanned copy of first page of contract between UIDAI and L 1 Identity Solutions Operating Company Pvt. Ltd. (page 18)
4. Letter from Vijay Bhalla, registrar CIC/SS/A/2012/001593/SH dated 03-09-2014 (page 19)
5. Letter from Vijay Bhalla, registrar CIC/SS/A/2012/003157/SH dated 14-10-2014 (page 19)
6. Screen shot of UIDAI webpage search results for its contractors (page 19)
7. EA name search of UIDAI website (page 20)
8. Scanned copy of clause 4.1.1 of Annexure 'E' to UIDAI contracts with BSPs (page 21)
9. Scanned copy of Clauses 15.1 of Annexure 'A' of the Contract between UIDAI and M/s. L1 Identity Solutions Operating Company Private Ltd. (page 24)
10. Scanned copy of Clauses 15.3 of Annexure 'A' of the Contract between UIDAI and M/s. L1 Identity Solutions Operating Company Private Ltd. (page 24)
11. Scanned copy of Clause 3.1 of Annexure 'B' of UIDAI's contract with M/s. L 1 Identity Solutions Operating Company Pvt. Ltd. (page 25)
12. 'Times of India' news report quoting CEO of UIDAI, Shri. Ajay Bhushan Pandey. (page 26)
13. US National Academies Research Report – "Biometric Recognition – Challenges and Opportunities" (pages 31 & 32)

14. Mathematical Proof Paper of Dr. Hans Mathews, Published in CIS Website (page 37)
15. The Executive Summary of the CAG report No. 2 (Civil) for year ended Mar 31, 2011, obtained through RTI is in the appendix. (page 88)
16. "Aadhaar" enabled frauds published in media - list compiled by Dr. Anupam Saraph (page 94)
17. UIDAI's RTI reply stating that the enrolment of an illegal immigrant, arrested while working in the Local Army HQ at Bengaluru, is a genuine enrolment. UIDAI reply No: K- 11013/100/2011 – RTI/Vol. IX/502/2014-15/1699 dated 12-11-2014 (page 107)
18. Page 171 of UIDAI's Counter-affidavit to My Writ Petition No: 37 of 2015, with Inadvertent Admission that 80 Million Enrollments (people's Names) Were Deleted as False/Duplicates
19. RTI reply from UIDAI dated 08-02-2016 on allegedly Fake and duplicate enrolments. (page 125)
20. RTI reply from UIDAI dated 25-05-2016 on allegedly Fake and duplicate enrolments. (page 125)
21. RTI Application of Author to UIDAI on Duplicate Enrollments
22. You Tube videos – List in Appendix with all URLs referred in the book (page lvii)

Documentary Evidence

RTI reply of Food and Civil Supplies Department Karnataka Government

OFFICE OF THE COMMISSIONER,
FOOD, CIVIL SUPPLIES AND CONSUMER AFFAIRS,
NO 8. CUNNINGHAM ROAD, BANGALORE. 560 052
Email: foodcomkar@gmail.com
Phone: 080 22262187, 22354857 fax 080-22267205.

No: CFS/AMC/RTI/50/2011-2012   Dated 22-01-2013

To,
Shri, Mathew Thomas,
#18 A, Adarsh Vista,
Basavanagar,
Marathahalli PO,
Bangalore 560037.

<u>ENDORSEMENT</u>

Sir,

Sub: Information provided under RTI Act 2005 Reg.,
Ref: 1) Under Secretary to Govt, FCS&CA, Bangalore letter
      Dated: 28/12/2012.
   2) Your application Dated: 09-01-2013.

****

Sl No	Information sought	Information
A	Number of fake ration cards detected in Karnataka State using UID/Aadhaar biometric data	There is no fake ration cards detected in Karnataka State using UID/Aadhaar biometric data, as the Department is not using UID/Aadhaar biometric data.
B	Number of fake ration cards detected in Karnataka State WITHOUT using UID/Aadhaar biometric data	Ineligible ration cards detected in Karnataka State is enclosed.
C	For each of the above cases at a and b. above, documents with the following information is requested i. Procedure adopted for deciding that these ration cards are fake	The procedure adopted to identify ineligible ration cards is by matching electric RR number along with the ration card in Urban area's & matching of house assesement number along with ration card in the Rural areas.
	ii. Designation of persons who decided that these ration cards are fake	After verification the Food Inspector decides if the ration card is eligible/ineligible.
	iii. Places where the fake ration cards were located found	Through out the State of Karnataka, ineligible ration cards are located.
	iv. Persons who were responsible for making the fake ration cards	It is the beneficiaries who are responsible for ineligible ration cards, they provide wrong electric RR

			number or wrong House Assement number.
	v.	Action taken against persons who made the fake ration cards and those responsible for proper implementation of, and/or prevention of corruption in public Distribution System.	As mentioned in coloumn (iv) it is the beneficiaries who are responsible for the existence of large ineligible ration cards.

Public Information Officer,
Food, Civil Supplies and
Consumer Affairs
Bangalore.

Page (2 of 3)

Govt. of KARNATAKA. Food and Civil Supplies & Consumer Affairs

ಕರ್ನಾಟಕ ಸರ್ಕಾರ
ಆಹಾರ, ನಾಗರಿಕ ಸರಬರಾಜು ಮತ್ತು ಗ್ರಾಹಕರ ವ್ಯವಹಾರಗಳ ಇಲಾಖೆ
FOOD, CIVIL SUPPLIES & CONSUMER AFFAIRS DEPARTMENT

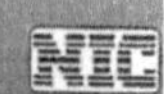

The Statistics as on : Jan 22 2013 3:00AM

REPORT ON DISTRICTWISE ~~ACTIVE RCs~~ *Suspended / canceled RC*

⊙ ALL ◯ RURAL ◯ URBAN ◯ IRA

◯ RCs Active ⊙ RCs SUSPENDED/CANCELLED

Details

District Name	AAY	APL	BPL	TOTAL
BAGALKOTE	4992	75713	58026	138731
BANGALORE	2710	164004	100341	267055
BANGALORE RURAL	2247	37917	38498	78662
BELGAUM	12267	215955	137336	365558
BELLARY	4749	118800	96532	220081
BIDAR	2529	111733	68232	182494
BIJAPUR	6392	93951	66731	167074
CHAMARAJA NAGARA	2686	30083	21231	54000
CHIKMAGALUR	2171	43268	35140	80579
CHITRADURGA	4604	58273	52141	115018
DAKSHINA KANNADA	1112	27370	10798	39280
DAVANAGERE	5295	122957	49878	178130
DHARWAR	2634	111882	50784	165300
GADAG	4348	61674	34796	100818
GULBARGA	8576	148039	71117	227732
HASSAN	3296	87109	58580	148985
HAVERI	4169	50928	39908	95005
KODAGU	1961	27627	34187	63775
KOLAR	3338	61854	39353	104545
KOPPAL	5298	64448	41530	111276
MANDYA	3576	69309	63258	136143
MYSORE	6674	139369	75770	221813
RAICHUR	9509	98256	70892	178657
SHIMOGA	4045	67246	42335	113626
TUMKUR	6122	106668	101536	214326
UDUPI	1400	18320	7238	26958
UTTARA KANNADA	1616	48431	42468	92515
CHIKKABALLAPURA	3965	44016	42164	90145
RAMANAGARA	3045	49288	43885	96218
YADGIR	6087	55382	39703	101172
BANGALORE CENTRAL	826	56552	7834	65212
BANGALORE EAST	406	150499	7757	158662
BANGALORE NORTH	353	134845	11004	146202
BANGALORE SOUTH	477	120885	5853	127215
BANGALORE WEST	384	187671	6239	194294
TOTAL	**133859**	**3060322**	**1673075**	**4867256**

RTI reply of UIDAI to Mr. Veeresh Malik Letter

No.F.12013/13/2011/RTI-UIDAI
Government of India
Planning Commission
Unique Identification Authority of India

2nd Floor, Tower-I, Jeevan Bharati Building
Connaught Circus, New Delhi 110001

Dated 21st July, 2011

ORDER NO. Appeal/3/2011

Name of the Appellant: Sh. Veeresh Malik

Address of the Appellant: D-61, Defence Colony, New Delhi-110024

Date of receipt of Application by CPIO: 15.3.2011
Interim Reply   18/3/11,21/4/11
Date of Order of the CPIO: 25.5.2011

Sub: **Order of First Appeal u/s 19 under RTI Act, 2005**

The appellant, vide his letter dated 02.06.2011 has raised the following Grounds of Appeal:

Ground of Appeal :

a) The reply of CPIO vide letter dated 25th of May, 2011 was found to be incomplete and casual in nature. In addition, learned CPIO has not provided information specifically as requested vide full name, address and websites of the foreign companies which are of US and non-US origin or control.

2.   In the first appeal, the appellant has sought the following relief:

"That the learned CPIO was kind enough vide his response dated 25th of May 2011 to provide information, but same was found to be incomplete, and casual in nature. In addition, learned CPIO has not provided information specifically as requested vide full name, address and websites of the foreign companies which are of US and non-US origin or control. Due diligence is requested to be exercised here in response, since many companies which claim to be American are actually registered in tax havens abroad, for example:- Google. It is therefore requested that suitable care be taken when providing me with this response".

Page (1 of 2)

3.	After careful consideration of facts and material on records, the order of the CPIO and the facts and Grounds of Appeal, the appeal is disposed off as under:

3.1	As regards Grounds (a) to (d) are concerned there is no dispute as information required has been provided to and has been duly acknowledged by the Appellant. However, with the CPIO's reply some other information collected from our different divisions have been added in this order (appeal). The following 3 Biometric Service Providers (BSPs) to UIDAI are added herewith.

    i)	Sathyam Computer Services/Sagem Morpho
    ii)	L I Identity Solutions
    iii)	Accenture Services

3.2	The above organizations responded to this organization's Expressions of Interest (EOI) and submitted their tenders for accepting the projects on the basis of fulfilling the following clauses:

a)	The prime respondent should have an office in India in the form of a Registered Office.
b)	If the Prime respondent does not have a registered office in India, then it should have a Branch office, Representative office, Sales office, or an office of its subsidiary company in India for the purpose of submission of the expressions of interest response.
c)	If the prime respondent is unable to meet the stated conditions, it shall submit a declaration/confirmation, stating that it shall have Registered Office in India for the purposes of signing of contracts with the UIDAI.

3.3	There are no means to verify whether the said companies/organizations are of US origin or not. As per our contractual terms & conditions, only the companies /organizations those who are registered in India can bid. Any further information in this regard can be obtained from the UIDAI public domain www.uidai.gov.in.

4.	In view of this, the information sought for by the applicant in his RTI First Appeal stands disposed off. In case Appellant wants to appeal against the appellate authority reply, he may file 2nd appeal to Central Information Commission within 90 days.

(Davinder Kumar)
Deputy Director General & Appellate Authority
Tele: 011-23752755

To,

Shri Veeresh Malik
D-61, Defence Colony
New Delhi 110 024

Copy to:	CPIO (Shri Ashish Kumar, ADG), UIDAI, New Delhi

Scanned copy of first page of Contract between UIDAI and L 1 Identity Solutions Operating Company Pvt. Ltd.

दिल्ली DELHI   344061

CONTRACT AGREEMENT

THIS CONTRACT AGREEMENT ("Agreement") made the 24th day of August 2010

BETWEEN

The **President of India** acting through the Director General, Unique Identification Authority of India (UIDAI) (hereinafter referred to as "Purchaser") which expression shall unless repugnant to the context or meaning thereof mean and be deemed to include its authorized agents, representatives and permitted assigns of the One Part.

AND

The Party **M/s L-1 Identity Solutions Operating Company Private Limited**, a company incorporated under the Indian Companies Act 1956 having its registered office at 2, Frontline Grandeur, 14 Walton Road, Bangalore 560001 (hereinafter referred to as "**L-1 India**"), a subsidiary of **L-1 Identity Solutions Operating Company**, a Delaware U.S.A. corporation (identified in Purchaser's Bid Document as the "Prime Consortium Member" and "Prime Bidder" and hereinafter referred to as **"Biometric Solution Provider"** or **"BSP"**), which expression shall unless repugnant to the context or meaning thereof mean and be deemed to include its successors and permitted assigns of the Other Part.

Page 1 of 4

Letter from Vijay Bhalla, registrar, dated 03-09-2014

Central Information Commission, New Delhi
File No. CIC/SS/A/2013/001593/SH
Right to Information Act-2005-Under Section (19)

Date of hearing	:	3rd September 2014
Date of decision	:	3rd September 2014

Name of the Appellant   :   Shri Methew Thomas,
18A, Adarsh Vista, Basavanagar,
Marathahalli P O, Bangalore - 560037

Name of the Public   :   Central Public Information Officer,
Authority/Respondent   Unique Identification Authority of India,
Planning Commission, 2nd Floor, Tower-I,
Jeevan Bharati Building, Connaught Circus,
New Delhi - 110 001

The Appellant was present at the NIC Studio, Bangalore.

On behalf of the Respondents, the following were present in person:-

1. Shri Subrata Das, Deputy Director.
2. Shri Mahabir Singh, Section Officer.
3. Shri Shambhu Choubey, Assistant.

Information Commissioner   :   **Shri Sharat Sabharwal**

This matter pertains to an appeal dated 24.5.2013 filed by the Appellant, in regard to his RTI application dated 10.4.2012, which was received by the Commission on 29.5.2013. It came up before us today. The Appellant submitted that his appeal concerning the same RTI application was heard earlier by the Commission. He further submitted that the Commission passed an interim order No. CIC/SS/A/2012/003157 dated 26.7.2013 and final order No. CIC/SS/A/2012/003157 dated 21.10.2013. The Appellant also submitted that the order of the Commission was complied with partially by the Respondents, because he was given only copies of contracts, but not the technical and commercial bids, forming annexures to the contracts. The Respondents submitted that these annexures were denied because the concerned third parties did not want this information to be disclosed

Page (1 of 2)

2.   The Appellant stated that he has written to the Commission earlier, complaining against non-compliance by the Respondents with the Commission's order dated 21.10.2013, mentioned above. In this context, he referred in particular to his letters dated 6.1.2014 and 6.8.2014.

3.   Having considered the records and the submissions made by both the parties, the Registry is directed to examine the matter concerning compliance with the order dated 21.10.2013 within two weeks of the issuance of this order. Further, since another appeal concerning the RTI application dated 10.4.2012 has already been examined by the Commission and an order passed thereon, we do not consider it necessary to issue a separate order on the appeal registered on File No. CIC/SS/A/2013/001593/SH.

4.   With the above observations, the appeal is disposed of.

5.   Copies of this order be given free of cost to the parties.

Sd/-
(Sharat Sabharwal)
Information Commissioner

Authenticated true copy. Additional copies of orders shall be supplied against application and payment of the charges prescribed under the Act to the CPIO of this Commission.

(Vijay Bhalla)
Deputy Registrar

Page (2 of 2)

Letter from Vijay Bhalla, registrar, dated 14-10-2014

Central Information Commission
Wing 'B', 2nd Floor
August Kranti Bhawan
Bhikaji Cama Place
New Delhi 110 066

CIC/SS/A/2012/003157/SH

October 14, 2014

Central Public Information Officer &
Deputy Director
Unique Identification Authority of India (UIDAI)
9th Floor, Tower I, Jeevan Bharat Building
Connaught Circus
New Delhi 110 001

Sir,

This refers to the Commission's order dated 03.09.2014 in Mathew Thomas v. UIDAI; Appeal No. CIC/SS/A/2013/001593 directing the Registry to examine the matter concerning compliance with the Commission's order dated 21.10.2013 in Appeal No. CIC/SS/A/2012/003157.

2. The matter was accordingly examined and placed before the Commission. I am directed to convey that you should, within **2 weeks** of receipt of this order, provide to the Appellant the limited information i.e. financial quotation/price quoted by the third party firms in the subject tender as disclosure of it would not inflict any harm to the competitive position of third party firms at this stage when the contract have already expired. As regards the remaining information concerning Technical Bid and Commercial Bid, It was observed that your decision (conveyed to the Appellant, Shri Mathew Thomas by letter No. F-12013/096/2012/RTI-UIDAI dated 20.12.2013) to deny this information to the Appellant after following the third party information procedure laid down in Section 11(1) of the RTI Act was in conformity with the decision of the High

Court of Delhi in BSNL v. Chander Sekhar; LPA No. 900/2010; date of decision 23.03.2012; Commission's Full Bench decision dated 20.05.2013 in Kuljit Singh and Anr. v. PFCL; and Commission's decision dated 1.09.2014 in Ajay Chadha v. Charak Palika Hospital, NDMC; date of decision 1.9.2014; Appeal No. CIC/DS/A/2013/001664-YA and CIC/DS/A/2013/001684-YA. Moreover, the Appellant has not established any larger public interest warranting the disclosure of information in question. Therefore, there shall be no disclosure with regard to the information concerning the Technical Bid and Commercial Bid as it falls under the exemption category of Section 8(1)(d) of the RTI Act.

3.   The matter is accordingly treated as closed.

(Vijay Bhalla)
Deputy Registrar

Copy to:

Shri Mathew Thomas
18 A, Adarsh Vista, Basavanagar,
Marathahalli PO
Bangalore 560 037

Page (2 of 2)

Screen shot of UIDAI webpage search results for its contractors

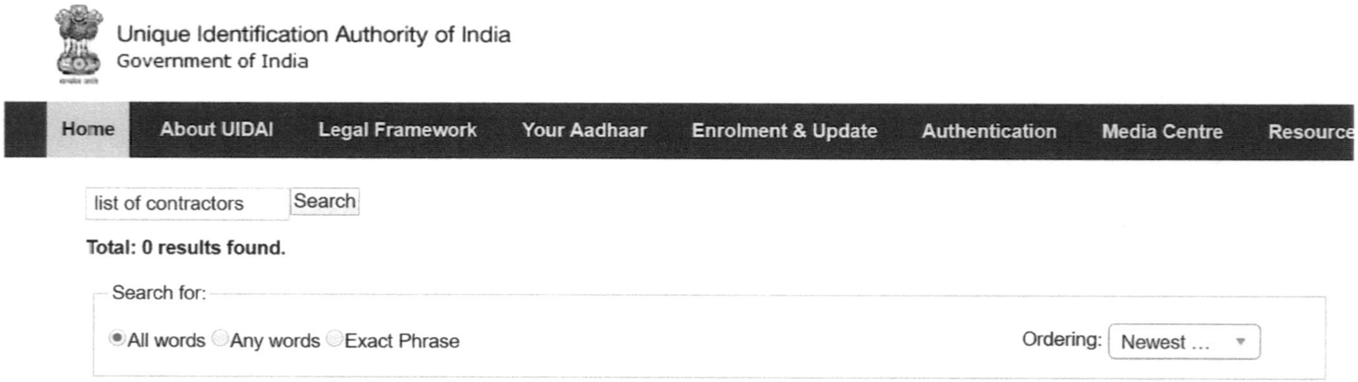

Unique Identification Authority of India
Government of India

| Home | About UIDAI | Legal Framework | Your Aadhaar | Enrolment & Update | Authentication | Media Centre | Resource |

list of contractors   Search

Total: 0 results found.

Search for:

◉ All words ○ Any words ○ Exact Phrase

Ordering: Newest …

EA name search of UIDAI website

Unique Identification Authority of India
Government of India

| Home | About UIDAI | Legal Framework | Your Aadhaar | Enrolment & Update | Authentication | Media Centre | Resour |

list of empaneled enr | Search

Total: 1 results found.

Search for:

⦿ All words ◯ Any words ◯ Exact Phrase

Ordering: Newest ... ▾

Display # 2(▾

1. Enrolment Agencies

... policies and guidelines, checklists, forms and templates issued by authority from time to time. Enrolment Agency Activities Procurement of Devices and other requirements as per Checklist for ...

Scanned copy of Clause 4.1.1. of Contract between M/s L1 ID Solutions and UIDAI

segmentation, image pre-processing, feature extraction and comparison score generation for fingerprint, iris and face modalities.

In summary, the following UID System modules utilize biometric components:

1. Multi-modal de-duplication in the enrollment server
2. Verification subsystem within the authentication server
3. Enrolment client
4. Manual checks and exception handling
5. Biometric sub-system monitoring and analysis

The functional requirements of the five areas are described, followed by the overall functions of the two biometric components.

4.1 UID System Requirements of the biometric components

4.1.1 Multi-modal Biometric de-duplication in the Enrolment Server

Considering the expected size of the de-duplication task, the UID enrolment server will utilize:

1. Multi-modal de-duplication. Multiple modalities — fingerprint and iris will be used for de-duplication. Face photograph is provided if the vendor desires to use it for de-duplication. *While certain demographical information is also provided, UIDAI provides no assurance of its accuracy.* Demographic information shall not be used for filtering during the de-duplication process, but this capability shall be preserved for potential implementation in later phases of the UID program. Each multi-modal de-duplication request will contain an indexing number (ReferenceID)[1] in addition to the multi-modal biometric and demographic data. In the event one or more duplicate enrolments is found, the ABIS will pass back the ReferenceID of the duplicates and the scaled comparison scores upon which the duplicate finding was based. The scaled fusion score returned with each duplicate found will have a range of [0, 100], with 0 indicating the least level of similarity and 100 as the highest level of similarity.

---

[1] ABIS will not be aware of the UID #, nor will it be aware of how UID #maps to reference ID or records in the reference DB.

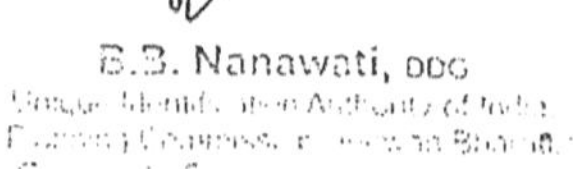

Scanned copy of Clause 15.1 of Annexure 'E' to UIDAI Contracts with BSPs

13.5 Records of Contract Documents:

13.5.1 M/s L-1 Identity Solutions Operating Company shall at all time make and keep sufficient copies of the Contract documents, manuals, reference material, drawings, specifications and any other document required by him to fulfill his duties under the Contract.

13.5.2 M/s L-1 Identity Solutions Operating Company shall keep at each Datacenter Site and UIDAI Location, adequate number of copies of all documents required to fulfill his duties under the Contract, in excess of his own requirement and those copies shall be available at all times for use by the Purchaser's Representative and/or by any other person authorized by the Purchaser's Representative.

14. Ownership and Retention of Documents

14.1 The Purchaser shall own the Documents, proposed by or for M/s L-1 Identity Solutions Operating Company arising out of or in connection with this Contract.

14.2 The Documents shall be retained by M/s L-1 Identity Solutions Operating Company not more than a period of 7 years as per Retention Policy of Government of India or any other policy that UIDAI may adopt in future.

14.3 Forthwith upon expiry or earlier termination of this Contract and at any other time on demand by the Purchaser, M/s L-1 Identity Solutions Operating Company shall deliver to the Purchaser all Documents provided by or originating from the Purchaser and all Documents produced by or from or for M/s L-1 Identity Solutions Operating Company in the course of performing the Services, unless otherwise directed in writing by the Purchaser at no additional cost. M/s L-1 Identity Solutions Operating Company shall not, without the prior written consent of the Purchaser store, copy, distribute or retain any such Documents.

15. Data and Hardware

15.1 By virtue of this Contract, M/s L-1 Identity Solutions Operating Company / The team of M/s L-1 Identity Solutions Operating Company may have access to personal information of the Purchaser and/or a third party or any resident of India, any other person covered within the ambit of any legislation as may be applicable. The Purchaser shall have the sole ownership of and the right to use, all such data in perpetuity including any data or other information pertaining to the residents of India that may be in the possession of M/s L-1 Identity Solutions Operating Company

Page (1 of 2)

Scanned copy of Clause 15.3 of Annexure 'A' of the Contract between UIDAI and M/s. L1 Identity Solutions Operating Company Private Ltd.

or The team of M/s L-1 Identity Solutions Operating Company in the course of performing the Services under this Contract.

15.2 The Purchaser shall have the sole ownership of and the right of use, proprietary Biometric templates of residents of India as created and maintained by M/s L-1 Identity Solutions Operating Company in the course of performing the Services under this Contract. In the event of termination or expiry of contract, M/s L-1 Identity Solutions Operating Company shall transfer all the proprietary templates to UIDAI in an electronic storage media in a form that is freely retrievable for reference and usage in future.

15.3 The Data shall be retained by M/s L-1 Identity Solutions Operating Company not more than a period of 7 years as per Retention Policy of Government of India or any other policy that UIDAI may adopt in future.

16. Indemnity

16.1 M/s L-1 Identity Solutions Operating Company shall execute and furnish to the Purchaser, a Deed of Indemnity in favour of the Purchaser in a form and manner acceptable to the Purchaser, indemnifying the Purchaser from and against any costs, loss, damages, expense, claims including those from third parties or liabilities of any kind howsoever suffered, arising or incurred inter alia during and after the Contract period out of:

   a.   any negligence or wrongful act or omission by M/s L-1 Identity Solutions Operating Company or the team of M/s L-1 Identity Solutions Operating Company or any third party associated with M/s L-1 Identity Solutions Operating Company in connection with or incidental to this Contract; or

   b.   any breach of any of the terms of the bid of M/s L-1 Identity Solutions Operating Company as agreed, the Bid and this Contract by M/s L-1 Identity Solutions Operating Company, the team of M/s L-1 Identity Solutions Operating Company or any third party.

   c.   any infringement of patent, trademark/copyright or industrial design rights arising from the use of the supplied goods and related services or any part thereof.

Page 29 of 65

B.B. Nanawati, bo;

Page (2 of 2)

Scanned copy of Clause 3.1 of Annexure 'B' of UIDAI's Contract with M/s. L 1 Identity Solutions Operating Company Pvt. Ltd.

2.   Escrow

2.1.   "Upon UID's written request, and pursuant to a mutually-agreeable, industry-standard escrow agreement, from the time of commencement of the contract for a period up to 2 years after expiry of contract, Biometric Solution Provider shall place in escrow: a copy of the source code for the Software, consisting of a full source language statement of the program or programs comprising the Software, in a form suitable for reproduction and use by computer; complete program maintenance documentation, including all technical manuals, release notes; and all other material necessary to allow a reasonably skilled programmer or analyst to understand, maintain, modify and enhance the Software without Biometric Solution Provider's assistance or reference to any other materials. The escrow agreement shall, at a minimum, provide for release of the source code to UID in the event Biometric Solution Provider ceases to do business as an ongoing concern or in the event of breach of contract by the Biometric Solution Provider. Biometric Solution Provider shall be responsible for all fees of the escrow agent."

3.   Privacy of data

3.1.   In course of the Agreement, the Biometric Solution Provider may collect, use, transfer, store or otherwise process (collectively, "process") information that pertains to specific individuals and can be linked to them ("personal data"). Biometric Solution Provider warrants that it shall process all personal data in accordance with applicable law and regulation. Biometric Solution Provider further warrants that it shall process such personal information only for the purposes of this Agreement, and shall not use or disclose such information, otherwise pursuant to purposes of the Agreement.

4.   Right for security clearance

4.1.   UID may execute background checks on any or all employees of the Biometric Solution Provider who are assigned to work on the project. Such background checks will include drug screening and checks for criminal activity, credit history checks, and checks on qualifications, suitability and experience of Biometric Solution Provider's employees before and/or during their assignment to the project under this Agreement.

5.   Opening of registered office in India

5.1.   The Biometric Solution Provider should have an office in India in the form of a registered office.

Page 6 of 7

D.D. Nanawati, ps.,

'Times of India' News Report Quoting CEO of UIDAI, Shri. Ajay Bhushan Pandey

https://timesofindia.indiatimes.com/business/india-business/contract-clauses-are-not-always-exercised-uidai/articleshow/60316437.cms

Contract clauses are not always exercised: UIDAI

Chethan Kumar| TNN | Sep 1, 2017, 02:45 IST

BENGALURU: Unique Identification Authority of India (UIDAI), while reiterating that Aadhaar data is secure, has said that contracts signed with firms are legal documents with contingency plans and that not all provisions are always exercised.

In a statement shared with TOI, which reported that contracts between UIDAI and foreign firms gave the latter access to biometric data, UIDAI said: "...Contracts in general are legal documents and often encompass a number of contingency provisions that may or may not be actually exercised during the execution of the contract but they are part of the contract."

The authority said it does not store data like passport or bank account numbers or licence and PAN details. "Hardware supplies are also tested twice before being put to use in the data centre and all applications running on IT hardware are secured through firewall, intrusion and data leakage prevention system, security incident and event management and identity, and access management system..."

"Processing access of biometric data... is, for eg, akin to processing access of confidential banking data of customers to the core banking solutions of some software companies and that does not mean that the customers' individual data has been handed over to these companies," it said.

US National Academies Research Report –
"Biometric Recognition – Challenges and Opportunities"

Biometrics is the automated recognition of individuals based on their behavioral and biological characteristics. It is a tool for establishing confidence that one is dealing with individuals who are already known (or not known)—and consequently that they belong to a group with certain rights (or to a group to be denied certain privileges). It relies on the presumption that individuals are physically and behaviorally distinctive in a number of ways. Figure S.1 illustrates the basic operations of a recognition process.

Biometric systems are used increasingly to recognize individuals and regulate access to physical spaces, information, services, and to other rights or benefits, including the ability to cross international borders. The motivations for using biometrics are diverse and often overlap. They include improving the convenience and efficiency of routine access transactions, reducing fraud, and enhancing public safety and national security. Questions persist, however, about the effectiveness of biometric systems as security or surveillance mechanisms, their usability and manageability, appropriateness in widely varying contexts, social impacts, effects on privacy, and legal and policy implications.

The following are the principal conclusions of this study:

• Human recognition systems are inherently probabilistic, and hence inherently fallible. The chance of error can be made small but not eliminated. System designers and operators should anticipate and plan for the occurrence of errors, even if errors are expected to be infrequent.

• The scientific basis of biometrics—from understanding the distributions of biometric traits within given populations to how humans

1

(Page 1 of 4)

Biometric Recognition: Challenges and Opportunities

2   *BIOMETRIC RECOGNITION*

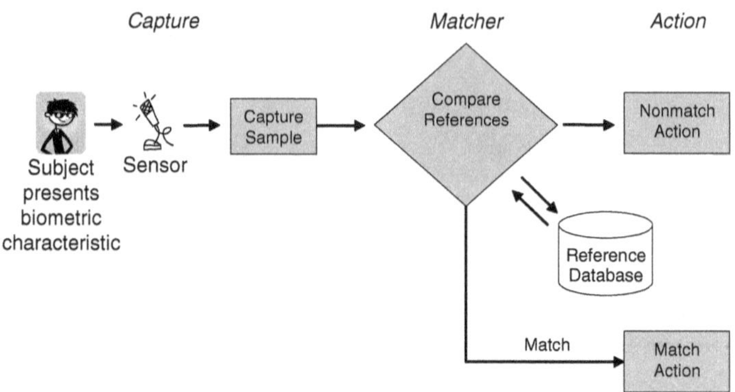

FIGURE S.1 Sample operation of a general biometric system. The two basic operations performed by a general biometric system are the capture and storage of enrollment (reference) biometric samples and the capture of new biometric samples and their comparison with corresponding reference samples (matching). This figure depicts the operation of a generic biometric system although some systems will differ in their particulars. The primary components for the purposes of this discussion are "capture," where the sensor collects biometric data from the subject to be recognized; the "reference database," where previously enrolled subjects' biometric data are held; the "matcher," which compares presented data to reference data in order to make a recognition decision; and "action," where the system recognition decision is revealed and actions are undertaken based on that decision.

interact with biometric systems—needs strengthening particularly as biometric technologies and systems are deployed in systems of national importance.

• Biometric systems incorporate complex definitional, technological, and operational choices, which are themselves embedded in larger technological and social contexts. Thus, systems-level considerations are critical to the success of biometric systems. Analyses of biometric systems' performance, effectiveness, trustworthiness, and suitability should take a broad systems perspective.

• Biometric systems should be designed and evaluated relative to their specific intended purposes and contexts rather than generically. Their effectiveness depends as much on the social context as it does on the underlying technology, operational environment, systems engineering, and testing regimes.

• The field of biometrics would benefit from more rigorous and comprehensive approaches to systems development, evaluation, and interpretation. Presumptions and burdens of proof arising from biometric

Biometric Recognition: Challenges and Opportunities

recognition should be based on solid, peer-reviewed studies of the performance of biometric recognition mechanisms.

FUNDAMENTALS OF BIOMETRIC RECOGNITION AND HUMAN INDIVIDUAL DISTINCTIVENESS

Biometric recognition systems are inherently probabilistic, and their performance needs to be assessed within the context of this fundamental and critical characteristic. Biometric recognition involves matching, within a tolerance of approximation, of observed biometric traits against previously collected data for a subject. Approximate matching is required due to the variations in biological attributes and behaviors both within and between persons.[1] Consequently, in contrast to the largely binary results associated with most information technology systems, biometric systems provide probabilistic results.

There are numerous sources of uncertainty and variation in biometric systems, including the following:

- *Variation within persons.* Biometric characteristics and the information captured by biometric systems may be affected by changes in age, environment, disease, stress, occupational factors, training and prompting, intentional alterations, sociocultural aspects of the situation in which the presentation occurs, changes in human interface with the system, and so on. As a result, each interaction of the individual with the system (at enrollment, identification, and so on) will be associated with different biometric information. Individuals attempting to thwart recognition for one reason or another also contribute to the inherent uncertainty in biometric systems.
- *Sensors.* Sensor age and calibration, how well the interface at any given time mitigates extraneous factors, and the sensitivity of sensor performance to variation in the ambient environment (such as light levels) all can play a role.
- *Feature extraction and matching algorithms.* Biometric characteristics cannot be directly compared but require stable and distinctive "features" to first be extracted from sensor outputs. Differences in feature extraction algorithms affect performance, with effects sometimes aggravated by requirements for achieving interoperability among proprietary systems. Differences between matching algorithms and comparison scoring mecha-

---

[1]For example, each finger of each person will generate a different fingerprint image every time it is observed due to presentation angle, pressure, dirt, moisture, different sensors, and so on. Thus each person can produce a large number of different impressions from a single finger—many of which will be close enough that good algorithms can match them to the correct finger source.

Biometric Recognition: Challenges and Opportunities

4   *BIOMETRIC RECOGNITION*

nisms, and how these interact with the preceding sources of variability of information acquired and features extracted, also contribute to variation in performance of different systems.

• *Data integrity.* Information may be degraded through legitimate data manipulation or transformation or degraded and/or corrupted owing to security breaches, mismanagement, inappropriate compression, or some other means. It may also be inappropriately applied to a context other than the one for which it was originally created, owing to mission creep (for example, using the data collected in a domain purely for the sake of convenience in a domain that demands high data integrity) or inappropriate re-use of information (for instance, captured biometric information might be incorrectly assumed to be of greater fidelity when transferred to a system where higher fidelity is the norm).

Many gaps exist in our understanding of the nature and extent of distinctiveness and stability of biometric traits across individuals and groups. No biometric characteristic is known to be entirely stable and distinctive across all groups. Biometric traits have fundamental statistical properties, distinctiveness, and differing degrees of stability under natural physiological conditions and environmental challenges, many aspects of which are not well understood, especially at large scales. Complicating matters, the underlying biological properties and distribution of biometric traits in a population are generally observed only through filters interposed by measurement processes and instruments and subsequent biometric feature extraction.

Thus, the development of a science of human individual distinctiveness is essential to effective and appropriate use of biometric recognition. Better understanding of biometric traits in human beings could be gained by carefully designed data collection and analysis. The biological underpinnings of physical distinctiveness and the stability of many biometric characteristics under natural physiological conditions and environmental challenges require further justification from basic biological and empirical studies. Importantly, the underlying distinctiveness of a biometric trait cannot be assessed apart from an understanding of the stability, accuracy, and inherent variability of a given measure.

Another fundamental characteristic of biometric recognition is that it requires decision making under uncertainty by both the automated recognition system and the human interpreters of its results. A biometric match represents not certain recognition but a probability of correct recognition, while a nonmatch represents a probability rather than a definitive conclusion that an individual is not known to the system. That is, some fraction of results from even the best-designed biometric system will be incorrect or indeterminate: both false matches and false nonmatches will occur. Moreover, assessing the validity of the match results, even given

Mathematical Proof Paper of Dr. Hans Mathews, Published in CIS Website

- **biometric identification: device specification and actual performance considered for the operations of the** UIDAI

  o   *hans varghese mathews*   *The Centre for Internet and Society, Bangalore*

o   **summary of findings**

1   A *biometric* is a numerized representation of some generic physical feature of an organism: and the biometric devices here are those intended for the *identification of individuals*. Such a device is supplied with a *specified error rate*: the probability that the biometrics of distinct individuals will *match*.[1] When more than one device is used, and a suite of biometrics is to identify an individual, the chance of such identification errors can be derived from the specified error rates of the individual devices: and for the matching procedure the UIDAI is following we compute $0.1155001 \cdot 10^{-11}$ as *the specified identification error*.[2] The error rates specified for biometric devices would be estimated under laborotary conditions, one expects, by their manufacturers: when they are used for the rapid identification of a large population, as in our case, their performance in the field might fall short of what their specified errors promise: and we find that

- *identification error in the field considerably exceeds, by a factor of 6 almost, the specified identification error for the matching procedure followed by the UIDAI.*

We are able to draw our conclusions by examining the result of an experiment performed by the UIDAI when 84 million citizens had been registered in their biometric database. The process of obtaining and storing biometrics is termed *enrollment*; and the stored suites of biometrics are called *templates*. The experiment estimated the chance of a *false positive match*: which occurs when the suite of biometrics of a new individual, one who is not actually enrolled, happens to match *some or other* stored template. The chance of a false positive match is the conditional probability, therefore, of a match occuring *given* that the individual is not enrolled: and it is usually termed the *false reject rate*. The rate depends on the number of individuals already enrolled. Write $\rho(n)$ for the false reject rate when n individuals have been enrolled: the specified identification error is the chance, now, that the biometrics of a new individual will match *any one* given template: and if ξ is the specified identification error then

$$\rho(n) \;=\; 1 - [1 - \xi]^n$$

Now for an identification error of $(0.1155001) \cdot 10^{-11}$ and an enrolled base of 84 million the false reject rate should be $(0.97020084) \cdot 10^{-4}$ at most: but the UIDAI got an estimate of $(0.57725) \cdot 10^{-3}$ from its experiment. The bound on this rate

---

[1]   Matching occurs when numerized representations are too similar: and similarity is usually decided by the *distance* between them falling below some *threshold*, for some appropriate measure of distance between the numerized representations the given device produces.

[2]   The UIDAI is using iris scanners and fingerprint scanners: and has made their specified error rates available to researchers at the Takshashila Institute: who have made them public. The specified error for their make of iris scanner has been repored as $1/13100$: the specified error for the fingerprint scanner as $1/500$. The UIDAI has not published its matching procedure: but our investigations have led us to conclude the following: a match is taken to occur if both irises match and *any one* digit also does.

comes from the relation $1 - [1 - \xi]^n \leq n \cdot \xi$, which holds for $0 < \xi < 1$ generally; from this, and from the relation between $\rho(n)$ and ξ above, one can get the bounds

$$\frac{\rho(n)}{n} \leq \xi \leq \frac{-\log[1 - \rho(n)]}{n}$$

We have estimated the identification error in the field by using the UIDAI's experimental value as a reliable operational estimate of $\rho(n)$: and $(0.687400801) \cdot 10^{-11}$ is our estimate of what ξ must be in the field.

2   The false reject rate is one measure of the operational accuracy, in the field, of a suite of biometric devices. A equally important measure is its converse: the conditional probability that an individual is *not enrolled,* actually, given a match between his or her biometrics and some or other stored template. We shall term this *mistaken identification:* and our principal finding is that

•   *the probability of mistaken identification rises considerably between the initial and final stages of enrollment: by a factor of 10, as it happens, between the first and last tenths of the population enrolled.*

We have proceeded here by estimating the total number of matches expected, and the number of false matches among these, for successive millions of individuals enrolled: for which we have used the lower of the bounds on $\rho(n)$ given by

$$n \cdot \xi \cdot \left[\frac{1 - \xi}{1 - \xi + n \cdot \xi} \right] \leq 1 - [1 - \xi]^n \leq n \cdot \xi$$

The actual numbers are not negligible. The UIDAI should expect a total of $534,010$ matches to occur for the first 100 million enrolled: out of which $34,180$ will be mistaken matches. But a total of $1,280,208$ matches are expected for the last 100 million enrolled: and among these fully $780,382$ would be mistaken matches. The discrepancy is even more extreme for small initial and final subsets: we estimate $50,325$ matches for the first 10 million, of which only 341 would be mistaken ones; but $13,1050$ matches are expected for the last 10 million, out of which $8,1607$ would be mistaken matches.[3]

3   When a match occurs the UIDAI must decide whether or not the individual is already enrolled: for which the templates matching that person's suite of biometrics must be examined. The amount of work here depends on how many templates will match a given suite of biometrics, generally, when a match does occcur. We get an upper bound of $10,922,437$ on the total number of matches when the entire population of 1.2 billion has been enrolled: of which $4,924,539$ would be mistaken ones. We estimate that only $11,267,203$ matching templates will have to examined, however, to decide which matches are mistaken: and our last finding is that

•   *only occasionally will more than one matching template have to be examined, when a match occurs, in order to decide whether or not that match is mistaken.*

---

[3]   The bounds above come from Professor Nico Temme of the CWI in The Netherlands: whose freely given help we gratefully acknowledge. To counts matches and mistaken matches one needs, besides identification error, the probability that enrolled individuals will try to register again; and one needs, as well, the chance of a match for an already enrolled person. The UIDAI has conducted an experiment which allows one to estimate the latter; and it has estimated to its satisfaction the former probability as well.

The Executive Summary of the CAG report No. 2 (Civil) for year ended Mar 31, 2011, obtained through RTI

Chapter 2

Performance Audit

Food, Civil Supplies and Consumer Affairs Department

2.1 Comprehensive Computerisation Project of the Department of Food, Civil Supplies and Consumer Affairs

Executive Summary

A comprehensive computerisation project to digitise the data collected through a house-to-house survey and issue computerised ration cards to the eligible families in the State was approved by Government (August 2005) for the Department of Food, Civil Supplies and Consumer Affairs. The project sought to eliminate ineligible ration cards, besides creating an effective distribution management system to ensure availability of rationed articles, reduce leakages and provide an efficient and real-time Management Information System.

The Department selected (March 2006) a partner under the Build, Operate and Transfer (BOT) model of Public-Private-Partnership (PPP) through a bidding process to implement the project over a period of five and a half years. However, Government's decision to adopt the PPP route had not been taken after considering all alternatives. Balanced sharing of risks between the Government and private sector partner had not been ensured for enduring success of the PPP arrangement and the choice of PPP was not taken after due diligence. The selection of the private partner and the qualifying procedures were flawed, resulting in selection of the partner who did not have the capacity to deliver.

The oversight over implementation of computerisation was so defective that the partner persistently bypassed the contracted procedures and carried on with the work in a totally uncontrolled environment. This resulted in an abnormal increase in the number of ration cards including those for the families below poverty line. The Department failed to enforce various provisions in the agreement resulting in several inadmissible payments to the partner, non-remittance/delayed remittance by the partner of the user charges collected from public *etc*. Although the partner was to complete the project set-up phase by October 2006, it remained incomplete even five years after the scheduled date of completion. After receiving a payment of ₹ 54.23 crore, the partner closed the operations prematurely in November 2010 without transferring any of the assets except the database of ration cards. An evaluation of the database by a third party showed that it was incomplete in many respects, suffered from many deficiencies and was not capable of preventing duplication of ration cards.

The Department had taken upon itself the responsibility of rectifying the mistakes in the database created by the partner. As the rectification process was still in progress, the process of issue, modification and deletion of ration cards in the State had come to a standstill since November 2010. Thus, various lapses of the Department/partner defeated the very objective of providing improved services to the public and protecting their interests adequately. The PPP project ended up as an example of doubtful value for money in a crucial area of governance.

"Aadhaar" Enabled Frauds Published in Media – List Compiled By Dr. Anupam Saraph

Publicly Reported Cases of Fake or Forged Aadhaar								
Title of article	Publication	Location	Date	Link	Fraud	How	Aadhaar in Database	Other documents
Challan in cheating, forgery case points to Aadhaar data breach	The Tribune	Chandigarh	17/04/18	http://www.tribuneindia.com/news/chandigarh/challan-in-cheating-forgery-case-points-to-aadhaar-data-breach/575238.html	Loans	Forged	N	Y
Aadhaar card scam busted, three arrested	The Times of India	Ahmedabad	14/04/18	https://timesofindia.indiatimes.com/city/ahmedabad/aadhaar-card-scam-busted-three-arrested/articleshow/63753633.cms	Aadhaar racket	Linkng of biometric with another persons documents	Y	N
40 bank accounts opened using forged documents in Mumbai, used for export-import business	Hindustan Times	Mumbai	31/03/18	https://www.hindustantimes.com/mumbai-news/40-bank-accounts-opened-using-forged-documents-in-mumbai-used-for-export-import-business/story-7JpH2wGBI4SwlIBnmhBdcL.html	Bank account	NA	Y	Y
Fake Aadhaar card in name of Bollywood actor used to book hotel room	Indian Express	Mumbai	29/03/18	http://indianexpress.com/article/india/fake-aadhaar-card-in-name-of-bollywood-actor-used-to-book-hotel-room-5115647/	Book hotel room	Forged	N	N
A fraud of another kind! Man opens fake bank branch in Uttar Pradesh's Ballia, arrested	Times Now	Ballia	29/03/18	http://www.timesnownews.com/the-buzz/article/karnataka-bank-uttar-pradesh-ballia-fake-branch-mulayam-nagar-fefna-area/212192	Opening bank branch	Obtained fake Aadhaar in alternate name.	Y	Y

Publicly Reported Cases of Fake or Forged Aadhaar								
Title of article	Publication	Location	Date	Link	Fraud	How	Aadhaar in Database	Other documents
Rohingya migrant, Andhra man get jail term for cheating	India Today	Hyderabad	28/03/18	https://www.indiatoday.in/pti-feed/story/rohingya-migrant-andhra-man-get-jail-term-for-cheating-1199878-2018-03-28?utm_source=inshorts&utm_medium=referral&utm_campaign=fullarticle	Illegal migrants	Fake documents	Y	N
Terror threat? Fake Aadhaar cards available for a mere Rs. 200	Zee News	Mumbai	27/03/18	http://zeenews.india.com/india/terror-threats-fake-aadhaar-cards-available-for-a-mere-rs-200-2094132.html	Train travel	Forged	N	N
Nepalese passengers forge Aadhaar, boarding passes to fly to Leh	DNA	Delhi	27/03/18	http://www.dnaindia.com/delhi/report-nepalese-passengers-forge-aadhaar-boarding-passes-to-fly-to-leh-2598003	Air travel	Forged	N	N
3 booked for making Aadhaar cards on forged documents	The Tribune	Moga	26/03/18	http://www.tribuneindia.com/news/punjab/3-booked-for-making-aadhaar-cards-on-forged-documents/563714.html	Aadhaar racket	Fake documents	Y	N
ATS detains man for making fake IDs for Bangladeshi trio	The Times of India	Pune	19/03/18	https://timesofindia.indiatimes.com/city/pune/ats-detains-man-for-making-fake-ids-for-bangladeshi-trio/articleshow/63359984.cms	Illegal migrants	NA	Y	Y
Bangladeshi national issued passport on fake documents, booked	The Times of India	Bareilly	18/03/18	https://timesofindia.indiatimes.com/city/bareilly/bangladeshi-national-issued-passport-on-fake-documents-booked/articleshow/63357920.cms	Passport	NA	Y	Y

Contd…

Publicly Reported Cases of Fake or Forged Aadhaar								
Title of article	Publication	Location	Date	Link	Fraud	How	Aadhaar in Database	Other documents
Man booked for forging Aadhaar, PAN to finance 30 two-wheelers in Doon	Hindustan Times	Dehradun	17/03/18	https://www.hindustantimes.com/dehradun/man-booked-for-forging-aadhaar-pan-to-finance-30-two-wheelers-in-doon/story-Vt8boDYJEbl9fCaOaaKivO.html	Loans	Fake documents	Y	Y
Rajasthan police bust racket using 'fake Aadhaar', computer hacking to help…	Times Now	Rajasthan	16/03/18	https://www.msn.com/en-in/money/other/rajasthan-police-bust-racket-using-%e2%80%98fake-aadhaar%e2%80%99-computer-hacking-to-help-candidates-clear-exam/vi-BBKituT?refvid=BBJKTpu	NA	NA	NA	NA
Four Rohingyas held by Balapur police for fake Aadhaar card	Deccan Chronicle	Hyderabad	08/03/18	https://www.deccanchronicle.com/nation/crime/080318/four-rohingyas-held-by-balapur-police-for-fake-aadhaar-card.html	Illegal migrants	Local brokers	Y	Y
B'deshi terrorists procuring forged Aadhaar, Pan cards: NIA lodges case	Business Standard	Kolkata	01/03/18	http://www.business-standard.com/article/pti-stories/b-deshi-terrorists-procuring-forged-aadhaar-pan-cards-nia-lodges-case-118030101044_1.html	Illegal migrants	NA	Y	Y
Junnar man clones Aadhaar cards to usurp land of two sisters, held	The Times of India	Pune	23/02/18	https://timesofindia.indiatimes.com/city/pune/junnar-man-clones-aadhaar-cards-to-usurp-land-of-two-sisters-held/articleshow/63035193.cms	Land	Cloned photographs	Y	N
3 held for Aadhaar fraud	The Telegraph	Guwhati	19/02/18	https://www.telegraphindia.com/states/north-east/3-held-for-aadhaar-fraud-209683	Aadhaar racket	Didn't have permission to enrol	Y	N

Publicly Reported Cases of Fake or Forged Aadhaar

Title of article	Publication	Location	Date	Link	Fraud	How	Aadhaar in Database	Other documents
Bengaluru medical seat fraud: Fake Aadhaar cards used to open bank accounts	The New Indian Express	Bengaluru	15/02/18	http://www.newindianexpress.com/cities/bengaluru/2018/feb/15/bengaluru-medical-seat-fraud-fake-aadhaar-cards-used-to-open-bank-accounts-1773527.html	Bank account	NA	NA	NA
Man arrested for making fake PAN and Aadhar card	The Times of India	Agra	15/02/18	https://timesofindia.indiatimes.com/city/agra/man-arrested-for-making-fake-pan-and-aadhar-card/articleshow/62936657.cms	Bank account	NA	NA	NA
Accused made hundreds of fake Aadhaar, PAN cards	The Hindu	Mumbai	14/02/18	http://www.thehindu.com/news/cities/mumbai/accused-made-hundreds-of-fake-aadhaar-pan-cards/article22746105.ece	Sim cards	Forged	N	Y
Shop making fake Aadhar cards & driving licences raided, 2 held	The Times of India	Mumbai	11/02/18	https://timesofindia.indiatimes.com/city/mumbai/shop-making-fake-aadhar-cards-driving-licences-raided-2-held/articleshow/62868271.cms	Aadhaar racket	NA	NA	NA
Madhya Pradesh: 'Aadhaar card forged for 2-wheeler loan'	The Times of India	Bhopal	28/01/18	https://timesofindia.indiatimes.com/city/bhopal/madhya-pradesh-aadhaar-card-forged-for-2-wheeler-loan/articleshow/62681117.cms	Loans	Forged	N	N
Seven held for getting mobiles financed on fake Aadhaar cards	The Tribune	Chandigarh	22/01/18	http://www.tribuneindia.com/news/chandigarh/seven-held-for-getting-mobiles-financed-on-fake-aadhaar-cards/532276.html	Business finance	Cloned photographs	Y	Y

Contd…

Publicly Reported Cases of Fake or Forged Aadhaar								
Title of article	Publication	Location	Date	Link	Fraud	How	Aadhaar in Database	Other documents
Four arrested for cheating, opening fake bank accounts	Millennium Post	Delhi	20/01/18	http://www.millenniumpost.in/delhi/four-arrested-for-cheating-opening-fake-bank-accounts-280687	Bank account	Forged	NA	NA
Fake Aadhaar ID Used to Sell Two Plots in Mumbai, One Arrest	The Quint	Mumbai	18/01/18	https://www.thequint.com/news/india/fake-aadhaar-id-used-to-sell-two-plots-in-mumbai-one-arrest	Land	NA	NA	NA
Two Uzbek women held, one with fake Aadhaar card	Millennium Post	Gurugram	18/01/18	http://www.millenniumpost.in/delhi/two-uzbek-women-held-one-with-fake-aadhaar-card-280424	Sex racket	NA	Y	N
CISF apprehends two passengers with fake Aadhaar cards in Delhi airport, raises security concerns	India Today	Delhi	09/01/18	https://www.indiatoday.in/india/story/cisf-passengers-fake-aadhaar-cards-delhi-airport-security-1131032-2018-01-09	Air travel	Forged	N	N
Duo try to use fake Aadhaar cards to enter jail, caught	The Times of India	Pune	06/01/18	https://discoverpune.com/pune-news/duo-try-to-use-fake-aadhaar-cards-to-enter-jail-caught-2/	Entering Jail	Forged	NA	NA
Andhra man tries to forge his Aadhaar to sell kidney, Guntur cops bust racket	The News Minute	Guntur	05/01/18	https://www.thenewsminute.com/article/andhra-man-tries-forge-his-aadhar-sell-kidney-guntur-cops-bust-racket-74209	Sell kidney	NA	NA	NA
Pak National with Aadhaar Card Arrested from Jaisalmer Air Base	The Quint	Jaisalmer	04/01/18	https://www.thequint.com/news/india/pakistani-national-with-aadhaar-card-arrested	Accessing Air Base	NA	Y	NA

Publicly Reported Cases of Fake or Forged Aadhaar								
Title of article	Publication	Location	Date	Link	Fraud	How	Aadhaar in Database	Other documents
Fake PAN, Aadhaar card racket busted in Uttar Pradesh's Shamli: Police	The New Indian Express	Shamli	24/12/17	http://www.newindianexpress.com/nation/2017/dec/24/fake-pan-aadhaar-card-racket-busted-in-uttar-pradeshs-shamli-police-1736112.html	Aadhaar racket	NA	NA	Y
Assam: Five held for making fake Aadhaar cards in Guwahati!	The North East Today	Guwahati	20/12/17	https://thenortheasttoday.com/assam-five-held-for-making-fake-aadhaar-cards-in-guwahati/	Aadhaar racket	NA	Y	Y
Illegal Bangladeshi immigrants held with Aadhaar cards	The Hindu	Bengaluru	18/12/17	http://www.thehindu.com/news/cities/bangalore/illegal-bangladeshi-immigrants-held-with-aadhaar-cards/article21859950.ece	Job application	Fake documents	Y	N
Assam UIDAI official involved in fake Aadhaar card job racket arrested	Time 8	Guwahati	17/12/17	https://www.time8.in/uidai-official-involved-in-fakee-aadhaar-card-job-racket-arrest/	Aadhaar racket	NA	NA	NA
Family Forged 11 Year Old Girl's Aadhaar Card In Order To Marry Her	India Times	Bulandshahr	16/12/17	https://www.indiatimes.com/news/india/family-forged-11-year-old-girl-s-aadhaar-card-in-order-to-marry-her-plus-five-other-important-news-329885.html	Marriage	Forged	Y	N
Fake documents, forged gazetted letters used to enrol for Aadhaar	The New Indian Express	Bengaluru	16/12/17	http://www.newindianexpress.com/states/karnataka/2017/dec/16/fake-documents-forged-gazetted-letters-used-to-enrol-for-aadhaar-1728704.html	Aadhaar racket	Fake documents	Y	N

Contd…

Publicly Reported Cases of Fake or Forged Aadhaar								
Title of article	Publication	Location	Date	Link	Fraud	How	Aadhaar in Database	Other documents
Prime suspect in fake Aadhaar racket held	The Times of India	Kolkata	14/12/17	https://timesofindia.indiatimes.com/city/kolkata/prime-suspect-in-fake-aadhaar-racket-held/articleshow/62061622.cms	Aadhaar racket	NA	NA	Y
Mumbai: Fake document racket busted in Bhayandar	The Free Press Journal	Mumbai	13/12/17	http://www.freepressjournal.in/mumbai/mumbai-fake-document-racket-busted-in-bhayandar/1185909	Aadhaar racket	Fake documents	Y	NA
Three held for Aadhaar card fraud	The Hindu	Chennai	13/12/17	http://www.thehindu.com/todays-paper/tp-national/tp-tamilnadu/three-held-for-aadhaar-card-fraud/article21569756.ece	Illegal migrants	Fake documents	Y	N
Lashkar-e-Toiba operative gets PAN, Aadhaar, passport in Bihar	The New Indian Express	Gopalganj	08/12/17	http://www.newindianexpress.com/nation/2017/dec/08/lashkar-e-toiba-operative-gets-pan-aadhaar-passport-in-bihar-1721653.html?utm_source=inshorts&utm_medium=referral&utm_campaign=fullarticle	Terrorist living in India	NA	Y	Y
Bangladeshi nationals with fake PAN, Aadhaar card nabbed	Meghalaya Times	West Garo Hills	29/11/17	http://www.meghalayatimes.info/index.php/front-page/32436-bangladeshi-nationals-with-fake-pan-aadhaar-card-nabbed	Illegal migrants	NA	NA	Y
Morphed Aadhaar cards were given to teens to cast vote: UIDAI	The Times of India	Agra	27/11/17	https://timesofindia.indiatimes.com/city/agra/morphed-aadhaar-cards-were-given-to-teens-to-cast-vote-uidai/articleshow/61824792.cms	Cast votes	Forged	N	N

Publicly Reported Cases of Fake or Forged Aadhaar								
Title of article	Publication	Location	Date	Link	Fraud	How	Aadhaar in Database	Other documents
Al-Qaeda terror suspect arrested in kolkata got fake Aadhaar card made in Karnataka	DNA	Kolkata	23/11/17	http://www.dnaindia.com/india/report-al-qaeda-terror-suspect-arrested-in-kolkata-got-fake-aadhaar-card-made-in-karnataka-2561987	Terrorist living in India	NA	Y	N
Five persons held on charges of generating fake Aadhaar cards	Nagaland Post	Dimapur	11/11/17	http://www.nagalandpost.com/ChannelNews/State/StateNews.aspx?news=TkVXUzEwMDEyMzcx-NA%3D%3D	Aadhaar racket	NA	Y	N
Minor with fake Aadhaar rescued	DNA	Mumbai	09/11/17	http://www.dnaindia.com/mumbai/report-minor-with-fake-aadhaar-rescued-2558765	Flesh trade racket	NA	Y	N
Apps create fake Aadhaar cards	Deccan Chronicle	Hyderabad	06/11/17	https://www.deccanchronicle.com/technology/in-other-news/061117/apps-create-fake-aadhaar-cards.html	Aadhaar racket	NA	NA	NA
Fake Aadhaar card gang busted, 2 arrested	The Tribune	Panchkula	02/11/17	http://www.tribuneindia.com/news/chandigarh/fake-aadhaar-card-gang-busted-2-arrested/491264.html	Aadhaar racket	NA	Y	N
Four held for making fake Aadhaar cards	The Tribune	Bathinda	31/10/17	http://www.tribuneindia.com/news/bathinda/four-held-for-making-fake-aadhaar-cards/489851.html	Land	NA	NA	N
Fake Aadhaar cards row: How Maharashtra government prevented payments to 10 lakh fraud accounts	Financial Express	Maharashtra	27/10/17	https://www.financialexpress.com/india-news/fake-aadhaar-cards-row-how-maharashtra-government-prevented-payments-to-10-lakh-fraud-accounts/908800/	NA	NA	NA	NA

Contd…

Publicly Reported Cases of Fake or Forged Aadhaar								
Title of article	**Publication**	**Location**	**Date**	**Link**	**Fraud**	**How**	**Aadhaar in Database**	**Other documents**
Dimapur police busts fake Aadhaar card racket	United News of India	Dimapur	12/10/17	http://www.uniindia.com/dimapur-police-busts-fake-aadhaar-card-racket/other/news/1016546.html?fromNewsdog=1&utm_source=NewsDog&utm_medium=referral	Aadhaar racket	Eye and finger scanner used to make fake Aadhaar	Y	N
Two held in Indore for making fake Aadhar cards	The Times of India	Indore	09/10/17	https://timesofindia.indiatimes.com/city/indore/two-held-in-indore-for-making-fake-aadhar-cards/articleshow/61006435.cms	Marriage	Forged	N	N
Fake 'originals' leave passport officials in a tight spot	The Hindu	Bengaluru	03/10/17	http://www.thehindu.com/news/cities/bangalore/fake-originals-leave-passport-officials-in-a-tight-spot/article19786888.ece	Illegal migrants	NA	Y	Y
Rot runs deep: Aadhaar, birth documents easily forged	The Times of India	Hyderabad	22/09/17	https://timesofindia.indiatimes.com/city/hyderabad/rot-runs-deep-aadhaar-birth-docus-easily-forged/articleshow/60788442.cms	Marriage	Online facility to correct details	Y	Y
Rohingya man held for forgery, holds Aadhaar, PAN cards	India Today	Hyderabad	12/09/17	https://www.indiatoday.in/pti-feed/story/rohingya-man-held-for-forgery-holds-aadhaar-pan-cards-1043375-2017-09-12	Illegal migrants	NA	Y	N
Fake Aadhaar card network busted in Kanpur	The Hindu	Kanpur	11/09/17	http://www.thehindu.com/news/national/uttar-pradesh-police-busts-fake-aadhaar-card-network/article19660140.ece	Aadhaar racket	Eye and finger scanner used to make fake Aadhaar	Y	N

Publicly Reported Cases of Fake or Forged Aadhaar								
Title of article	**Publication**	**Location**	**Date**	**Link**	**Fraud**	**How**	**Aadhaar in Database**	**Other documents**
Three Pakistanis issued Aadhaar based on fake papers	The Indian Express	New Delhi	04/08/17	http://indianexpress.com/article/india/three-pakistanis-issued-aadhaar-based-on-fake-papers-4782484/	Illegal migrants	Fake documents	Y	N
Pakistani narcotic smuggler held in TN had travelled across India with two fake Aadhaar cards	The Times of India	Madurai	23/07/17	https://timesofindia.indiatimes.com/city/chennai/pakistani-narcotic-smuggler-held-in-tn-had-travelled-across-india-with-two-duplicate-aadhaar-cards/articleshow/59724246.cms	Illegal migrants	NA	NA	NA
Aadhaar centre owner, 4 others held for issuing cards against fake documents	The Times of India	Bengaluru	16/06/17	https://timesofindia.indiatimes.com/city/bengaluru/aadhaar-centre-owner-4-others-held-for-issuing-cards-against-fake-documents/articleshow/59167846.cms	Aadhaar racket	Fake documents	Y	N
Agents Provide Fake Aadhar Card With Real Train Ticket in Patna	News 18	Patna	05/06/17	https://www.news18.com/news/india/agents-provide-fake-aadhar-card-with-real-train-ticket-in-patna-1423109.html	Aadhaar racket	NA	NA	NA
Two held for running fake Aadhaar card racket	Zee Business	Delhi	02/06/17	http://www.zeebiz.com/india/news-dl-aadhaar-arrest-17118	Aadhaar racket	NA	N	NA
Rail cops uncover fake Aadhar scam	The Asian Age	Mumbai	31/05/17	http://www.asianage.com/metros/mumbai/310517/rail-cops-uncover-fake-aadhar-scam.html	Train travel	Forged	N	N

Contd…

Publicly Reported Cases of Fake or Forged Aadhaar								
Title of article	Publication	Location	Date	Link	Fraud	How	Aadhaar in Database	Other documents
Bengaluru: Fake Aadhaar, forged IDs land Indo-Pak couple in jail	Hindustan Times	Bengaluru	31/05/17	https://www.hindustantimes.com/india-news/bengaluru-fake-aadhaar-forged-ids-land-indo-pak-couple-in-jail/story-5G0hqMJHmkrX1XKx98fhkI.html	Illegal migrants	Fake documents	Y	N
After Karnataka, Pakistani national with fake Aadhaar card arrested from Haryana's Bahadurgarh	News X	Bahadurgarh	26/05/17	https://www.newsx.com/national/64539-after-karnataka-pakistani-national-with-fake-aadhaar-card-arrested-in-bahadurgarh	Illegal migrants	Fake documents	Y	Y
Bangla man held with Aadhaar card, Indian 'passport	The Times of India	Mumbai	17/05/17	https://timesofindia.indiatimes.com/city/mumbai/bangla-man-held-with-aadhaar-card-indian-passport/articleshow/58706177.cms	Illegal migrants	NA	Y	Y
Rajasthan ATS nabs 11 impersonators, forged Aadhaar cards recovered	The Times of India	Udaipur	30/04/17	https://timesofindia.indiatimes.com/city/udaipur/rajasthan-ats-nabs-11-impersonators-forged-aadhaar-cards-recovered/articleshow/58449371.cms	Exams	Forged	N	N
A man arrested for issuing Aadhar cards on the basis of forged documents allegedly committed suicide in police lock-up.	Ahmedabad Mirror	Ahmedabad	28/04/17	http://ahmedabadmirror.indiatimes.com/ahmedabad/crime/man-commits-suicide-at-gu-police-lock-up/articleshow/58405842.cms	Aadhaar racket	Fake documents	Y	N

Publicly Reported Cases of Fake or Forged Aadhaar								
Title of article	Publication	Location	Date	Link	Fraud	How	Aadhaar in Database	Other documents
Jobless engineer made over 100 fake Aadhaar cards	The Times of India	Ahmedabad	28/04/17	https://timesofindia.indiatimes.com/city/ahmedabad/jobless-engineer-made-over-100-fake-aadhaar-cards/articleshow/58406979.cms	Aadhaar racket	Forged	N	N
Indore: Fake mobile financing gang busted, 11 arrested	The Free Press Journal	Indore	06/04/17	http://www.freepressjournal.in/indore/indore-fake-mobile-financing-gang-busted-11-arrested/1047047	Loans	NA	NA	NA
Delhi realtor breaks into businessman's a/c with fake Aadhaar card, steals Rs. 2.5 lakh	The Times of India	Mumbai	06/02/17	https://timesofindia.indiatimes.com/city/mumbai/delhi-realtor-breaks-into-businessmans-a/c-with-fake-aadhaar-card-steals-rs-2-5-lakh/articleshow/56991835.cms	Phishing Scam	NA	NA	NA
MFIs distribute loans on fake Aadhaar, election cards	The Times of India	Nagpur	31/01/17	https://timesofindia.indiatimes.com/city/nagpur/mfis-distribute-loans-on-fake-aadhaar-election-cards/articleshow/56879742.cms	Loans	NA	NA	NA
Nine held in Aadhaar racket bust	The Telegraph	Kolkata	20/12/16	https://www.telegraphindia.com/1161220/jsp/calcutta/story_125700.jsp	Aadhaar racket	Eye and finger scanner used to make fake Aadhaar	Y	N
Racket in Fake Aadhaar	Deccan Chronicle	Bengaluru	03/12/16	https://www.pressreader.com/india/deccan-chronicle/20161203/281771333808164	Sim cards	Forged	N	N
'If Lord Hanuman can get an Aadhaar number, why can't a Pakistani spy?'	Scroll.in	NA	03/11/16	https://scroll.in/article/820536/if-lord-hanuman-can-get-an-aadhaar-number-why-cant-a-pakistani-spy	Illegal migrants	Fake documents	Y	NA

Contd...

Publicly Reported Cases of Fake or Forged Aadhaar								
Title of article	Publication	Location	Date	Link	Fraud	How	Aadhaar in Database	Other documents
Fake Aadhaar numbers used in PDS	Deccan Herald	Bengaluru	13/10/16	https://www.deccanherald.com/content/575504/fake-aadhaar-numbers-used-pds.html	Siphon PDS grains	Forged	N	N
Fake Aadhaar troubles passport officials in city	The Times of India	Visakhapatnam	27/08/16	https://timesofindia.indiatimes.com/city/visakhapatnam/Fake-Aadhaar-troubles-passport-officials-in-city/articleshow/53881455.cms	Passport	Forged	N	N
Three held for forging Aadhar card documents	India Today	Mumbai	01/08/16	https://www.indiatoday.in/pti-feed/story/three-held-for-forging-aadhar-card-documents-676986-2016-08-01	Aadhaar racket	Fake documents	Y	Y
Spammed with snail mail, man uncovers Aadhaar card fraud	Mumbai Mirror	Mumbai	27/07/16	https://mumbaimirror.indiatimes.com/mumbai/crime/spammed-with-snail-mail-man-uncovers-aadhaar-card-fraud/articleshow/53358970.cms	Aadhaar racket	Fake documents	Y	N
Man files plaint against wife for forging his Aadhaar card	The Times of India	Aurangabad	10/07/16	https://timesofindia.indiatimes.com/city/aurangabad/Man-files-plaint-against-wife-for-forging-his-Aadhaar-card/articleshow/53138891.cms	Book hotel room	Forged	N	N
Touts forge Aadhaar IDs to get confirmed berths	The Times of India	Mumbai	09/07/16	http://epaperbeta.timesofindia.com/Article.aspx?eid=31804&articlexml=Touts-forge-Aadhaar-IDs-to-get-confirmed-berths-09072016002022	Train travel	Forged	N	N
Food Dept detects 6L Fake Aadhaar card holders	The Pioneer	Ranchi	25/06/16	http://www.dailypioneer.com/STATE-EDITIONS/ranchi/food-dept-detects-6l-fake-aadhaar-card-holders.html	Siphon PDS grains	NA	NA	NA

Publicly Reported Cases of Fake or Forged Aadhaar

Title of article	Publication	Location	Date	Link	Fraud	How	Aadhaar in Database	Other documents
Seizure of 5,000 fake Aadhaar cards worries WB authorities	E-Gov	Malda	18/05/16	http://egov.eletsonline.com/2016/05/seizure-of-5000-fake-aadhaar-cards-worries-wb-authorities/	Aadhaar racket	Forged	N	N
Aadhaar card scam busted	The Hindu	Delhi	17/05/16	http://www.thehindu.com/news/national/other-states/aadhaar-card-scam-busted/article8608804.ece	Aadhaar racket	Forged	N	N
Jaish-e-Mohammed terrorist from PoK caught, Aadhaar card recovered from him	The Economic Times	Srinagar	15/05/16	https://economictimes.indiatimes.com/news/defence/jaish-e-mohammed-terrorist-from-pok-caught-aadhaar-card-recovered-from-him/articleshow/52279688.cms	Illegal migrants	NA	NA	NA
Alarm over seizure of fake passports from illegal Bangladeshi immigrants	The Hindu	Mumbai	16/11/15	http://www.thehindu.com/news/national/alarm-over-seizure-of-fake-passports-from-illegal-bangladeshi-immigrants/article7880927.ece	Passport	NA	NA	NA
Agency issues fake Aadhaar cards with UIDAI data	The Times of India	Bengaluru	15/09/15	https://timesofindia.indiatimes.com/city/bengaluru/Agency-issues-fake-Aadhaar-cards-with-UIDAI-data/articleshow/48965176.cms	Aadhaar racket	Forged	NA	NA
Man makes Aadhar card for dog 'Tommy Singh', arrested	The Indian Express	Bhind	05/07/15	http://indianexpress.com/article/trending/man-arrested-for-getting-aadhar-card-made-for-dog/	Aadhaar racket	NA	Y	N
South Mumbai RTO stumbles upon fake driving licence scam	Mid-Day	Mumbai	04/07/15	https://www.mid-day.com/articles/south-mumbai-rto-stumbles-upon-fake-driving-licence-scam/16342197	Drivers License	Forged	N	Y

Contd...

Publicly Reported Cases of Fake or Forged Aadhaar								
Title of article	Publication	Location	Date	Link	Fraud	How	Aadhaar in Database	Other documents
Man Arrested for Making 'Fake' Aadhaar Cards	NDTV	Chandigarh	02/07/15	https://www.ndtv.com/chandigarh-news/man-arrested-for-making-fake-aadhaar-cards-777341	Aadhaar racket	Forged	N	N
16 held in Aadhaar card scam	The Times of India	Gudivada	31/10/14	http://www.thehindu.com/todays-paper/tp-national/tp-andhrapradesh/16-held-in-aadhaar-card-scam/article6551082.ece	PDS grains	NA	NA	NA
Bangladeshi man in fake ID card racket	The Telegraph	Kolkata	27/10/14	https://www.telegraphindia.com/1141027/jsp/calcutta/story_18967131.jsp	Aadhaar racket	Forged	NA	Y
Four held for making fake Aadhaar cards	The Times of India	Kanpur	27/06/14	https://timesofindia.indiatimes.com/city/kanpur/Four-held-for-making-fake-Aadhaar-cards/articleshow/37303353.cms	Aadhaar racket	NA	NA	NA
Illegal immigrants can 'buy' Aadhaar for Rs. 500: Sting operation	The Times of India	Delhi	25/03/14	https://timesofindia.indiatimes.com/india/Illegal-immigrants-can-buy-Aadhaar-for-Rs-500-Sting-operation/articleshow/32624851.cms	Aadhaar racket	NA	Y	NA
Duo used fake documents to get AADHAR, PAN cards for clients	Mid-Day	Mumbai	19/01/13	https://www.mid-day.com/articles/duo-used-fake-documents-to-get-aadhar-pan-cards-for-clients/197188	Aadhaar racket	Fake documents	NA	N
Seven booked in Aadhaar fraud	The Times of India	Hyderabad	17/06/12	https://timesofindia.indiatimes.com/city/hyderabad/Seven-booked-in-Aadhaar-fraud/articleshow/14190401.cms	Aadhaar racket	NA	Y	NA

Publicly Reported Cases of Fake or Forged Aadhaar								
Title of article	Publication	Location	Date	Link	Fraud	How	Aadhaar in Database	Other documents
Aadhaar card scam unearthed in Hyderabad	The Times of India	Hyderabad	27/04/12	https://timesofindia.indiatimes.com/india/Aadhaar-card-scam-unearthed-in-Hyderabad/articleshow/12888048.cms	Siphon PDS grains	Forged	NA	NA
Cobrapost exposes how illegal immigrants easily avail Aadhaar cards	The Firstpost	Delhi	25/03/12	https://www.firstpost.com/india/cobrapost-exposes-how-illegal-immigrants-easily-avail-aadhaar-cards-1449057.html	Aadhaar racket	Fake documents	Y	Y
Pakistan Spy Mehmood Akhtar with "Aadhaar card"	Times of India	Delhi	27/10/16	https://timesofindia.indiatimes.com/india/Pakistan-spy-Mehmood-Akhtar-told-to-leave-India-within-48-hours-MEA/articleshow/55093786.cms		Had LPG connection & Bank account		

UIDAI's RTI Reply Stating That the Enrolment of An Illegal Immigrant, Arrested While Working in the Local Army HQ at Bengaluru, is a Genuine Enrolment

भारत सरकार, योजना आयोग, भारतीय विशिष्ट पहचान प्राधिकरण

Government of India, Planning Commission, Unique Identification Authority of India

संख्या ४९, खानिज भवन, रेस कोर्स रोड, बेंगलूर - ५६० ००१

No.49, 3rd Floor, South Wing, Khanija Bhavan, Race Course Road, Bangalore – 560 001

No.K-11013/100/2011-RTI/Vol.IX/502/2014-15/1699   Dated 12th November, 2014

Shri Mathew Thomas,
No.18-A, Adarsh Vista,
Basavanagar,
BANGALORE – 560 037.

Sir,

Sub: Reply under Right to Information Act, 2005

With reference to your RTI application received through UIDAI, HQ on 16.10.2014 seeking information on newspaper article appearing in Indian Express on 20.02.2014, point-wise reply to your queries are given below:

Sl. No.	Information sought	Reply
1.	It was reported in Indian Express newspaper on 20.02.2014 that 9 illegal immigrants working in the local Army HQ at Bangalore were arrested and two of them were found in possession of Aadhaar letter. Copy of any investigation report you have carried out to determine how these illegal immigrants were issued Aadhaar.	This office had received a letter from Inspector of Police, Cubbon Park Police Station on 22.02.2014 requesting to confirm genuineness of Aadhaar of two persons and information as to the enrolment agency and documents provided by them. The required information was provided to the Inspector of Police on 24.04.2014. Copy attached.
2.	Copy of any document showing action taken by you to prevent recurrence of such serious / dangerous errors	Aadhaars issued to the two persons referred by Inspector of Police were found to be genuine and enrolments were carried out on the basis of accepted PoI / PoA document. Hence question of action does not arise.
3.	Name and address of enrolment agency from whose enrolment centre the enrolment of the above persons was done	Mars Telecom Systems Pvt. Ltd., No.8-2-293/82/B/95 Road: 1 Jubilee Hills, Hyderabad – 500 033.
4.	Copy of any document with information on action taken by you against the enrolment agency	No such document as enrolments were carried out on the basis of accepted PoI / PoA document.

If you are not satisfied with the reply, you may appeal to the Appellate Authority, UIDAI, RO, Bangalore within 30 days of receipt of this letter. The address and contact number of the appellate authority is given below:

Ms. E. P. Nivedita, I.A. & A.S., Assistant Director General & Appellate Authority, UIDAI, Regional Office, Bangalore, No.49, Khanija Bhavan, 3rd Floor, South Wing, Race Course Road, BANGALORE 560 001. Tel: 91—80-22343482. e-mail: **nivedita.pe@uidai.net.in**

Yours faithfully,

(K. Thirumal)
Deputy Director & CPIO,
UIDAI, R.O., Bangalore.

Page (2 of 2)

Page 171 of UIDAI's Counter-affidavit to My Writ Petition No: 37 of 2015, with Inadvertent Admission that 80 Million Enrollments (people's Names) Were Deleted as False/Duplicates

171

lxxvi. That the contents of paragraph no. 6 (lxxvi) of the Writ Petition are wrong, false, misconceived and denied. It is submitted that no .Aadhaar ID is generated at the stage of enrolment as alluded to in the paragraph. In case any malpractice is noticed or reported, action is initiated against the enrolment agencies as well as the operators. The Respondent undertakes concurrent evaluation of the enrolments and has performance monitoring in place. A wrong enrolment packet does not necessarily lead to the generation of the entire UID Scheme. There are several stages like de-duplication, quality checks etc. to assess the veracity of each enrolment packet. A total of 8 crore enrolment packets have been rejected for false or duplicate enrolments. Each enrolment packet is fully trackable and the operator and enrolment agency of any such irregular packet is liable for omission / commission.

It is reiterated that in the referred case, the matter was duly investigated by the Respondent. The operators/supervisors who were identified were immediately blacklisted and enrolment agencies were directed to take action against erring staff. Some of

RTI Reply from UIDAI dated 08-02-2016 on Allegedly Fake and Duplicate Enrolments

Government of India
Planning Commission
Unique Identification Authority of India
Technology Centre, Bangalore – 560 103

Ref: TC-UID/ADMIN/RTI /06/Vol iv/2012/63   dated 08/02/2013

To
Sri.Mathew Thomas
18,A,Adarsh Vista, BasavaNagar,
Bangalore 560 037

Sub: Information under Right to Information Act 2005
Ref: Letter No.K-11013/100/2011-RTI/Vol III/77/2012-13/1135 dated 31/12/2012
....

        With reference to the above cited letter the following information is furnished.

1. No.of duplicate identities detected during de-duplication in all enrolments done so far with   state-wise breakup

Reply: Number of duplicate identities detected and rejected sofar is 7755388. However, Statewise breakup is not available.

2. Name , designation and address of persons who decided that these identities were duplicates:

Reply: De-duplidcation is done by an automated system

3. Role of M/s Morpho Trust in identifying duplicate identities:

Reply: M/s Morpho is a consortium member of one of the Biometric Solution Providers – M/s Mahindra Satyam offering De-Duplication service for the UIDAI enrolment program.

4. Action Taken by UIDAI upon detection of duplicate identities:

Reply: The duplicate/Second enrolement is rejected and letter to the resident sent regarding the rejection.

5. Number of persons whose biometrics could not be captured together with reasons for failure to capture the data in all enrolments done in UID scheme

Reply: This can be divided into two categories viz.

a. Infants upto 5 Years: Around 70 Lakhs and these cases are accepted through cross check with the guardian biometrics

b. True biometric exception cases : These are around 5 lakhs. Guidelines are drawn to process these cases through manual inspection through the Quality Team

6. Action taken in case of Shri.B.S.Yeddyurappa, former chief minister of Karnataka

Reply: As per section 8(1) of RTI ACT,2005 the information relating to a third party can not shared.

7. Results of actions taken in cases where there was failure to enrol in the UID database due to failure to capture biometric data.

Reply: Genuinue Biometric exceptions with supervisor approval at the time of enrolement are processed for Aadhaar generation remaining are rejected.

.....2

Page (1 of 2)

Government of India
Planning Commission
Unique Identification Authority of India
Technology Centre, Bangalore – 560 103

AADHAAR

8. Number of persons who were not enrolled due to furnishing false documents for identity proof or address proof
   Reply: Details are not available with Tech Centre,Bangalore
9. Actions taken against persons who furnished such false identity and address documents with results of actions
   Reply : No such cases are available with Tech Centre, Bangalore

Venkat Rao K.
(ADG & CPIO)

Page (2 of 2)

RTI Reply from UIDAI dated 25-05-2016 on Allegedly Fake and Duplicate Enrolments

GOVERNMENT OF INDIA
Ministry of Communications & IT
Department of Electronics & Information Technology (DeitY)
Unique Identification Authority of India
TECHNOLOGY CENTRE
Bengaluru-560092

Ref: TC-UID/Admin/RTI/06/Vol XXII/2015-2016 / 26   Date: 24.05.2016

To

Shri. Mathew Thomas
18A, Adarsh Vista, Basavanagar
Marathahalli P.O, Bangalore-560037.

     Sub: Information w.r.t RTI Application of Shri. Mathew Thomas - Reg
     Ref: F.No.12013/312-315/2016-RTI/UIDAI dated 25.04.2016.

With reference to the above RTI Query of Shri. Mathew Thomas the following information is furnished.

a) Please inform the total number of false or duplicate enrollments that have been rejected in all UID/Aadhaar enrollments so far.
   Reply: As on 8th May, 2016, 6,45,70,593 enrollments are rejected under the reason codes for MDD_Fail _for_duplicate and DBD_Fail_for Duplicate.

b) Please inform how many of these were false enrollments and how many were duplicate enrollments.
   Reply: No information available with respect to false enrollments available.

c) Please inform how it was determined whether the enrollment was false or duplicate. i.e the criteria used to distinguish between a false enrolment and a duplicate enrollment.
   Reply: Duplicate enrollments are detected by means of demographic and biometric de-duplication checks. No information available with respect to false enrollments.

d) Please provide any document which contains the information requested in sub-paragraphs a to c above.
   Reply: No documents available in this office.

e) Please inform whether the persons whose enrollments were rejected as false or duplicate were informed about your decision to reject the enrollment.
   Reply: Enrollments rejected/in process/Aadhaar generated along with hold/reject reason codes are available in the uidai.resident.net.in portal for status check to residents. Reject SMS is also being sent to affected residents.

f) Please inform whether any of the persons whose enrollments were rejected either as false or duplicate appealed against your decision to reject the enrollment and if so, how many such appeals were received and how were they resolved.
   Reply: All the grievances received from the residents are disposed off in the prescribed manner. No records of such categorization are maintained at this office separately.

Page (1 of 2)

If you are not satisfied with the reply you may appeal to the Appellate Authority in UIDAI,Technology Centre, Bangalore within 30days from the receipt of the letter. The address of the Appellate Authority is given below:

Shri. Sirish Choudhary, Assistant Director General & Appellate Authority
UIDAI Technology Centre, Government of India,
Aadhaar Complex, NTI Layout, Tatanagar, Kodigehalli, Bangalore-560092

(K. Maneesha Raman)
Dy. Director & CPIO

Copy to: Shri. Pramod Kumar, Dy.Director & Nodal CPIO,2nd Floor, Tower-I, Jeevan Bharati Building , Connaught Circus, New Delhi-110 001. W.r.t ltr no F.No.12013/312-315/2016-RTI/UIDAI dated 25.04.2016.

(K. Maneesha Raman)
Dy. Director & CPIO

Page (2 of 2)

RTI Application of Author to UIDAI on Duplicate Enrollments

अधपत्रा COUNTERFOIL

इसे फाइलकर प्रेषक अपने पास रख ले।
To be detached and kept
by the Sender.

पोस्टल आर्डर

₹ 10

POSTAL ORDER

किसे अदा करना
To whom payable _Dy. Director_
& CPIO, Technology Centre
किस डाकघर में _UIDAI - 607_
At what Office ___________

क्या इसे क्रास किया है
Whether crossed ___________

भेजने की तारीख
Date sent _2/6/2016._

38F 358323

File No: RTI/UIDAI/False & Duplicate Enrollments – 2
Thursday, June 2, 2016

APPLICATION UNDER SECTION 6(1)
OF THE RIGHT TO INFORMATION ACT, 2005

Quote our file reference in all your replies

Permit me to inspect files held by you relevant to the subject matter of this RTI

Applicant		Mathew Thomas
		18 A, Adarsh Vista, Basavanagar, Marathahalli P O, Bangalore 560037

The information/ documents required:

a. duplicate enrolments detected using the Automated Biometric Identification System (ABIS)?

b. Does ABIS generate any print record? If so, please furnish a copy of such a record for a period, say for any week, for example, 1 Jan 2015 to 7 Jan 2015 containing duplicates identified by ABIS.

c. If not, please print the output of ABIS for a period, say for any week, for example, 1 Jan 2015 to 7 Jan 2015 containing duplicates identified by ABIS.

d. Does ABIS use demographic information for de-duplication?

e. Were manual checks carried out before the decision to declare an enrolment as a duplicate one done? If so, please furnish a copy of any manual check report.

f. Who is the authority to decide that an enrolment is a duplicate one?

g. Is there any record kept of duplicate enrolments, declared as such and signed by the competent authority? If so, please furnish a copy of such a signed record declaring enrolments as duplicates for any period?

h. Did UIDAI receive any appeal against an enrolment declared as duplicate?

i. If so, how was the appeal disposed of?

j. Are the appeals received electronically or in hard copy or both and is the disposal recorded anywhere either digitally or otherwise.

k. If no record is maintained of appeals and disposal the reasons for not keeping such a record may be furnished

l. Please furnish copy of the prescribed manner (protocol or laid down procedure) for disposal of such appeals.

m. Please furnish a copy of any one such appeal and its disposal.

n. Is ABIS capable of detecting a false enrolment? A false enrolment is defined as one where either biometric (using another person's biometrics) and / or demographic and / or nationality information is deliberately falsified

4. Year to which the document pertains	2010 to 2016
5. Designation and address of the Public Information Officer	Ms. K. Maneesha Raman, Dy. Director & CPIO, Technology Center, UIDAI, Government of India, Ministry of Communications and IT, Department of Electronics & Information Technology (DeitY), Aadhaar Complex, NTI Layout, Tata Nagar, Kodigehalli, Bengaluru 560092
Particulars of initial fee of Rs. 10 paid	Indian Postal Order Number: 38F 358 323

BANGALORE

DATE: Thursday, June 2, 2016

SIGNATURE OF THE APPLICANT

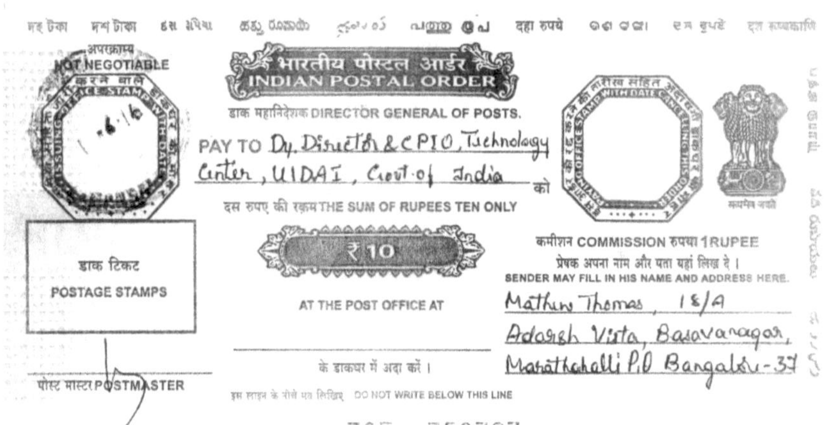
NOT NEGOTIABLE
भारतीय पोस्टल ऑर्डर
INDIAN POSTAL ORDER
डाक महानिदेशक DIRECTOR GENERAL OF POSTS.
PAY TO Dy. Director & CPIO, Technology Center, UIDAI, Govt. of India को
दस रुपए की रकम THE SUM OF RUPEES TEN ONLY
₹ 10
कमीशन COMMISSION रुपया 1 RUPEE
प्रेषक अपना नाम और पता यहाँ लिखे दे ।
SENDER MAY FILL IN HIS NAME AND ADDRESS HERE.
Mathew Thomas, 18/A
Adarsh Vista, Basavanagar,
Marathahalli P.O Bangalore-37
डाक टिकट
POSTAGE STAMPS
AT THE POST OFFICE AT
के डाकघर में अदा करें ।
पोस्ट मास्टर POSTMASTER
इस लाइन के नीचे मत लिखिए DO NOT WRITE BELOW THIS LINE
38F   358323

SP DOMLUR <560071>
EK258270293IN
Counter No:1,OP-Code:RAMANJ
To:K MANEESHA RAMAN,
    SAHAKARANAGAR, PIN:560092
From:MATHEW THOMAS , BG 37
Wt:15grams.
Amt:17.00 ,06/06/2016 ,12:35
Taxes:Rs.2.00<<Track on www.indiapost.gov.in>>
India Post

List of URLs

1. 'Aadhaar' Trust: https://economictimes.indiatimes.com/peoples-power/articleshow/24993826.cms?intenttarget=no
2. https://timesofindia.indiatimes.com/city/bangalore/Dharam-govt-will-reboot-BATF/articleshow/804693.cms?referral=PM
3. http://www.toxicswatch.org/2013/09/why-nilekani-gave-contacts-to-safran.html Nilekani took ID World award at Milan workshop in 2010
4. https://www.dawn.com/news/1341807 NADRA awarded contracts at huge cost
5. https://en.wikipedia.org/wiki/Tariq_Malik NADRA chief received ID World award in 2009
6. https://cis-india.org/internet-governance/uid-summary-of-findings.pdf/view Hans Mathews - False Matches increase by factor of 6 or 10
7. https://www.thetimes.co.uk/article/id-cards-are-the-ultimate-identity-theft-r3xwdp0wzhz Ian Angell 'Times Online' 7 Mar 2008
8. http://www.lse.ac.uk/researchandexpertise/experts/profile.aspx?KeyValue=i.angell%40lse.ac.uk Ian Angell Profile
9. https://www.pressreader.com/india/the-times-of-india-mumbai-edition/20171111/282411284599613 UIDAI CEO article - "Getting rid of ghosts: 'Aadhaar' is a foundation for new clean India, not a surveillance state"
10. https://www.aarp.org/work/social-security/info-06-2012/social-security-card-non-citizen.html Can I Get a Social Security Card If I'm Not a U.S. Citizen?
11. https://en.wikipedia.org/wiki/Social_Security_number Social Security was originally a universal tax, but when Medicare was passed in 1965, objecting religious groups in existence prior to 1951 were allowed to opt out of the system.[15] Because of this, not every American is part of the Social Security program, and not everyone has a number. However, a social security number

is required for parents to claim their children as dependents for federal income tax purposes,[12] and the Internal Revenue Service requires all corporations to obtain SSNs (or alternative identifying numbers) from their employees, as described below. Social Security cards printed from January 1946 until January 1972 expressly stated that people should not use the number and card for identification.[17] Since nearly everyone in the United States now has an SSN, it became convenient to use it anyway and the message was removed.[18] Since then, Social Security numbers have become de facto national identification numbers.[2] Although some people do not have an SSN assigned to them, it is becoming increasingly difficult to engage in legitimate financial activities such as applying for a loan or a bank account without one.[19] While the government cannot require an individual to disclose their SSN without a legal basis, companies may refuse to provide service to an individual who does not provide an SSN.[20][21] The card on which an SSN is issued is still not suitable for primary identification as it has no photograph, no physical description and no birth date. All it does is confirm that a particular number has been issued to a particular name. Instead, a driver's license or state ID card is used as an identification for adults.

12. http://www.dematerialisedid.com/BCSL/Drown.html David Moss - India's ID card scheme – drowning in a sea of false positives – Mar 2011

13. http://www.zdnet.com/article/id-card-will-drown-in-a-billion-mismatches/ ID card 'will drown in a billion mismatches' By Nick Heath | September 26, 2008

14. http://www.dematerialisedid.com/BCSL/Tulipmania.html Tulipmania and the Home Office David Moss

15. http://www.newswithviews.com/Devvy/kidd27.htm HOW THE GOVERNMENT LIES ABOUT SOCIAL SECURITY

16. https://www.fool.com/retirement/2017/05/08/the-3-biggest-lies-youve-been-told-about-social-se.aspx The 3 Biggest Lies You've Been Told About Social Security (and Believed)

17. http://www.thehindu.com/news/national/Tembhli-becomes-first-Aadhar-village-in-India/article13673162.ece Tembhli becomes first Aadhar village in India TEMBHLI (NANDURBAR DISTRICT):, SEPTEMBER 29, 2010 14:14 IST

18. https://www.google.co.in/search?safe=active&dcr=0&source=hp&ei=TrM-JWvSAGcj9vgTet5WYCw&q=how+the+government+lies+about+social+security+devvy&oq=ho&gs_l=psy-ab.1.0.35i39k1l2j0i67k-1l3j0j0i131k1l3j0.1636.3939.0.9341.3.2.0.0.0.0.140.273.0j2.2.0......0....1.1.64.psy-ab...1.2.273.0...46j0i46k1.0.SNfK_unaMIw Google search SSN

19. https://www.fool.com/retirement/2017/05/08/the-3-biggest-lies-youve-been-told-about-social-se.aspx The 3 Biggest Lies You've Been Told About Social Security (and Believed)

20. INSAF Campaign 2017 <http://www.insafindia.com/2017/11/why-im-saying-no-to-aadhaar-join.html>

21. http://www.thehindu.com/news/national/Tembhli-back-to-square-one-as-labourers-leave-for-Gujarat/article15765221.ece Tembhli back to square one as labourers leave for Gujarat TEMBHLI(NANDURBAR):, OCTOBER 02, 2010 03:04 IST

22. https://en.wikipedia.org/wiki/Pay_By_Touch Pay By Touch

23. http://www.zdnet.com/article/id-card-will-drown-in-a-billion-mismatches/ ID card 'will drown in a billion mismatches'

24. http://www.dmossesq.com/2015/09/so-where-are-we-on-astrology-13-years.html So where are we on astrology? 13 years late, UK government promises biometrics strategy by end 2015. Why? David Moss

25. https://www.google.co.in/search?safe=active&dcr=0&source=hp&ei=pKIJWom6PMiBvgTc_b3QAQ&q=prof+john+daugman&oq=prof+john+daugman&gs_l=psy-ab.3...33i160k1.15528.24938.0.27165.23.21.0.0.0.0.283.2610.8j11j2.21.0......0....1.1.64.psy-ab...2.21.2602.0...0j35i39k1j0i131k1j0i20i263k1j0i10k1j33i21k1.0.M8gXLyTn1Bw Google search – Daugman

26. http://sphewu.info/john-daugman-algorithm-ljp/ John Daugman Algorithm

27. http://www.lse.ac.uk/researchandexpertise/experts/profile.aspx?KeyValue=i.angell%40lse.ac.uk Ian Angell "id cards are the ultimate identity theft"

28. http://eprints.lse.ac.uk/741/1/PressRelease_5-09-05.pdf An assessment of UK Identity Cards Bill and its Implications: ID Cards UK's High Tech Scheme is High Risk

29. UBCC <https://uidai.gov.in/images/loksabha/LS_USQ_1131_answered_on_08022017.pdf>

30. The grapes of rot: Govt bought 56,000 quintals of wheat, only to waste. Bangalore Mirror21-11-2017 http://bangaloremirror.indiatimes.com/bangalore/cover-story/the-grapes-of-rot-govt-bought-56000-quintals-of-wheat-only-to-waste/articleshow/61730952.cms?

31. Police Puts 'Starvation Death Victim' in the Dock for Fudging 'Aadhaar' ET 23-12-2017 <https://economictimes.indiatimes.com/news/politics-and-nation/police-puts-starvation-death-victim-in-the-dock-for-fudging-aadhaar/articleshow/62215261.cms>

32. One of earliest anti-Sham ID, called, 'Aadhaar' campaign's – Bangalore 20-04-2010 <https://m.facebook.com/notes/pramod-biligiri/uid-and-fundamental-rights-a-workshop/396414903887/>

33. Identity Cards Act 2006 <https://en.wikipedia.org/wiki/Identity_Cards_Act_2006#Legislative_progress>

34. U.K. "NO2ID" https://en.wikipedia.org/wiki/NO2ID

35. The Difference Engine: Dubious security <https://www.economist.com/blogs/babbage/2010/10/biometrics>

36. Mathew Thomas Interview by Kshitij Urs – 1 https://youtu.be/J8YtkVf2cjY

37. Mathew Thomas Interview by Kshitij Urs – 2 https://www.youtube.com/watch?v=Nu6rrSt6Koo&t=841s

38. Mathew Thomas Interview by Kshitij Urs – 3 <https://www.youtube.com/watch?v=tweCG9se2hw&t=491s>

39. Mathew Thomas Azim Premji University 2012 – Examination of Concerns <https://www.youtube.com/watch?v=T-LYL9JzeI8&t=626s>

40. At Money Life Foundation - "Medicine Worse than the Disease" <https://www.youtube.com/watch?v=De4h9e79m5Q>

41. Cobra Post Expose of Sham ID, called, 'Aadhaar' <https://www.youtube.com/watch?v=Hrpajgws7So&list=PLZ8AgVRbddAvktP_eGC9sZ8oOrG75F_3T>

42. Mathew Thomas – Technical Aspects of Sham ID, called, 'Aadhaar' <https://www.youtube.com/watch?v=1q7JCoRHuio&t=81s&index=3&list=PLZ8AgVRbddAvktP_eGC9sZ8oOrG75F_3T>

43. UID Fraud Exposed by 'Headlines Today' <https://www.youtube.com/watch?v=G4NhhZQP68Y&t=6s&index=5&list=PLZ8AgVRbddAvktP_eGC9sZ8oOrG75F_3T>

44. Narendra Modi – Election Speech against Sham ID, called, 'Aadhaar' - 2014 <https://www.youtube.com/watch?v=bofF8zKT-E8&list=PLZ8Ag VRbddAvktP_eGC9sZ8oOrG75F_3T&index=6>

45. Narendra Modi – His 'U' Turn after Election <https://youtu.be/leI8RVd-s_4>

46. Aadhaar Trust 'Business Today – 17-08-2003 <http://archives.digitaltoday. in/businesstoday/20030817/cover1.html>

47. Why Nilekani gave contacts to Safran Group & took awards from it 05-09-2013 <http://www.toxicswatch.org/2013/09/why-nilekani-gave-contacts-to-safran.html>

48. Tariq Malik NADRA's Chief – Wikipedia Profile <https://en.wikipedia.org/wiki/Tariq_Malik>

49. Pakistan completes biometric re-verification of 72 million SIMs 27-02-2015 <http://www.planetbiometrics.com/article-details/i/2752/>

50. Pakistan turns to biometrics for banking 18-11-2014 <http://www.planetbiometrics.com/article-details/i/2409/>

51. Pakistan spy Mehmood Akhtar told to leave India within 48 hours: MEA – TOI 27-10-2016 <https://timesofindia.indiatimes.com/india/Pakistan-spy-Mehmood-Akhtar-told-to-leave-India-within-48-hours-MEA/articleshow/55093786.cms>

52. JeM terrorist from PoK caught, Aadhaar card recovered from him <https://www.indiatoday.in/pti-feed/story/jem-terrorist-from-pok-caught-aadhaar-card-recovered-from-him-608935-2016-05-15>

53. More people in Pakistani mission may be involved in ISI spy ring: police – DC – 27-10-2016 <https://www.deccanchronicle.com/nation/current-affairs/271016/more-people-in-pakistani-mission-may-be-involved-in-isi-spy-ring-police.html>

54. Pak national caught entering Jaisalmer Air Force station, four others arrested from Barmer – HT – 03-01-2018 <https://www.hindustantimes.com/jaipur/pak-national-caught-entering-jaisalmer-air-force-station-four-others-arrested-from-barmer/story-LdvyP0ImQS4Xl6UPaOvpRI.html>

55. Aadhaar in the hand of spies <https://fountainink.in/reportage/aadhaar-in-the-hand-of-spies->

56. Apple CEO Tim Cook meets Modi, launches updated version of 'Narendra Modi mobile app' <https://www.gadgetsnow.com/tech-news/Apple-CEO-Tim-Cook-meets-Modi-launches-updated-version-of-Narendra-Modi-mobile-app/articleshow/52373043.cms?>

57. Globalise identity, not aadhaar: Using one single database and identity management scheme for everything will not work <https://blogs.timesofindia. indiatimes.com/toi-edit-page/globalise-identity-not-aadhaar-using-one-single-database-and-identity-management-scheme-for-everything-will-not-work/>

58. Equifax – John Oliver – SSN data stolen <https://youtu.be/mPjgRKW_Jmk>

59. Despite the comparisons, India's Aadhaar project is nothing like America's Social Security Number <https://scroll.in/article/823570/despite-the-comparisons-indias-aadhaar-project-is-nothing-like-americas-social-security-number>

60. **Searching for beneficiaries of subsidies and benefits** <https://medium. com/@anupamsaraph/searching-for-beneficiaries-of-subsidies-and-benefits-560835b8afaf>

61. Playing Dice With Criminal Sentences: The Influence of Irrelevant Anchors on Experts' Judicial Decision Making http://journals.sagepub.com/doi/abs/10.1177/0146167205282152

62. Extraneous factors in judicial decisions <http://www.pnas.org/content/108/17/6889.full>

63. US National Academies Research Report – "Biometric Recognition – Challenges and Opportunities" https://www.nap.edu/login.php?record_id=12720

64. UID Summary – Dr. Hans Mathews – for CIS <https://cis-india.org/internet-governance/uid-summary-of-findings.pdf/view>